RETIREMENT 901

A Comprehensive Seminar for Senior Faculty and Staff

Clay Schoenfeld
Emeritus Professor and Dean, University of Wisconsin-Madison
Contributing Editor, *Administrator*, *Academic Leader*, *Professional Scholar*

Foreword by

James A. Fosdick, University of Wisconsin-Madison
Emeritus Professor, Journalism/Mass Communication

Magna Publications, Inc.
2718 Dryden Drive
Madison, WI 53704-3086
608/246-3580
1993

Retirement 901: A Comprehensive Seminar for Senior Faculty and Staff

Library of Congress Cataloging-in-Publication Data

Schoenfeld, Clay, 1924 -

Retirement 901: a comprehensive seminar for senior faculty and staff / Clay Schoenfeld: foreword by James A. Fosdick.

p. cm.

Includes bibliographical references and index.

ISBN 0-912150-25-4

1. College teachers—United States—Retirement. 2. Universities and colleges—United States—Faculty Retirement. I. Title. II. Title: Retirement nine hundred one.

LB2334.S32 1993

331.25'22—dc20 92-62443

CIP

6-6-96 dso

Printed in The United States of America

Library of Congress Catalog Card Number: 92-62443

ISBN: 0-912150-25-4

Magna Publications, Inc.
2718 Dryden Drive
Madison, WI 53704-3086
608/246-3580

Also by Clay Schoenfeld:

The University and Its Publics, 1954
Effective Feature Writing, 1960
The Shape of Summer Sessions to Come (Ed.), 1961
Publicity Media and Methods, 1963
Year-Round Education (with Neil Schmitz), 1964
University Extension (with Theodore J. Shannon), 1965
Wisconsin Sideroads to Somewhere, 1966
The American University in Summer (with Donald Zillman), 1967
Cabins, Conservation, and Fun, 1968
Canada Goose Management (Ed., with Ruth Hine), 1968, 1977
Outlines of Environmental Education (Ed.), 1971
Everybody's Ecology, 1971
Interpreting Environmental Issues (Ed.), 1972
Human Dimensions in Wildlife Programs (Ed., with John C. Hendee), 1973
The Outreach University, 1977
Public School and Public Action Environmental Education Programs (Ed., with John Disinger), 1977
If You Want to Be a Badger, 1977
Environmental Studies Programs in Colleges and Universities (Ed., with John Disinger), 1978
Environmental Education in Action —I and *II* (with John Disinger), 1977, 1978
Wildlife Management in Wilderness (with John C. Hendee), 1978, 1980
Public Involvement in Environmental Policy (Ed., with John Disinger), 1979
Down Wisconsin Sideroads, 1979
Environmental Communication Research and Commentary (with Renee Guillierie), 1979
The Environmental Communication Ecosystem, 1981
Effective Feature Writing (with Karen S. Diegmueller), 1982
Ribbands of Blue, 1984
Wisconsin (with Michael Weimer), 1985, 1990
Interpreting Public Issues (with Robert J. Griffin, Dayle H. Molen, and James F. Scotton), 1991
Mentor in a Manual: Climbing the Academic Ladder to Tenure (with Robert Magnan), 1992

CONTENTS

FOREWORD

Retirement and Aging: Sentence or Opportunity?

James A. Fosdick, University of Wisconsin-Madison Emeritus
Professor of Journalism and Mass Communication

Different occurrences can trigger one's realization that age is creeping up. It might be a more frequent ache, or a more persistent one. It could be when someone you consider a contemporary offers you a seat on a crowded bus. It could be memory slippage (when a stranger asks you your name, do you reply, "How soon do you need to know?"). In my case, I think it was when our oldest grandson declared his imminent marriage plans.

Retirement from 43 years of work didn't do it. That was a voluntary act and, overall, a pleasant transition. Nope, it must have been the shock of knowing that perhaps in a year or so my spouse Polly and I could be *great*-grandparents.

Actually, there is good news and bad news about retiring and aging. Since retiring and aging do not occur at precisely the same time, it is important to consider them separately. The outlook — "flavor," if you will — of this Foreward is definitely optimistic and supported by some statistics and especially by the considered opinions and analyses of several writers who have spent significant portions of their professional careers studying the topic and its implications for individuals and the society — such as the author of this book.

Such an outlook stimulates me to discard the theory of disengagement expressed by a couple of writers in 1961.

According to this theory, older people desire certain forms of social isolation; that is, they consciously and deliberately seek a reduction in social contacts and achieve successful and satisfying aging by withdrawing from society. This is the idea expressed by Shakespeare's King Lear when he bequeathed his kingdom and his regal responsibilities to his two elder daughters with the declaration: "Tis our fast intent to shake all cares and business from our age, conferring them on younger strengths while we, unburdened, crawl toward death."

A more sociable attitude is that expressed by the writer of a recent magazine article entitled "Zip, Zest, and Ginger" (*The Key*, Fall 1991, 109: 3). Marjorie Cross Bird makes the point, supported by the U.S. Census and other accepted sources, "that aging is in style ... a lot of people are doing it. More and more of us are becoming seasoned citizens. Like ginger, we have some flavor; we add interest to what otherwise might be bland." In short, we have a lot to contribute to society.

We can remember when:

- There were no bumper stickers making position statements.
- T-shirts and sweatshirts had absolutely nothing to say.
- Some of us were shocked to hear Clark Gable use THAT word in *Gone With the Wind.*
- We could converse with teenagers not plugged into Walkmans.
- Turtles were neither Ninja nor mutant nor teen-aged.
- "Far out" meant a long way from here, not "cool."
- "Cool" meant a temperature, not "very good."
- "Good" meant "good," and "bad" didn't (mean "good," that is).

And our memory's getting longer. Consider this: by the year 2030, the entire baby boom generation will be senior citizens ... and one out of every two baby boomers may eventually need long-term health care. If we consider those over 65 to be senior citizens (yes, a term that many don't particularly like), their percentages in the total U.S. population, which hit 12.6% in 1990, are projected to be: 13% in 2000, 13.9% in 2010, 17.7% in 2020, and 21.8% in 2030 (Census Bureau figures). Each day more than 1,600 Americans reach age 65. In the 40 years between 1990 and 2030, the proportion of the population over 65 will grow 75%—quite an increase!

Contrast these figures with the fact that in 1900, people over 65 contributed less than 4% of the U.S. population, and the life expectancy of children born that year was about 48 years. The U.S. isn't the only nation experiencing an Aging Boom. It's worldwide. Nearly every nation in the world today already shows signs of a population explosion among its aged, or will in the next few years.

If we call "aged" a country with at least 7% of its population over 65 (in this age group), as the United Nations does, then the U.S., all the European nations, and Japan fit this category. Most of the developing nations of the world are catching up. Within the next 30-40 years, nearly all nations of the world will have reached the 7% standard. The UN has predicted that more than 1.21 billion people will have reached age 60 by 2025. The Aging Boom is upon us, and the world has never witnessed anything like it.

The Aging Boom, however, is not expected to proceed at the same rate throughout the world. According to Earl F. Foell ("Rewriting the Baby Boom") in *World Monitor* magazine (September 1991):

> More than 90% of the babies born on earth from now until the end of the century will be born in Third World nations ... and the populations of the United States, Europe, Japan, what we have been used to calling the Soviet Union, and the East Asian Tiger nations (South Korea, Taiwan, Hong Kong, and Singapore) will be graying.

Implications of these shifts in demographics are many, and I don't intend to try to deal with all of them here. One possibility is that more responsibility may devolve upon the "graying" populations of the developed nations. The retirement horizon may recede. At least the U.S. seems to be changing from a period in which the elderly have been set aside, excluded from work and careers, turned out to pasture like race-horses that have stopped winning, to a period in which calendar age is recognized as irrelevant to the potential for useful and significant participation in society.

This continued participation in full-time work and career has always been the norm for many, of course. Politics, the professions (medical and other systematic research, law and the judiciary, and more recently teaching), and business provide numerous examples. But for most people, the expectations and the practice have been different. The third phase of life, complete retirement (following phase 1, growing up and preparing for work and career; and phase 2, earning a living and perhaps raising a family) has begun in the seventh decade of life. Already we see golden parachutes inducing some to retire earlier ... and postponement of retirement by others who haven't lost interest in their work or who have retooled themselves for a career change. This flexibility in the deadline for retirement is partly dependent on attitudes held by the aging themselves and by the public at large.

One of the best-known long-workers and non-retirers was Thomas Edison. He patented his first invention in 1868, when he was 21, and received his last patent when he was 81. As a matter of fact, he applied for a patent (to extract rubber from goldenrod) when he was 83, one year before he died.

Attitudes toward aging can be real or imaginary. So-called "sociogenic aging" (or aging which has no physical basis) is the role our folklore, prejudices, and misconceptions about age impose on "the old." Sociogenic aging is imaginary or imposed aging. Simply a change of attitude can abolish it.

In his Foreword to Charles Russell's book, *Good News About Aging*

(John Wiley & Sons, 1989), James Birren (of the University of Southern California) repeats Russell's implied question, "How do you want to spend the second half of life?" with an illustration and comment.

> Certainly it is longer than most of us expected it to be, and it would seem to be full of more opportunities. A 102-year-old woman visited the Gerontology Center that I directed for many years. When I was introduced to her, I asked her why she came to the university's center. She said that she was curious about what a gerontology center did. I then asked her how she came to the university. She said that she took a bus. Then I asked her with whom did she come, and she said that she came alone.
>
> Does this fit your concept of the elderly? Curiosity motivated a 102-year-old person to take a bus across Los Angeles to see what a university was doing in gerontology.

According to a Louis Harris poll commissioned in 1974 by The National Council on Aging (summarized by Ronald and Beatrice Gross, and Sylvia Seidman, in *The New Old: Struggling for Decent Aging*, Anchor/Doubleday, 1978), pollsters found a significant disparity between what the *general public believes* old age is like and what the elderly report they have actually experienced.

Among the revelations of this pioneering study are:

- Most older people believe that their condition in life is better, economically and socially, than the general public believes it to be (despite the fact that many older people are in desperate straits).
- Most older Americans have both the desire and the potential to be productive, contributing members of society.
- Old people are themselves primary victims of stereotyped ways of perceiving aging and the aged.
- 86% of Americans agree that people should not be forced to retire because of age.

Fear of crime was the only problem any sizeable number of older people considered a serious problem, and only one-quarter of the older people considered crime a serious problem for their generation.

Another body of research, Charles Russell's *The General Social Survey (GSS), 1972-1986: The State of the American People*, also studied different age groups' attitudes toward aging and life. Among the questions asked was, "When a person has a disease that cannot be cured, do you think doctors should be allowed to end the patient's life by some painless means if the patient and his family request it?"

At ages 18-24, 71% of the group answered "yes," while 26% were opposed. At 85+, however, only 39% agreed and 53% were opposed, demonstrating one of the greatest differences between the very young and the very old in the entire survey.

Attitudes still need to change. Plenty of evidence shows that older people enjoy life, but many of the general public still think we have little to rejoice about in advanced maturity. Never mind the proof that the old are more relaxed and count more happy people among them than do the young, or that the most difficult time of life is probably from the teens to the mid-30s — many still think it's no fun to be old.

Things are often not as bad as pessimists expect them to be.

Probably because of an inheritance of folklore and stereotypes which have led many to dread old age, coupled with a youth/energy/sports worship which seems to come naturally to most Americans, we have apparently forgotten the dignity and prestige accorded elders in biblical times and in early Greece. Even in olden times, however, there was a dichotomy of attitudes toward aging; some called it "the worst of times," while others considered it "the best of times." These feelings probably reflected the writers' own experiences with old age, just as many in any stage of life will interpret the meaning of life purely from their own experience rather than from a broader, more representative perspective.

As reported in Russell's *Good News About Aging* (John Wiley & Sons, 1989), among the Greek thinkers who took a particularly dreary view of life was Aristotle, who lived around 350 B.C. and is said to have been the first scientific student of human society and experience. He believed that young persons fall into permissible errors because they incline to enthusiasm and excess. The old, however, have more serious faults that grow out of their experience with the inevitable misfortunes of life. They are suspicious. They live by shrewdness and calculation rather than by moral values. They are rigid, small-minded, cynical, ungenerous, cowardly, and shameless. They appear self-controlled only because they lack passion, not because they have become wise. Aristotle concluded that such faults should disqualify the old from holding political office.

Given the varying attitudes about old age which have existed for centuries, we should not be surprised to learn that the 1974 Harris survey found significant disparities between problems attributed to the 65-plus and what older people themselves identify as very serious problems. Anticipated problems include poor health, fear of crime, loneliness, not enough money to live on, feeling neglected, dependent or burdensome, boredom, lack of adequate medical care, too little education, not enough to do to keep busy, too few friends, poor housing, not enough job opportunities, lack of transportation, and inadequate clothing.

That these problems, and a host of others, do indeed exist for many older Americans was substantiated by the survey of people 65 and older. However, when the problems attributed to the 65-plus were compared with what older people themselves identify as very serious problems, there were in most cases enormous discrepancies in degree. According to the Harris survey, the first and smaller figure is what older people reported from their experience, and the second is what the general public *anticipated* or *expected.*

- Fear of crime (23%, 50%)
- Poor health (21%, 51%)
- Not enough money to live on (15%, 62%)
- Loneliness (12%, 60%)
- Not enough medical care (10%, 44%)
- Not enough education (8%, 20%)
- Not feeling needed (7%, 54%)
- Not enough to do to keep busy (6%, 37%)

Older people questioned in the survey may have been reluctant to identify their problems as "very serious." Yet when the analysis went a step further and included definitions of "somewhat serious" in personal experience, there still remained, in most cases, considerable differences between the actual experience and the severity of problems expected by the public at large.

We should conclude from this that, although problems do exist for older people, the same problems do not exist for *all* older persons, substantiating the fact that the aged are a *mixed* group. The elderly constitute a group because of their chronological age, but factors more powerful than age alone determine the conditions of their later years. For about one in three of the elderly poor, serious health problems, not enough money, and fear of crime make life a difficult struggle indeed. In three areas, problems stand out as more serious for the 80-plus than for those in their 60s: poor health, loneliness, and not feeling needed. In addition, judging by responses to questions in the Harris survey, poverty and race appear to generate more of the very-serious problems than old age itself. It appears that the "problems of aging" may not be problems of aging so much as they are problems of fulfilling needs that all adults have.

Some of these can be solved, or prepared for, by the individuals themselves; others require the cooperation and love of family and friends or the larger society. Slightly more than one-third of the 65s-or-over said their life now was better than they had expected, almost half said it was about as they expected, and only 11% reported it worse than they expected.

As has been mentioned, some of the greatest disparities in attitudes about aging are between the youngest and the oldest age groups. Whether one wants to call this evidence of the "generation gap" or not, explanations of the disparities are worth pursuing. One explanation seems to be the obvious cohort orientation of each group ... that is to say, the differences in the life experiences of the younger and older people sampled in the Harris survey. The older population experienced the Great Depression of the early 30s as youngsters. I vividly recall that my mother stretched our food dollars by preparing homemade potato soup, rice pudding, homemade biscuits, and imaginative re-dos of leftovers from the Sunday roast or fried chicken ... a chicken, by the way, which was often purchased (or obtained from Grandpa's farm) "on the hoof" and slaughtered by my father in the back yard of our middle-class home. My mother usually did the plucking, after dipping the carcass in boiling water. Also, I can recall our Sunday relaxation (no TV, of course, and no radio either in my earliest years) consisting of a motor car ride through the less fortunate neighborhoods of Muncie, Indiana, or Toledo, Ohio. I am convinced this was to make the three of us a little less discouraged about our financial straits.

What I mean to say is that many of today's older population probably feel pretty good about their lot because it is so much better than the life they used to lead as children. On the other hand, the current younger generation, who may have read about the Depression but did not experience it, has developed a life-style conditioned by credit cards, supermarkets loaded with goodies, education supplemented by audiovisual aids and computers, and teachers who themselves did not grow up in the Depression. Is the current recession sufficiently deep and pervasive to condition working adults to the modifications in life style sometimes experienced during retirement? How will *they* adjust to aging and retirement? Will they accommodate as well as the current aging retirees seem to have done?

Given the current state of the U.S. economy (including the federal deficit) and the increasing likelihood that Social Security income and other mandated benefits may not keep pace with inflation and the perceived needs of future retirees, today's working people may find they need to rely on their own savings and investments for retirement to an even greater extent than did those now experiencing their retirement years. Will they be able to do this? In addition to my suggestion that one explanation for the accommodation to or the contented acceptance of retirement and aging by the older people included in the Harris and GSS surveys is their life experience, it seems likely that many in this group have in specific ways prepared themselves for their third stage of life.

According to surveys, majorities of the total public, young and old, agree on seven "very important steps people should take" in preparing for their later years:

- Ensure medical care is available (88%)
- Prepare a will (81%)
- Build up savings (80%)
- Learn about pensions and Social Security benefits (80%)
- Buy your own home (70%)
- Develop hobbies, leisure-time activities (64%)
- Decide whether you want to move or stay where you are (50%)

In addition, 31% believe it is very important to "plan new part-time or full-time jobs." Although it did not appear in the survey responses, one important addition to any prescription for successful aging should include the admonition for one to continue (or initiate, if one has not been doing so) to engage in regular, if moderate, exercise. With retirement often comes an inclination to decrease one's physical activity.

After all, isn't that what retirement's all about ... the opportunity to "take it easy"?

Scientists who study the aging process know that the effects of time can be slowed, and in some instances reversed, by such simple things as exercise. University of Wisconsin-Madison Professor of Preventive Medicine Everett Smith has accumulated persuasive evidence that the best elixir for our aging bones is weight-bearing exercise such as walking, jogging, tennis, and dancing.

After one has recovered from the Big Change of retiring from a daily job, has enjoyed several days or weeks of not having to get to the office or the classroom at 7:50 a.m., and perhaps has even collected the first retirement checks, the challenge to fill time presents itself. If the recent retiree has faithfully taken the seven or eight important steps recommended earlier, any worries about retirement should have been minimized. Hobbies and other leisure activities can be pursued with a greater feeling of freedom, you can proceed with the change in residence (even to Florida as many have done to avoid northern winters!) or begin the new part-time or full-time job. Doesn't this sound exciting?!

However, on the unlikely chance that you're still feeling bored and useless, let me remind you of a couple of useful activities for the extra time and energy you may have. Two rewarding activities which help make life worth living for many retired folk are a return to the classroom for learning something new ... and volunteering their time and services for a worthwhile cause. As Irving Berlin, that prolonged and delightful songsmith once put it: "Age is no mark of merit unless you do something constructive with it."

Many colleges and universities have been courting the older student for several years, in part because of declining enrollments and the need to justify public and private financial support of staffs and facilities which had grown to accommodate the baby boom generation as it moved through the system. Some campuses even permitted free enrollment in classes, on an audit (non-credit) basis. According to a recent newspaper story, several colleges are actively recruiting foreign students to maintain enrollment levels. (It may be worthwhile to read *The Older Adult as Learner,* by D. Barry Lumsden, Hemisphere Publications, 1958.)

An interesting and amusing story about older adults in the classroom appeared in a newspaper story a few years ago. The account reported on one Harry Gersh. He was the second generation of his family to go to Harvard — the *first* was his son. It seems Gersh enrolled as a first-year student at the age of 63, and at last reports was not only achieving grades well above the average, but having a marvelous time. He was quoted as saying that the only realistic problem he saw in going through four years of undergraduate study and earning his bachelor's degree was money.

"My son had it much easier," he said. "He had a rich father!"

But perhaps the most impressive of the "other activities" of the older generation is volunteer work. Many consider this one of the great prerogatives and contributions of age. Research has shown that volunteers among the old have greater life satisfaction and a greater will to live than their peers. Mother Teresa and Albert Schweitzer are among the most widely known, but there are many enthusiastic volunteers ... in political, religious, social service, environmental, and medical organizations. (See *Elders in Rebellion: A Guide to Senior Activism,* by Lou Cottin, Anchor Press, 1979.)

But let me move to a specific program designed for those alert and able persons in the third phase of their lives.

Elderhostel is a special educational venture for older adults, organized in 1975 by Marty Knowlton, a social activist and educator, who linked the European hosteling concept with the residential emphasis of the Scandinavian Folk Schools. The nonprofit enterprise has grown from a few hundred hostelers on a handful of New England college campuses into an international network of 1,800 participating institutions. There are programs in every American state and Canadian province as well as in more than 45 foreign countries. Last year almost one-quarter million people enrolled in Elderhostel. (For more detailed coverage, read *Elderhostels: The Students' Choice*, by Mildred Hyman, Muir Publications/ Norton & Co.)

Although each program is unique, the pattern has changed little over the years. A typical domestic (U.S.) program includes:

- six nights, usually starting Sunday afternoon and ending Saturday morning;
- three academic courses that each meet for 1½ hours daily, scheduled so that you may take all three;
- simple but comfortable dormitory or conference center accommodations;
- some extracurricular activities.

All you need to qualify is an inquiring mind. Elderhostel isn't a group tour. The focus is on academics; you're a student-in-residence for the week. However, attendance is not taken, and if you want to skip a session, it won't reduce your course grade ... because there are none; everybody passes and gets a certificate!

The price is right ... almost cheaper than living at home, except for your travel costs to and from the campus or other location you have selected. Polly and I have often signed up for two different Elderhostels in the same general location, to prolong our visit to the area ... and to avoid a little more winter weather. There is also an International Elderhostel program, which offers a unique opportunity to experience different cultures. More than 25,000 older students will attend one of these foreign programs this year. The format is a bit different from those in the U.S. Some include one or two weeks at a single study site, but most are two, three, or four weeks long, with each week spent at a different site. This may be in the same or in different countries. Also, international programs usually feature one significant area of study or course per week. Classes are conducted in English, and most classes are held in the morning, complemented by course-related field trips and excursions.

While I don't want to bore you with statistics, you might want to know what kinds of folks participate in these programs. The following facts are from a 1989 survey:

- 61% are female, 39% are male;
- 50% are 70 years or older, 31% are between 65 and 69, and 19% are 64 or younger;
- 70% are married, 20% widowed;
- 69% are retired completely;
- 46% have a four-year college degree or more, 20% have a master's degree;
- 67% attended their most recent Elderhostel programs with a spouse or relative, 27% attended with a friend;
- 78% were completely satisfied with the last Elderhostel program they attended; 2% were somewhat dissatisfied;
- courses offered and location were a major factor in selecting programs for more than 70% of those surveyed; sleeping and bathroom arrangements were also given significant consideration;
- 27% traveled between 200 and 500 miles to their last program, 25% traveled between 500 and 1,000 miles, and 32% traveled more than 1,000 miles;
- regular activities for many of the hostelers surveyed include: academic courses, watching or listening to public television or radio, and community service and volunteer work.

Obviously, the mix of people makes for interesting discussions and, occasionally, lasting relationships.

Let me conclude by telling you about an episode that occurred at one of the Elderhostels on Jekyll Island, off the coast of Georgia. In mid-afternoon I had taken off for a round of golf at a nearby course. Polly said she'd meet me at the Laundromat near our living quarters, which were villas, some of which were occupied by vacationers not participating in the Elderhostel. While waiting for the washer cycle to be completed, Polly had been describing the program to one of the women, a vacationer but not one of our group. When I walked into the Laundromat, this spritely woman spied my name badge and inquired:

"Oh, I see your badge! Are you one of those *elderly hostages*, too?!"

References

Cottin, Lou, 1979. *Elders in Rebellion: A Guide to Senior Activism* (Garden City, NY: Anchor Press).

Gross, Ronald & Beatrice, and Sylvia Seidman, 1978. *The New Old: Struggling for Decent Aging* (Garden City, NY: Anchor Press/ Doubleday Press).

Hyman, Mildred, 1989. *Elderhostels: The Students' Choice* (Santa Fe: Muir Publications/Norton & Co).

Lumsden, D. Barry, 1985. *The Older Adult As Learner: Aspects of Educational Gerontology* (Washington: Hemisphere Publs./Harper & Row).

Russell, Charles H., *et al.*, 1989. *Good News About Aging* (New York: John Wiley & Sons).

Russell, Charles H., and Inger Megaard, 1988. *The General Social Survey, 1972-1986: The State of the American People* (New York: Springer-Verlag).

Schwed, Peter, 1977. *Hanging in There! How to Resist Retirement from Life and Avoid Being Put Out to Pasture* (Boston: Houghton Mifflin).

PREFACE

If current demographic assumptions are correct, the number of academics retiring or contemplating retirement between 1994 and 2004 will greatly exceed any past figure and may well exceed any future figure for a single decade.

There are three principal reasons for this phenomenon:

First, the rather massive cohort of college and university academic personnel brought on in the 1955-1964 decade to bolster an exploding higher education establishment — these graying faculty and staff are now entering the zone of "normal" retirement age.

Second, under federal statutes, all institution-imposed mandatory retirement age policies become illegal as of January 1, 1994, rendering retirement age for all academics a matter of personal choice.

Third, current pressing environmental factors complicate that personal choice — an uncertain economy; the increasing longevity of both men and women and hence a genuine prospect for a second career, paid or unpaid; Social Security regulations about to postpone "full retirement age" beyond 65; volatile Medicare policies and federal/state tax laws; changing financial vehicles for retirement savings and payouts; individual, institutional, and government restlessness over the control and management of pension assets — all adding up to an erosion of convention regarding retirement norms, leaving many senior faculty and staff somewhat at sea without a rudder, so to speak.

The unprecedented percentage of older people in the general population has given rise to an outpouring of advice for present and potential retirees from a wide range of professional and amateur individuals and agencies. Yet the experiences, motivations, and needs of academic personnel are sufficiently unique that generalizations about retirement in the broad — why, when, where, and how — don't quite fit the campus climate.

Hence, this handbook, written for senior academic faculty and staff by one of your own.

Based on wide-ranging conversations with academic types around the country, on the latest pinpoint research, on a thorough literature review, and on personal experience, *Retirement 901* addresses concisely the five generic concerns agitating any academic approaching retirement:

- Determining an optimal retirement age
- Ensuring an adequate income stream

- Providing for continuing, affordable health care
- Developing abiding activities for self-fulfillment
- Planning and putting together a graceful retirement picture

Among the more common sentiments of retirees is this: "Oh, if I only had known then what I know now!" Meaning that prompt preparation is the *sine qua non* of a successful life after campus days are over. While this "survey course" can't provide highly individualized answers to what is after all a highly personal process, it is confidently an intensely practical guide to what questions to ask, what options to consider, what pitfalls to avoid, and what aspirations to harbor.

The "quickie quizzes" at the close of each chapter will help focus your attention on important procedures, and the references and recommended readings alone may be worth the "seminar fee."

One of the reviewers of this book in manuscript form was John Disinger, professor, School of Natural Resources, The Ohio State University. His broad-ranging comments and confessions illuminate its principal points:

> The most helpful feature of this book is the clear identification of topics of appropriate concern to the potential retiree; that is, what are the particular items of which he/she is obligated to become aware in his/her enlightened self-interest. Since I personally am at the age (nearly 62) where my own retirement is somewhere near but not yet scheduled, I need to know what I need to know. You have identified them chapter and verse.
>
> Another helpful feature: You have avoided pronouncements of the "Now hear this, this is it, gang!" variety. Rather, your recurring refrain — "These are generalizations; your individual case may be, and probably is, different" — is initially frustrating, but ultimately revelatory.
>
> As I read the manuscript, I found myself wishing that you would take me by the the hand and tell me what always works. But it is clear that nothing always works. However, the options — the choices — you present clearly.
>
> I've found nothing that contradicts my personal knowledge and experience. I will, however, check back at intervals after my retirement to find out if you advised me well. If you did not, you will hear from me loud and clear.
>
> What's missing? Nothing of which I'm aware. What's superfluous? Nothing.
>
> Nothing in your draft is inappropriate or offensive. Quite the contrary.

> This is a very fine piece of work. It should be accessible to all faculty, including many younger than me. Though I have made some efforts at developing a retirement nest egg for some time, I do wish that I had taken it a bit more seriously — and put more into it — in my younger days.
>
> More importantly, I think that all of us need to decide what we are going to do, how we will spend our time productively and enjoyably, as we get older; I am only now beginning to address that one. I do know some retirees who literally have nothing to do, and it clearly is not good for them or anyone who knows them.
>
> I didn't start thinking about post-retirement activities until quite recently, and now I'm attempting to make up for lost time — thanks to *Retirement 901*.

In addition to Professor Disinger, for invaluable professional counsel and technical assistance I'm vastly indebted to the following people:

Chapter 1: W. Lee Hansen, University of Wisconsin-Madison professor of economics, member of the American Association of University Professors Committee on Retirement, and co-editor, *The End of Mandatory Retirement* (San Francisco: Jossey-Bass, 1989); the late Richard M. Millard, president emeritus, the Council on Postsecondary Accreditation.

Chapter 2: William Haight III, publisher, Magna Publications; W. Lee Hansen; Ron J. Konkol, Social Security Administration staff specialist; Charles O. Kroncke, dean, School of Management, University of Texas-Dallas; John R. Pike, former Wisconsin Investment Board executive director; Richard Ranney, Indiana investment company executive and advisor to universities; Myron Stevens, attorney of counsel.

Chapter 3: Maurice Kiley, Illinois insurance company executive and consultant to state and federal governments; Earl Thayer, former executive director, Wisconsin Medical Society; Dr. David T. Watts, clinical professor of geriatrics, University of Wisconsin Hospital and Clinics.

Chapter 4: James A. Fosdick, emeritus professor of journalism and mass communication, University of Wisconsin-Madison; and Polly Fosdick.

All Chapters: Larry D. Clark, dean, College of Arts and Science, University of Missouri-Columbia; Robert Dick, recently retired community development communications specialist, University of Wisconsin System Extension, and Lois Dick; John Disinger, professor, School of Natural Resources, The Ohio State University; Robert J. Griffin, professor, Marquette University College of Communication, Journalism, and Performing Arts; William E. Haight II, retired professor of mass communication, Michigan State University; John C. Hendee, dean, College of Forestry, Wildlife, and Range Sciences, University of Idaho; John Long, retired adjunct professor of English, Loyola University; Magna Publications editorial staff: Marilyn Annucci, Charles Bryan, Doris Green, Robert Magnan, and Mary Lou Santovec; Robert F. Meier, chair, sociology, Iowa State University; Dayle Molen, emeritus professor of journalism, California State University-Fresno; Rudolf J. H. Schafer, recently retired environmental education staff specialist, California State Department of Education; Sheryl Stateler Smith, government bulletins technical editor; and Wilson B. Thiede, emeritus outreach provost, University of Wisconsin System.

CS

Madison, WI

November 1992

1

Answering the Big Question: When Should I Retire?

Faculty Retirement Norms

Conventional age in academia, end of mandatory retirement, and factors influencing your timing.

The Three "Triple-A" Essentials

Adequate income stream, affordable health care, and activities for self-fulfillment.

Making Prompt Preparations

Retirement planning — why, when, and how? Check your attitude.

Quickie Quiz

References

"Trust yourself. ... You know more than you think you do. ... Don't take too seriously all that the neighbors say. Don't be overawed by what the experts say. Don't be afraid to trust your own common sense." Aren't those comforting words of advice? Recognize them? If you're a member of what's called "the GI generation," you probably read them some 40 years ago. That's how Dr. Benjamin Harrison Spock began his famous best-seller, *Common Sense Baby and Child Care* (1946).

Dr. Spock was the uncontested guru of that whole generation, vastly simplifying the problems of parenting. No matter what the puzzlement, Dr. Spock proclaimed, wait a minute in confidence and they'll go away. Sure enough, most of them actually did.

Now, some 40 years later, that same generation — and their "baby boomer" progeny — perceive a new set of puzzlement. So we seek new handy-dandy guidebooks in the style of Dr. Spock. There aren't many on the market.

As you're well aware, barring love, war, and taxes, no topic so intrigues today's print journalists, paperback authors, and prime-time commentators as that congeries of problems and possibilities known, precisely or not, as "the graying of America." Unfortunately, unlike Dr. Spock, all those savants seem to take a savage delight in trying to make any journey over the hill an enormously complicated trip.

An example:

My public library branch has just inaugurated a new shelf (between "Automotive Care" and "Seven-Day Fiction") labeled "Senior Citizen Reading." It features a hard-cover tome, as hefty as an unabridged dictionary, titled *Complete Guide to the Golden Years*. The first word of its first chapter is (so help me) "Whereas." To go on from there, you need a lawyer for a translator.

It doesn't have to be that way, least of all for past or present denizens of campuses, familiar with cogent lecture outlines, tested laboratory protocol, self-governing agendas, computerized purchasing procedures, and so on. Without eschewing the presentation of essential data, we propose to make this guide as pragmatic and lively as its topic.

Let's start out with a quote from a latter-day Dr. Spock (no, not that Star Trek Spock):

> What's the 'turnover' point in your retirement picture? At that point, taking all factors into consideration, there is no reason for continuing to work.

> I see the retirement picture in terms of control and options. That is to say, the ideal is to have a comfortable degree of control over one's life, and a reasonable range of options which might be exercised.
>
> For example, let's say I would like to go to Alaska and do some back country hiking and fishing. What factors would determine whether or not I could do so? Physical health and condition; legal, professional, and social constraints and entanglements; finances; and perhaps other factors would enter into the picture.
>
> Obviously, if I were wheel-chair bound with a bad heart condition, dependent on relatives, and had little or no income, I would not have sufficient control over my life or resources to exercise the Alaska option. On the other hand, if I had an adequate income stream, were in good health, and sought outdoor recreation for self-fulfillment, I'd call my travel agent right away.
>
> Isn't that what retirement's all about — balancing restraints and opportunities? (Schafer 1992)

So writes Rudolph J. H. Schafer, a fellow retiree from academe in California. Schafer may have distilled the whole discussion of retirement down to its nub. But on the hunch that there's worthwhile detail to add, here goes.

For years the vast majority — at least 85% — of America's institutions of higher education have had a mandatory retirement age for their faculty and staff. Then, in a series of Age Discrimination in Employment acts and amendments beginning in 1967, the federal Congress began to look askance at the practice, culminating in a 1986 law proscribing mandatory retirement on the basis of age as of Jan. 1, 1994.

As a matter of fact, according to information from the American Council on Education (Luke 1992), legislatures have already "uncapped" all colleges and universities in nine states, and all public colleges and universities in another 13 states. (Readers will know if they're in one of those 22 states or in a state contemplating eliminating mandatory retirement in advance of the federal deadline.)

So faculty and staff can now begin to exercise uninhibited freedom of choice over the age at which they retire — at least so far as institutional rules are concerned. Which leads to a number of questions hitherto unposed by academics.

FACULTY RETIREMENT NORMS

What's Been the Conventional Age of Retirement?

Surveying country-wide some 100 colleges and universities offering at least the baccalaureate, Pennsylvania State University scholars Michael J. Dooris and G. Gregory Lozier (1991) found that the average age of faculty at retirement in the period 1982-1988 was 64. That figure differed only very slightly whether an institution had a mandatory retirement age of 65 (63.8) or of 70 (64.3), whether the institution was independent (65.3) or public (63.5), whether the institution was baccalaureate (63.5), comprehensive (63.6), or doctoral (64.3), whether the institution had a defined-benefit retirement plan (63.1) or a defined-contribution program (65.3), whether the institution was in the Northeast or Midwest (64 and 64.9, respectively) or in the South or West (63.6 and 63.2, respectively), or whether in that time frame an institution had changed its mandatory retirement age from 65 to 70 (63.8 to 63.8) or from 65 to none (64.7 to 63.6).

Surveying 518 retired faculty from those same institutions, Dooris and Lozier found that for a full 80% of the respondents any mandatory retirement age was not a significant factor in their decision when to retire, but that 17% indicated they might have stayed on if mandatory retirement policies had not been in effect.

"Who are the people among us with the most experience in solving unprecedented problems, the people most likely to have seen more of the world, mastered or at least dabbled in more specialties, learned to distinguish the candor from the cant, the people with the most time for reflection and the most to reflect about? The answer leaps to the eye: They are, on the average, those who have lived longer." — Harland Cleveland, *The Knowledge Executive* (New York: Truman Talley, 1985)

The Teachers Insurance and Annuity Association/College Retirement Equities Fund (TIAA-CREF 1990) found that, among their annuitants who retired in 1988, 42.7% were under age 65, 25.6% were 65, 19.2% were between 66 and 69, and 12.4% started their annuities at 70 or later.

A special committee on academic retirement (Hammond and Morgan, 1991) reported to the National Research Council in 1991 that "few faculty at uncapped institutions choose to continue working past age 70, ... and in Florida the average retirement age for all university employees (the state retirement system cannot separate data on faculty) has remained remarkably stable at around age 63 since the state eliminated mandatory retirement in 1976."

In an even more recent survey of 19,000 retirees from 120 institutions, the National Association of College and University Business Officers (NACUBO) and TIAA-CREF (1991) found that 49% had retired before

65, 24% at age 65, 15% between ages 66 and 69, and 5% over 70.

All of these recent data merely confirm the prediction made by Karen C. Holden and W. Lee Hansen (1989) in the classic studies they assembled indicating that in academe "uncapping the mandatory retirement age is unlikely to alter retirement age by much." How do these retirement-age data from academe compare with data from out there in "the real world"? Says Mark Hayworth, professor of gerontology and sociology at the University of Southern California's Andrus Gerontology Center: "The average age of retirement (among American workers) now stands at a little above 60. ... The trend toward earlier retirement should continue in the 1990s. It is fed by the greater availability of pension programs, more working spouses, and greater accumulation of household wealth (1992)."

David Wise, professor of political economy at Harvard University's Kennedy School of Government, is even more ebullient. He estimates that about 75% of the workers in private-sector companies with guaranteed pension plans retire before age 62, and some often well before that (Davis 1992). But academics tend not to be so eager to quit.

So, for what it's worth, if you want to go with the flow of the data, you'll retire between the ages of 60 and 68. But remember, there's now no rule that says so.

What Factors Have Seemed to Influence Retirees in the Past?

While retirement is a very personal decision, you may find it helpful to know what factors are reported to have influenced retirement decisions for colleagues who've preceded you.

Dooris and Lozier, surveying in 1987-88 those 518 retired faculty representing 101 public and private baccalaureate, comprehensive, and doctoral colleges and universities literally from Maine to California, asked them to rate on a six-point Likert scale the importance of 18 factors in their decision to retire — when and how. (The average faculty retirement age at the institutions surveyed ranged from 62.7 to 64.7; the age span among respondents at the time of the survey was from 55 to 70-plus.)

Here are the results of the survey

(6 = very important, 1 = not important):

Overall financial status	4.4
Eligibility for full retirement benefits	4.4
Desirability of more personal/family time	4.1
Other interests	3.5

(6 = very important, 1 = not important):

Working conditions or policies	2.9
Availability of early retirement incentive benefits	2.6
Personal health	2.5
Annual salary increases	2.2
Availability of emeritus benefits	2.2
Mandatory retirement policies	2.1
Other employment opportunities, including self-employment	2.0
Health of a spouse	1.9
Administrative pressure	1.8
State of the economy	1.8
Interaction with co-workers	1.7
Budget cutbacks	1.7
Curricular revisions	1.6
Timing of spouse's retirement	1.5

(The researchers might have posed other options; for example, "Perceived burnout" or "Research grants expired," but it's unlikely that such insertions would have changed the overall expressions.)

As you can see, money seems to talk: the two most important factors influencing avowed retirement decisions on the part of the faculty cohort were related to finances. So, if your overriding concern in arriving at a "when and how" decision is your financial condition upon retirement, you've got a lot of company.

Interestingly enough, when the researchers examined their data in more detail, they found that

- for one-fifth of the respondents, the three most highly rated factors weren't important at all;
- 17% indicated they would have stayed on the payroll indefinitely if mandatory retirement had been uncapped at the time;
- "working conditions and policies" figured heavily in the decision of faculty in agriculture and library science;
- female faculty, regardless of discipline, were more likely than males to indicate that working conditions and policies were key factors affecting their retirement decisions;
- and early retirement incentive benefits were the most important factor for over 20% of the cohort.

If you're feeling tired and ready to quit, you're simply in tune with the times, says Harvard economist Juliet Schor (1991). Americans are working longer hours than they used to — a month's worth of hours more than just 20 years ago, according to Schor's research. She doesn't say so, but "get ahead" academics may be among the leading workaholics.

As we say, retirement is a very personal affair, with different strokes for different folks. While it's nice to know how the rest of the world thinks, you shouldn't allow any sort of peer pressure to warp your own individual approach to one of the most important decisions of your life.

If somebody suggests that aging faculty tend to "run out of gas," you can quote from a 1992 study to the contrary.

Assuming teaching effectiveness can be measured by student evaluations — and a growing body of data says that's true — then in most disciplines at a representative research university, senior faculty don't seem to lose their edge.

As a matter of fact, scores actually improve for professors in the humanities and the social sciences as they approach retirement age. It is only in the biological and physical sciences that evaluations decline with age, and then only marginally.

According to researchers at Ohio State University, "It appears that the impending uncapping of retirement age for tenured faculty raises no major concerns for dramatic deterioration in teaching effectiveness in an aging professoriate. ... Such concerns are unfounded" (Kinney and Smith 1992).

A recent Associated Press story confirms this research ("Age Appears No Barrier to Leadership: Studies Find Chronological Age Not Good Predictor of Job Performance," June 8, 1992). The story quotes two university researchers: one at Eastern Montana College who found no significant differences in leadership capabilities among 1,600 young and old managers in 17 varied organizations; the other at Pennsylvania State University who found public safety might actually be enhanced by encouraging experienced public service officers to stay on the job rather than retire.

What Handwriting Do You Read on the Wall?

Environmental factors, both institutional and personal, may impinge on your freedom of choice.

- Oscar M. Ruebhausen speculates about some of the forces that may be at work on you:

- You may yearn for new challenges, a new career, a new climate, or even new colleagues.
- You may wish to retire not because you think you have lost competence, but because you have achieved that measure of psychological security, economic independence, and personal dignity that enables you to say, "I don't want to be bossed any more" — not by provosts, deans, colleagues, or students.

On the other hand, as Ruebhausen points out:

- Students may cease to sign up for your classes or seminars.
- Your research grant funds may run dry.
- There may no longer be calls for your institutional, professional, or public services.
- Your area of expertise may decline in relevance.
- You may be disinclined to adapt to high-tech classrooms, laboratories, libraries, or offices.
- A static or declining financial condition at your institution may cry out for staff reductions, or room could be made on the roster for persons of greater professional potential, for women, for minorities, or for younger people (Ruebhausen, 1990).
- After hearing from 1,500 retired academics, Mario A. Milletti reports that while most of them are comparatively well off, in good health, and satisfied with retirement, others wish they had delayed retirement to better confront inflation and the high cost of prolonged illness (Milletti 1989).

- John W. Creswell *et al.*, after interviewing a large cross section of department chairs, lists such signs that indicate readiness for retirement from active campus careers:
  - Dissatisfaction with work roles or assignments — "There was very little professional will left in this individual."
  - Lack or loss of enthusiasm, getting stale, or suffering burnout — "He started to come to the campus late and withdrew into himself."
  - Performing minimal duties, doing only what crosses their desks — "This person taught classes and that's about all he did."
  - Negative attitude — "He was perceived by others as not having a positive attitude; a chip on his shoulder all the time (Creswell 1990)."

- Claiming that "recent studies show faculty members beyond 60 often ... taper off as scholars," Dean Mary P. Richards suggests ways department chairs can nudge older professors into retirement:
  - Trot out any available early-retirement incentives.
  - Talk about the joys of extracurricular activities.
  - Discuss arrangements for continued informal associations.
  - Play hardball in merit reviews.
  - Enlist a neutral person to handle terminal negotiations.

Any senior faculty member experiencing this sort of massaging will recognize the handwriting on the wall for sure (Richards 1992).

- Robert Boice, director of the faculty instructional support office and professor of psychology at SUNY-Stony Brook, after surveying department chairs, lists these characteristics of some aging professors: inactivity as scholars; shirk committees, student advising; opposition to department functioning; social isolation from colleagues; unfriendliness toward chair; source of student complaints; explosive with colleagues/students; suspicious/paranoid behavior.

While some of these attributes may be solely in the mind of your chair, if you suspect in any way you're guilty, maybe it's time to sign out (Boice 1992).

- On the other hand, you may be recognized as a late bloomer whose spirit belies your age. At 69 you're at the peak in perception, and you don't want to leave either the work you still can do well or the perks that go along with professing. You want to quit while you're ahead, but you don't think now's quite the time.
- Above all, the relative generosity of many pension programs, increasing longevity, the growing public recognition that "senior citizens aren't out of it," multiplying cases of working spouses contributing to wherewithal — all conspire to prove there can be life after academe — provided you don't let any perceived sudden loss of status get you down.

As Jack Nicklaus, legendary golf pro, once said, "I know when it is I want to quit — but I'm not sure I'll recognize it when I get there."

The trick is to read the handwriting on the wall — the good, the bad, the indifferent — and respond accordingly. (For more information on this topic, you might want to read Albert Rees' and Sharon Smith's *Faculty Retirement in the Arts and Sciences,* 1991.

THE THREE "TRIPLE-A" ESSENTIALS

To an extent as surprising as it is gratifying, both empirical and anecdotal data agree on the basic considerations that make the difference between a satisfying retirement and one fraught with frustrations. I'll introduce them here in general terms, then examine them in more detail in the proceeding chapters.

Adequate Income Stream

There is, of course, no precise income stream volume that will meet the goal of each retiring faculty/staff member. There are, however, some principles that the Commission on College Retirement concludes are basic to the achievement of your pension goal:

First, a pension plan should provide income for the lifetimes of you and your spouse.

Second, a pension plan should provide income that, when added to other sources of support available to the family, allows you to maintain a standard of living comparable to that which you enjoyed immediately prior to retirement. Social Security benefits, spousal earnings, savings, and income from other assets are all important contributors to your retirement income security.

Third, a pension plan for college and university personnel should be portable; that is, notwithstanding job changes, any pension plan of which you are the beneficiary should follow you into any new position without any penalty.

Fourth, a pension plan should provide you with reasonable flexibility in the selection of (1) the managers to whom your funds are entrusted for investment, (2) the investment objectives for which your funds are invested, and (3) the agency(ies) that will provide your lifetime annuity.

Fifth, financial information and planning services should be available to help you make better decisions about the level, composition, investment, and payout of core pension accumulations (Ruebhausen 1990).

Those five Commission standards constitute one ideal against which you can measure your own pension program status. If your situation falls short in some regards, you may or may not have the time or the latitude to effect improvements, but at least now you know what to look at.

Any readers interested in a more detailed "statement of principles on academic retirement and insurance plans" may consult the document by that name first published by the American Association of University

Professors and the Association of American Colleges in 1950, revised in 1958, 1969, 1980, and, more recently, 1988.

Harvard's Wise warns that the bloom of retirement and leisure can fade in the face of economic realities, forcing retirees to take another job, usually part-time and typically paying about half what the old position did — if insurance plans are less than satisfactory.

He warns particularly about the lure of "golden parachute" buy-outs — early retirement incentives. A lump-sum payment that seems large at the time may be quite inadequate when averaged over the remaining years of a retiree's life. Given rising life expectancy, that period can be quite extended.

Lee Cuba, a Massachusetts sociologist studying retirement patterns on Cape Cod, sounds much the same note: For all too many people, the euphoria of retirement is followed by the shock of discovering that they're unable to do the things they always dreamed of doing when retired.

Worse, it may not even be possible to maintain the lifestyle they had when employed. They borrowed against pension plans to educate the kids; then when they go to retire they find themselves with no assets and a big debt to pay off.

So, when do you retire? At the point in your economic life when work becomes optional (Davis 1992).

(*For a full discussion of the economics of retirement, see Chapter 2.*)

Affordable Health Care

Security in retirement is more than a recurring monthly income. It is also the ability to meet highly unpredictable costs stemming from illness and/or a need for long-term care.

In all likelihood, nothing in your spectrum of retirement concerns is surrounded with so much uncertainty as this topic, and much of that uncertainty is beyond your control.

At a minimum, here are some questions you ought to be asking:

- Can I continue to be a member of the group health insurance plan(s) which covers me before retirement? Can a surviving spouse?
- Will my institution contribute all or any premium costs, or will I be on my own?
- Will my coverage erode? Could stringent cost-containment strategies by health insurance companies lead to curtailments in actual coverage?

- Will my coverage be portable or will it be restricted to a site-specific HMO?
- Can I supplement my basic medical and hospital coverage with specialized policies? Should I?
- To what extent will Medicare help?
- Will my campus help alleviate the health care cost/benefit crunch? Will the problem finally be solved through some form of a national health care/health insurance system?
- Will Medicaid come to my rescue?
- What about long-term care through a hospice service or in a nursing home?
- Assuming I'm well covered in terms of insurance, will adequate-to-excellent medical and hospital care be available?

As you can see, when it comes to health care, it can be a jungle out there. But judicious planning can help meet your requirements. (For more on this topic, you might want to read Mark Blum's "The Health Care Conundrum," in *Academe*, May-June 1991, pp. 13-15.)

However you view your health care situation, you need to plan. Health care costs are escalating at an alarming rate, due in part to new diagnostic and treatment interventions, many of them the fruits of university laboratory and hospital research.

A simple example: An X-ray costs about $75, magnetic resonance imagery (MRI) about $1,300. Yet no self-respecting doctor today would decline to use advanced MRI. Besides, the patient doesn't care; insurance picks up the tab.

It may be impossible to curb health care costs without also limiting new technologies that can enhance human health and well-being, says William R. Schwartz, physician and health policy analyst at Tufts University Medical School. According to Schwartz:

> Cuts in waste and inappropriate care are not great enough to keep up with the health care system's relentless 5%-a-year cost increases after inflation attributed to technology and other factors. If you want to fully exploit the revolution in biomedical research, you've got to pay the price (Rich 1992).

The net result to you and me: it'll cost more and more money to keep us going.

(*For a full discussion of health care issues, see Chapter 3.*)

Abiding Activities for Self-Fulfillment

Fruitful and rewarding retirement calls for more than an adequate, steady income stream — more than the maintenance of physical health or the ability to meet the potentially catastrophic costs of long-term care. Essential to you — and important for your fellow human beings — is the maintenance of your sense of identity, dignity, and self-worth.

Nothing can be so destructive as a sudden loss of status. One day you're Doctor, Professor, Dean, Assistant to the Associate Provost, or whatever; the next day you're just SSN 393-03-5705. One day you're shouting, "I'm free at last!" The next, you're wallowing in aimless idleness.

It doesn't have to be that way. Through imaginative planning and active pursuit, you can be all you want to be in terms of continued activity.

For example, you and your institution can team up to help preserve your sense of status and mutually beneficial contributions. Consider the following suggestions of the Commission on College Retirement:

- Continue part-time in your department or office
- Participate in ongoing research programs
- Perform in an area different from your preretirement career
- Teach or administer at another college or university
- Present noncredit or retiree courses and seminars
- Act as a consultant to your office or a related office
- Serve as a campus spokesperson to campus constituencies
- Work with student groups (Ruebhausen 1990)

But your fulfilling activities needn't be linked to your former or a similar institution. Indeed, you may find it exhilarating to turn your back, on your old haunts and march breast forward, like Tennyson's Ulysses, to "sail beyond the sunset, and the baths of all the western stars, ... strong of will, to strive, to seek, to find, and not to yield" to any thought or suggestion that you're "over the hill."

Retirees are right to be prepared for a future outside the culture and support system of academe to which they're accustomed, according to Steven Berglas, a psychologist at McLean Hospital in Belmont, Massachusetts:

> Retirement is seen as a reward for competency and prior service, but some retirees don't consider the consequent depression that can set in when they're no longer manifesting that competency.

> The two factors for well-being are love or respect and self-esteem, and retirees often feel deprived of respect when they stop producing. They've lost power and the feedback of someone saying, "Hey, you did a good job!" They start demanding from a spouse the gratification they got from working and burden the hell out of her or him).
>
> Berglas advises retirees to make a gradual transition from full-time work to total retirement: "Move into a mentoring role of some sort or find a skill-based avocation, something where you're manifesting competence" (Davis 1992).

About one-third of older employees who choose early retirement rather than looking for a new job regret their decision within the first six months, according to Challenger, Gray & Christmas, a Chicago-based outplacement firm that reports early retirees often become bored and miss co-workers.

Say the editors of *Parade Magazine* in their July 26, 1992, issue under a "Rethinking Retirement" headline: "Never having to work again might seem like a dream come true, but it's the attitude that sours most quickly once a person has retired."

One reviewer comments, "Don't be surprised if your approach to retirement evolves over time. At first you may be intent on hanging on to your campus 'security blanket.' Later on you'll be only too happy to shove off."

Perhaps Harlan Cleveland, University of Minnesota Emeritus Dean of the Hubert H. Humphrey Institute of Public Affairs, has it right:

> The very word "retirement" is obsolete. It implies withdrawal. We need a new word; for lack of a better one, I suggest the phrase Alan Pifer and others have been trying to popularize: "The third stage of life."
>
> (By outlawing mandatory retirement) Congress has declared retirement to be a social disease. Congress, reflecting what must be an overwhelming national concensus, has by unanimous vote started a complicated process of eradicating it.

Cleveland points out that Matilda White Riley, an emeritus professor of sociology, has called retirement "a socially constructed phase of life — certainly not a 'natural phenomenon'" — and predicts that increasing numbers of older faculty members will continue fruitful careers into a period that can extend to approximately one-quarter of their adult lives (1987).

At its worst, retirement — that third stage of life — can be like the running down of a tired clock. At its best, it can approach or be the best years of your life. The choice is almost entirely yours.

(*Chapter 4 suggests a dozen-plus tested azimuths for you to consider.*)

MAKING PROMPT PREPARATIONS

Let's eavesdrop on a conversation between two fairly young women in either an OOM (Officers Open Mess) or an NCOC (Non-Commissioned Officers Club) on any Army post in the U.S. Asks one soldier of the other, "How many do you have?" The reply: "Six." (Translation: "Six years until retirement after 30 years of service.")

Now let's eavesdrop on a conversation between two relatively young investment bankers in a restaurant among Wall Street skyscrapers. Asks one of the other, "How many do you have?" The reply, "Six hundred." (Translation: "Six hundred units of a thriving stock annuity fund.")

And now let's eavesdrop on a conversation between two fairly young chemistry professors in a campus student union cafeteria.

Asks one, "How many do you have?" The reply: "Six." (Translation: "Six Ph.D.-candidate research assistants or six teaching assistants for a large lecture course."

For some reason or other, unlike people in other pursuits academicians either tend to make few plans for the morrow or tend not to talk about them much if they do.

Why this should be so, we can only speculate. For one thing, professors may be so single-mindedly devoted to their teaching, research, and service responsibilities that they subordinate personal concerns. Or, more likely, because they never went into academia for money anyway, they may somehow think simply that the fates will provide. Perhaps by osmosis, academic staff seem to acquire somewhat the same *gestalt*, although not to the same degree.

Whatever, many seem to have an aversion to contemplating retirement, much less to engaging in much retirement planning.

And that's unfortunate. But in your own case you can address that tendency.

Why Is Retirement Planning So Important?

As the Commission on College Retirement reports: Planning is vital to the faculty/staff member in order to prepare for the post-retirement years, to organize a life of reduced stress, to launch a new career, or to take advantage of other opportunities for personal growth and enjoyment. With planning, for example, faculty/staff members can maximize their post-retirement income stream, arrange for available and affordable health care, and fully develop opportunities for desired continuing activity, paid or unpaid. ... Only with planning can there be reasonable assurance that retirement will, in fact, be a career change and not merely a cessation of activity (Ruebhausen 1990).

Career planning is certainly not alien to an academic. You plotted your early stages — what courses to take as an undergraduate, where to do your graduate work and under whom, what research area to concentrate on and what dissertation topic to select, what type of institution to join as an assistant professor or staff member, and so on. Winding down your college career should be the subject of equal planning.

As Confucius is often quoted, "One should be as careful at the end as at the beginning."

Incidentally, in that recent NACUBO/TIAA-CREF survey, retirees who reported they were "satisfied" with retirement were more likely than not to have thoroughly prepared.

When Should You Start Retirement Planning?

Ideally, a person should at least start thinking about the dimensions of retirement when he or she first recognizes that the present has a future — in the fourth grade, say, or certainly by the age of puberty.

All right, such a statement is both facetious and unrealistic. It's not unrealistic, however, to say that there comes a time well before any usual retirement age when it's the soul of practicality to look ahead and sketch out retirement strategies.

True, the longer you wait the more accurately you'll be able to estimate that crucial "replacement ratio" — how much of your preretirement annual income you'll need to replace with retirement income in order to maintain your standard of living. And the longer you wait the less likely you'll be so consumed by thinking about retirement that you divert yourself from what's going on in some of the best years of your career.

On the other hand, the longer you postpone retirement planning, the less opportunity you have to stockpile retirement /income, ensure continuing health care, and work out the details of self-fulfilling years to come. Indeed, tardy planning can lead to a debilitating final period of active duty.

A realistic age at which to begin serious retirement planning will vary considerably from person to person, of course, depending on an array of individual circumstances. But let's say that, on average, you should begin to get your ducks in order by age 55. At or about that age, with any luck, you'll have enough disposable income so that through investments you can influence significantly your retirement income stream. You'll have a grasp on health matters. You'll have maturing ideas about how and where you want to spend your time after leaving the campus, and an interval in which to start solid planning about how to turn those ideas into realities when retirement years arrive.

One reviewer remonstrates: "I think 55 is too late. I'd start planning when kids are ready to fly. The longer you plan and save, the better retirement will be."

The succeeding chapters will provide details on planning to meet your three essential retirement goals. But here let's foreshadow those coming chapters with some sage words of advice from Andrew Tobias on the when and how of retirement planning. "These are the basic rules," he says:

1. Start!
2. Save!
3. Invest under the shelter of a tax-deferred retirement account.
4. If you're young, invest in stocks.
5. Don't rush to put your money in the market when prices are high.
6. As retirement nears, begin to take less risk.
7. Don't get hung up on the fine points of saving. Just do it.
8. Don't put your savings someplace you'll later regret.
9. Stick to a plan. Becoming a nation of savers instead of a nation of spenders is one of the most important things we can do.
10. Volunteer your time now, when you're vigorous and healthy, in return for "time dollars" that will entitle you to assistance when you need it (Tobias 1992).

Alone, or Not?

With any luck, you won't be on your own in your retirement planning. More and more colleges and universities have developed or are developing enlightened counseling/assistance programs to help ease the transition from employment to retirement for their staff and faculty.

The National Association of College and University Business Officers suggests that such a program include these components:

- Workshops and informational sessions for staff and faculty members and their spouses
- Financial planning assistance
- Manuals outlining benefits and applicable taxes
- Communications with retirees through newsletters and invitations to campus events
- Organizations for retirees
- Continued relations between current and retired staff and faculty (TIAA-CREF 1991)

Check it out with your institution's personnel/benefits office. You may be pleasantly surprised at the advice available. If there's none, perhaps you could help energize a reform effort.

There's certainly plenty of room for improvement. In the recent NACUBO/TIAA-CREF survey, only about 23% of all retirees responding said that they had received exit counseling from their colleges and universities.

Some institutions don't do much of a job of keeping track of their former employees, says Professor Thomas Blank of the University of Connecticut's School of Family Studies: "There's a sort of corporate conservatism that says, 'If we don't find out, we won't have to do anything about it and we won't have to tell anybody.' "

There's the other extreme, of course — the perpetual pleas to pledge to a capital fund drive to replace Old Main Hall. One of my senior colleagues, feeling all tapped out, finally wrote "Deceased" on one such envelope and sent it back. His "heirs" got a nice letter of condolence from the head of the campus foundation — and the suggestion that they set up a scholarship fund.

There's growing evidence, however, that at least some institutions are providing counseling for their senior personnel. For example, at Oregon State University in spring 1992, staff and faculty contemplating retirement could attend a series of seminars on "Preparing to Retire in the Next Few Years," "Long-Term Health Care Insurance," "Tax-Deferred Investments," and "Tenure Relinquishment."

(*Succeeding chapters will discuss all four topics.*)

Half Empty or Half Full?

The strategies and tactics — and certainly the attitudes — you bring to planning for and pulling off your retirement can depend a good deal on your view of your world and where it's going; in other words, on whether you see the glass as half empty or half full.

It's easy to summon up pessimistic data:

- The economy has grown at a puny 0.5% since 1988.
- Housing starts in 1991 reached their lowest point since 1945.
- Between June 1990 and December 1991, total employment dropped nationally by more than 3 million jobs.
- In 1980, America received $29 billion in net income from its overseas investments; by 1989, payments to foreign holders of U.S. assets exceeded receipts from U.S. foreign investments by more than $900 million.
- The income of the median family grew 111% in real terms between 1947 and 1973; it grew by only 8% in the period from 1973 to 1990.
- The violent crime rate rose from 364 to 732 per 100,000 people from 1970 to 1990.
- The number of inmates in federal and state prisons rose from 212,953 in 1960 to 680,809 in 1989.
- The number of single-parent-with-children families rose 25% between 1980 and 1989.
- The U.S. infant mortality rate is 16th among industrialized nations.
- Productivity growth increased nearly 3% annually from 1947 to 1970; since then growth has averaged only about 1%.
- The proportion of 25- to 29-year-olds who had completed college was lower in 1989 than in 1977.
- The upper class has been getting richer, the lower class poorer, the middle class stagnant (Dionne 1992).
- Federal debt amassed between 1978 and 1981: $1.1 trillion. Added since 1982: $3 trillion. Rate that debt was growing in mid-1992: $11,574 per second. Last budget surplus: 1969. Amount budgeted for interest on the debt in 1993: $315 billion. Portion of budget spent for interest on the debt, 21%. Portion for defense, 19% (*U.S. News & World Report*, June 22, 1992).

Enough already, you say. How about some optimistic data? OK:

- Housing prices may have risen, but the typical house now has more than twice as much living space as in 1950 — and fewer occupants.
- In 1971, only 35% of households had more than one car; now 53% do. Only 28% of us had more than one TV; now 71% do. Some 26% of

households now have personal computers, and 79% have VCRs; those products didn't exist in 1971.

- Between 1950 and 1970, median family income rose 89%; since then it's increased only 13%, but that's still a rise of one-seventh.
- About 31% of families now have incomes exceeding $50,000 (in 1990 dollars); that's up from 19% in 1970 — a 60% increase in two decades.
- Low mortgage rates today make housing more affordable than at any time since the 1970s.
- In 1940, more than one-fifth of the population still lived on farms, less than one-third of the farms had electric lights, and only one-tenth had a flush toilet.
- Among all Americans, more than half of the households didn't have a refrigerator and 58% lacked central heating in 1940.
- About 64% of Americans are homeowners now, up from 44% before 1941.
- Life has gotten easier in many ways — jet travel, air conditioning, interstate highways, direct long-distance dialing, automatic washers and dryers, antibiotics — all postwar developments.
- Beyond these material gains, postwar society represents a major advance in four ways: more economic stability, less discrimination, alleviation of suffering among the old and the poor (from 9% of the population covered by health insurance in 1940 to 87% in 1989), more open avenues to higher education (from 7% of 20-to 24-year-olds in school in 1940 to 27% in 1989) (Samuelson 1992).

What tea leaves you read and how you read them can affect whether you're a worrywart, a cockeyed optimist, or something in between. For example, recent polls indicate that people old enough to have experienced the Great Depression tend to see recessions deepening and the U.S. economy in serious decline. "Their memories make them very sensitive because they understand how Social Security and Medicare rely on a productive economy," says Deborah Chollett, a Georgia State University economist. "They worry about what awaits their children and grandchildren." Polls also suggest that members of the baby boomer generation can have quite different attitudes. Perhaps because they've never felt any really hard knocks, they tend not to be so shaken up by doomsday soundbites on TV (Vilbig 1992).

Whatever your own faith and fashion, they can play a part in determining how you face providing for those three essentials for a successful retirement: adequate income stream, affordable health care, and self-fulfilling activities. I wouldn't presume to suggest what stance you ought to take, but I will suggest that you acknowledge frankly and honestly where you're coming from and how that may impact on your decision-making. There's no fun in fooling yourself!

Quickie Quiz

Use the last 15 minutes of this class time to write succinct answers to the following questions, and then turn in your papers to the proctor at the exit:

1. What is the "normal" retirement age at your institution?

2. Is there an overt institutional incentive program encouraging early retirement?

3. Are there any covert institutional constraints on postponing retirement?

4. Do you have an opportunity to continue part-time?

5. What are the advantages to you personally in retiring at 60 or earlier? At 62? At 65? At 70 or later? Disadvantages in each case?

6. How do you feel, deep down, about retiring?

7. If you're married, what is your spouse's attitude?

8. Have you made any retirement plans or are you drifting into it?

9. What handwriting do you read on your wall?

10. Do you really want to max this course, or just get by with a "C"?

References

Boice, Robert, 1992. "Problems Most Commonly Listed by Chair," *Academic Leader*, July, p. 2.

Cleveland, Harlan, 1987. "The Abolition of Retirement," *Change*, November/December, pp. 8-10.

Creswell, John W., *et al.*, 1990. *The Academic Chairperson's Handbook*, (Lincoln: University of Nebraska Press).

Davis, William A., 1992. "Early Retirement Means Second Career for Many," *Boston Globe*, July 19, p. 1A.

Dionne, E. J., Jr., 1992. "Lies, Damned Lies, and Politics," *The Washington Post National Weekly Edition*, Feb. 3-9, pp. 23-24.

Dooris, Michael J., and Gregory Lozier, 1991. *Faculty Retirement Projections Beyond 1994* (Boulder, CO: Western Interstate Commission for Higher Education).

Hammond, Brett P., and Harriet P. Morgan, Eds., 1991. *Ending Mandatory Retirement for Tenured Faculty: The Consequences for Higher Education* (Washington, DC: National Academy Press).

Hayworth, Mark, 1992. Quoted in Judith Waldrop, "Old Money," *American Demographics*, April, p. 26.

Holden, Karen C., and W. Lee Hansen, Eds., 1989. *The End of Mandatory Retirement: Effects of Higher Education*, New Directions for Higher Education #65, Spring (San Francisco: Jossey-Bass).

Kinney, D., and S. Smith, 1992. "Age and Teaching Performance," *Journal of Higher Education*, May-June, pp. 282-302.

Luke, Gina G., 1992. Personal correspondence in author's files, March 31.

Milletti, Mario A., 1989. *Voices of Experience: 1500 People Talk About Retirement* (New York: TIAA-CREF).

Rees, Albert, and Sharon Smith, 1991. *Faculty Retirement in the Arts and Sciences* (Princeton, NJ:Princeton University Press).

Rich, Spencer, 1992. "Is High Tech Medicine Too Pricey?" *The Washington Post National Weekly Edition*, July 20-26, p. 33.

Richards, Mary P., 1992. "Counseling Faculty Members About Retirement," *The Department Chair*, Spring, pp. 1, 15.

Ruebhausen, Oscar M., Ed., 1990. *Pension and Retirement Policies in Colleges and Universities* (San Francisco: Jossey-Bass).

Samuelson, Robert J., 1992. "How Our American Dream Unraveled," *Newsweek*, March 2, pp. 32-39.

Schaffer, Rudolph, J. H.,1992. Personal correspondence in author's files.

Schor, Juliet, 1991. *The Overworked American* (Bristol, VT: Basic Books).

TIAA-CREF, 1991. "The NACUBO/TIAA-CREF Survey of College and University Retirees," *Research Dialogues*, October.

TIAA-CREF, 1990. "Income and Other Factors in Delayed Retirement," *Research Dialogues*, January.

Tobias, Andrew, 1992. "Money: When to Start Planning and How," *Parade Magazine*, April 26, pp. 10-11.

U.S. News and World Report, 1992. "Money Clip," June 22, p. 25.

Vilbig, Peter, 1992. Maturity News Service, March 9.

2

Ensuring an Adequate Income Stream

Adopting a Philosophical Position

A starting point for successful financial planning.

Figuring Out How Much You're Going to Need

The good news and the bad.

Assessing Your Group Annuity(ies)

Retirement/Pension Plans, individual investment strategies, yearly retirement incentives, and other potential benefits.

Making Sense Out of Social Security

Answers to frequently posed questions, and other information.

Putting Frosting on the Cake with a TDA

Advantages, drawbacks, and how to read the ratings.

Collecting Collateral Perks

COLAs, cut rates, paid-up life insurance, liquidated mortgages, disappearing dependents, and spousal income.

Extending Your Career

Inspiring examples and helping hands on campus.

Cutting the Cost of Living

Generous advice on frugality.

Watching Out for Bulls and Bears

Still have some venture capital to play with?

Recognizing Taxes Shall Always Be With You

How to trigger an audit.

Taking Care of Kith and Kin

Trusts, lawyers and legacies, and estate planning.

Sifting and Winnowing Advice

Financial advice — the wheat vs. the chaff.

Some Benedictory Strategies

Pre-retirement do's, post-retirement do's, all-the-time do's.

Quickie Quiz

References

As common sense tells us and we've seen from the experiences of others, the bottom line in retirement planning lies in doing your very best to make sure you'll have the financial wherewithal to maintain — maybe even enhance — the scale of lifestyle to which you're accustomed or to which you aspire. Certainly you hope to avoid in your retirement years a sword of declining resources hanging over your head and/or that of your loved one(s).

So volatile are economic conditions over which we have little or no control, and so varied are individual circumstances, that it's impossible to make plans with scientific accuracy. But together we can sharpen the precision of your planning a good deal by making some reasonable assumptions and adhering to some sound principles.

ADOPTING A PHILOSOPHICAL POSITION

Douglas Osterheld, Emeritus Associate Vice President of the University of Wisconsin System, who has presided over considerable amounts of public and personal money, claims it is "painfully apparent how varied are the financial planning considerations affecting each individual." Still, he says he believes there are "four elements of 'a basic philosophical position' that each of us must resolve as we seek to relate 'personal conduct just before and during retirement life' to fiscal techniques":

1. An American ethic has generally been, for most of "the GI generation," one of accumulating resources over their employed lives. But retirement may call for varied strategies — not only of continuing to add to resources "in the form of investments that promise to cushion inflationary pressures but also of utilizing existing resources to augment annual income."
2. Each of us has a "comfort zone" — a necessary feeling of security that differs quite markedly for each of us and that dictates the level of risk-taking we can tolerate with respect to the amount of secure savings we require "in the bank" as well as the sort of "playing the market" we can indulge in. In turn, the level of risk-taking with venture capital each of us can handle with equanimity will "be dependent in part on the kind of annuity options we've chosen."
3. Are we going to plan to sequester reserves "for someone who will succeed us"? Or are we going to "spend down that which we've accumulated?" What we "intend to do for benefactors of our estate" will significantly affect our financial planning.
4. A starting point for any financial planning "must be the lifestyle you and your spouse will hope to achieve." This in turn will impinge on

the standard of living you want to have and where you want to live. And "any financial plan worthy of the name will reflect (a) the existence and persistence of inflation, and (b) the ever-increasing span of retirement years that must be covered.

In Osterheld's book, *Financial Planning for Retirement*, you can find five detailed worksheets that Osterheld says constitute the "guts" of your financial planning:

- comparative spendable income — now and in retirement,
- expenses now and in retirement,
- projected retirement cash flow,
- net worth,
- and five-year income projection beyond the initial retirement year, which could well be stretched to 10 years (Osterheld 1984).

(You'll find a simplified worksheet on estimated retirement income and costs at the end of this chapter under the "Quickie Quiz" section.)

With Osterheld's plea for a "philosophical position," University of Texas-Dallas School of Management Dean Charles O. Kroncke strongly concurs: "One cannot properly plan an economic future until the question of 'What will I be when I grow up?' is answered."

FIGURING OUT HOW MUCH YOU'RE GOING TO NEED

In the first year of your retirement, how much stable income are you going to require to meet your anticipated needs and/or wants?

Unless you're scandalously wealthy, that's a fundamental figure for you to determine as reasonably as possible. The further you are from your chosen retirement age, the less accurately you'll be able to estimate that figure; on the other hand, the more chances you may have to adjust that figure to fit changing circumstances.

Right now we have to set up a little scenario for illustrative purposes. It won't fit your situation exactly, but it will give you some ideas on how you can ensure your own adequate retirement income stream.

Here's what we're going to assume:

You're a full professor, age 55, who plans to retire at age 65. Your current academic-year salary is $50,000. You obviously aren't living high on the hog, but you aren't in financial straits either. So if you can retain the same relationship between income and outgo in the years ahead, you'll be OK.

To begin your planning, you have to guestimate what your annual base salary will be at age 65 in the final months of active duty 10 years from now.

First, look back and recall what your salary was 10 years ago when you were 45. Let's say it was $25,000. That means your salary has doubled in 10 years. Is it realistic to assume your salary will double again in the next 10 years to $100,000? Hardly. Remember, you were the happy recipient of some healthy boosts in those years, particularly when you moved from associate to full professor.

So, look ahead and assume that, given tightened economic conditions, you'll be lucky to receive only modest annual increases in the coming decade, making your salary $70,000 at age 65. That may be conservative or optimistic. Who knows?

Let's split the difference between the two approximations and say your final active-duty annual salary will be $85,000.

With that as a working figure, what will your income actually be in your first **post-retirement year?** Will that be enough to sustain your present lifestyle?

First, the Good News

If you're an average person, you won't need as much income in your initial retirement years as you do now to support the lifestyle to which you're accustomed as you do now. Financial-planning experts used to say two-thirds would do it; now they're more apt to say 75%-80%. Splitting the difference again would make your requisite initial retirement income about $62,000.

Why don't you need as much relative income in retirement as you do now? Principally because, with any luck, you'll be out from under some big-ticket expenditures that aren't apt to recur:

For instances:

- The mortgage on your residence could be all paid up.
- Your offspring could be out of college and independent.
- You may no longer be contributing to a savings plan.
- You could be in a lower tax bracket and/or some of your income could be tax-free.
- Any life insurance policies could be paid up.
- Commuting-to-work expenses are no more.

- Unless you change dimensions, clothing costs should take a nose-dive once you no longer have to look presentable day after day.
- You're finally home free from credit-card and other debts — maybe.
- You have an investment paying enough interest to cover the cost of a new car every few years — you hope.
- Other seldom-in-a-lifetime outlays could be past, never likely to return, such as a very expensive vacation or two, or even building a vacation retreat.
- Various "senior citizen" monetary perks will kick in.

Remember: not all of these "for instances" will fit your situation, but with good fortune at least some of them will apply. (*More about bonuses later in the chapter.*)

Now for the Bad News

Assuming that about 75%-80% of your final salary will ensure an adequate income in your initial retirement years, will that be enough for the long haul? Most likely, no. **You've got to provide for exigencies.**

For instances again:

- **Inflation**. When high rates of inflation are combined with earlier retirement and increased longevity, the value of unindexed pension benefits falls drastically. Even a relatively mild rate of inflation, such as 3%, will cut purchasing power nearly in half over a 20-year period. If inflation averages 5% a year, as it did for the last decade or so, an income that would cover your expenses during the first year of your retirement would soon be sadly insufficient. For example, assume inflation were to average 5% for the first 10 years of retirement; that would mean you would need $16,000-plus at the end of the tenth year to purchase the same items you bought for $10,000 in your first year.
- **Taxes** — federal, state, and local. While under present regulations your income taxes may drop upon retirement; that's no guarantee they'll remain so. State sales taxes, local real estate taxes, various excise taxes — they all can be on an escalator.
- **Interest/dividend rates.** The same generous interest rates and dividend returns that helped build up your pension kitty and other equities in the "greed is good" era are not likely to be around in 10 years, if the current economic climate is any barometer. So you've got to downscale your anticipated income accordingly. (On the other hand, of course, any forms of investment paying an annual dividend may be

sufficient to counter the effects of lower interest earnings in an era of decreased inflation. It's a crap shoot.)

- **Catastrophic health costs.** With a sound health insurance planning program, you should be able to protect yourself well from most health-care costs in your retirement years — except for long-term care. That could be devastating, unless you self-insure or take out a special policy, either of which can remove a sizeable chunk from your income.
- **Parental support.** Depending on their circumstances, you might have to come to the rescue of your folks in small or large ways.
- **Offspring support.** Much more likely you'll have to help your children or your grandchildren if they're to attain your level of education or lifestyle. For the first time in history, a generation of Americans can't look forward with any assurance to the economic self-sufficiency of their parents or grandparents. You could well have to assist with term life insurance premiums, a down payment on a home, college tuition, maternity and/or child care, a lingering illness — you name it and it could happen — needs that can't wait for the probate of your estate.
- **Recession/stagflation/depression.** Not to be an alarmist, but anybody these days who doesn't factor in the worst in retirment planning, to some extent at least, is whistling in the dark. Even a small sustained dip in the economy can lower the market value of any real estate you own. A larger regional decline could wipe out money you've stashed away in some investment. A serious depression could jeopardize your whole retirement scheme.
- **That confusing CPI.** Whatever you do in your guestimating, don't let present and projected Consumer Price Indexes deceive you. The federal government calculates a monthly CPI on the basis of the ups-and-downs in the cost of a fixed market-basket of goods and services, but the goods and services in the government's basket may not be those you're purchasing, either today or in 10 years.

For example, if you'll look back on that list of items you probably are now consuming but probably won't after you'll retire, you'll notice it includes a home, and gasoline and clothes in quantity — goods whose prices have stabilized or even declined in recent years. Now look at the list of expenses you'll probably be facing after retirement. It includes medical services — costs which have been rising at a shocking rate and show no inclination of abating.

The point is, if the government's CPI reflects overall inflation, that doesn't mean your personal CPI will. In other words, the weighting of items in an average consumer's market-basket that tilts toward goods can be quite different from the weighting of items in a retired person's basket that tilts toward services, which tend to rise faster than the general CPI.

Will your good news balance out your bad news?

To answer that question you must go back and pose a couple of other crucial questions:

- What will my retirement income be — at year 1 and down the pike?
- What will my financial needs/wants be in retirement?
- If the former doesn't match the latter, what can I do about it?

Read on.

ASSESSING YOUR GROUP ANNUITY(IES)

For most faculty and academic staff, the core of their retirement incomes will come from annuities paid out by the funds or companies into which they and/or their institutions have made monthly contributions over the years of employment.

What type of plan you are in, for how long, and what form of payout you elect will have a significant effect on the amount and longevity of your take-home pay (pension) in retirement.

For example, a pioneering survey, exploring what journalism and mass communication faculty retirees are receiving in benefits and perks from or through the institutions they served, shows "there are often wide, inexplicable variations in the range and quality of rewards provided. How retirees fare seems often to be a matter of chance; some retired are rich in economic and related advantages, others grossly deprived" (Jaffe 1992).

Types of Retirement/Pension Plans

Retirement/pension (the terms are interchangeable) plans for college employees come in a variety of shapes and sizes.

Controls

Public institutions tend to be under plans allied with either teachers or other public employees, managed by a government instrumentality. Private institutions tend to be under either a self-funded or trusteed plan, a commercial insurance company plan, a church pension plan, or TIAA-CREF (Teachers Insurance and Annuity Association/College Retirement Equities Fund).

The last is far and away the biggest. Indeed, a number of public institutions use TIAA-CREF as a supplement, as an alternative, or even as their sole plan. TIAA-CREF is in fact two not-for-profit companies, albeit with a single "top board" of trustees. TIAA was set up in 1918 by the Carnegie Foundation for the Advancement of Teaching to serve the college world; CREF, its affiliate, was formed by TIAA in 1952. Together these two highly regarded funds hold over a billion dollars in trust for hundreds of thousands of academic personnel. At the time of retirement their TIAA-CREF savings will represent their major asset from a lifetime of work.

Policies

Although there are all sorts of permutations on this basic distinction, public plans tend to be what are called *defined-benefit* plans. That is, in exchange for agreed-upon monthly deposits, the fund management guarantees to pay out predictable retirement benefits that are frequently at least partially indexed for inflation after retirement.

Private or quasi-private plans, on the other hand, tend to be *defined-contribution* plans. That is, while the amount of input is prescribed, the payout is not, so participants can either profit from rising economic tides or bear significant financial risk, the amount of annual benefits varying considerably depending on the investment performance of management's portfolios.

These are generalities. Some public fund policies can be defined-contribution type, while some private or quasi-private fund policies can be the defined-benefit type. So check yours out.[1]

Personal Options

If you're in a public pension plan, you'll likely have very little, if any, control over how or where your money is invested, other than perhaps to be able to choose between a fixed or variable strategy, unless elected officials on your ostensible behalf set certain public-interest restrictions on public investment boards. If you're in a commercial or quasi-private plan, you may or may not have considerable latitude.

[1]Under the federal Tax Reform Act of 1986, defined-benefit retirement plans may pay no more than $90,000 or 100% of the employee's average compensation during the three highest-earning years (whichever amounts to less), while defined-contribution plans may contribute no more than $30,000 or 25% of the employee's compensation annually (whichever is less). The defined-benefit limit can rise according to changes in the Consumer Price Index, but the defined-contribution limit is frozen until a 4:1 ratio in those limits is reached (Sumberg, Alfred D., "Tax Changes, Retirement, and Pensions," in Holden and Hansen, Eds., 1989, *The End of Mandatory Retirement*, Jossey-Bass: San Francisco; p. 11).

For example, before the Commission on College Retirement and other entities entered the lists, TIAA-CREF was one of the more rigid plans in terms of allowing individuals to move their money around. Following a 1990 reform, however, TIAA-CREF now offers a wide range of individual investment options. TIAA is a traditional conservative fixed annuity plan. CREF variable funds offer these possibilities: a stock account, a money market account, a bond market account, a "social choice" account giving special consideration to certain social criteria, and a new global equities account. And you can be in only one, all six simultaneously, or any variation thereof.

Pros and Cons

While it may well be unreasonable for you to switch retirement plans now, you may still be interested in the major advantages and disadvantages of both types, if only to advise new colleagues.

Public pension plans tend to be site-specific. That is, you can't take it with you, other than at your salary level when you leave. On the other hand, you tend to be vested quickly in a public plan.

Some public pension plans are seriously underfunded; for example, in Massachusetts, unfunded liabilities total in the billions and represent a significant claim on future tax resources. In other states, legislators faced with making confiscatory tax increases are looking with covetous eyes on the prospect of invading public-employee pension funds.

On the other hand, as you've seen, public defined-benefit plans provide a sure, fixed percentage of your closing salary levels as a retirement pension. But you don't have much choice about how and where your money is invested.

Commercial or quasi-private retirement plans tend to be more portable. That is, you can move your participation from institution to institution without missing a beat, provided all the institutions involved have contracts with the same vendor(s). On the other hand, vesting tends to be delayed somewhat. Although such funds are not subject to political invasion, any variable-benefit policies are subject to the whims of the marketplace. But you often can dictate to some degree an individual investment strategy.

As the midway barker says, you pays your money and you takes your chances.

Individual Investment Strategies

Assuming you're in TIAA-CREF or a similar retirement plan offering individually guided investment options, there are several principles you ought to consider, according to TIAA-CREF itself:

- Don't play poker with your eating money. Retirement plans aren't like the investments you might make with discretionary income. They're something else — the guts of your savings.
- The greater the reward, the greater the risk. Investing in the market in a stock account **can** pay off. For example, CREF funds invested in common stocks had a total investment gain of 24.3% during the 12 months ending Aug. 31, 1991. On the other hand, similar funds took a licking in the late 1970s, and could again.
- Don't put all your eggs in one basket. Diversification is a way to cover risky investments with relatively sure things.
- Hold 'em; don't fold 'em. The concept of market timing isn't for amateurs — or even professionals. Persistence helps you diversify over time, eliminating temporary ups and downs. And it allows you to relax instead of trying to out-guess Wall Street.
- March to the beat of your own drummer. Reallocate or transfer among accounts because **you** — your personal circumstances — change.
- The nearer you are to your chosen retirement date, the more conservative you should become. Leave aggressive investment to younger people, who have time to make up for any losses. Start securing whatever gains you have made over the decades by reducing the risks you take in later years (1991).

Remember, we're talking here about playing around with your basic pension funds. The same guidelines may not apply to investments made with any venture capital you may have. (*We talk about that later*.) And, if you're in a pension plan that allows you only limited or no individual investment options, relax, enjoy, and take what comes. You may wind up better off than a colleague who acts on periodic tips from "Wall Street Week" on PBS.

Inputs

Retirement/pension plans tend to use one of two contribution rates: the level-percentage approach, in which the contribution rate is a uniform percent of salary, or the step-rate approach, in which a higher contribution rate is applied to the portion of salary above the Social Security wage base. Contributions are usually paid jointly by the institution and the individual, with the institution typically paying the larger share. On the other hand, you may be in a plan in which contributions are shared equally, or in which the institution picks up the whole tab.

The big difference to you is this: when you start drawing your retirement benefit, you'll of course be subject to income tax on the part that your institution contributed plus its investment earnings. Whether you have to pay taxes on the share you contributed will depend on whether it was an after-tax salary deduction contribution or a before-tax salary reduction contribution. You've already paid taxes on the former so you'll be taxed on only its investment earnings. The latter and its earnings are all subject to income tax.

Payouts

The size of your monthly benefit check (annuity) will depend on a number of factors:

Type of Retirement Plan

If you're in a **fixed** plan, your annuity typically will be based on a formula utilizing (a) an average of your three highest years of earnings, (b) number of years of creditable service, and (c) a percentage figure ranging from about 1.5% to 2.5%. The resulting annuity will be guaranteed never to decrease, but it may increase in any year depending on the fund's investment success. If you're in a **variable** plan, your annuity is based strictly on the performance of the funds you and/or the managers have invested in over your period of service.

You may be in both types of plans simultaneously or at various periods of your life.

Length of Service

Obviously, the longer you're in either type of plan, the more deposits you will have had working for you, and that will be reflected in your annuity.

Age at Retirement

Higher monthly benefit checks come with older ages of retirement because of the shorter life expectancy over which monthly benefit payments are to be made.

In defined-contribution plans, the upward benefit leverage due to the mortality factor is usually greater than other factors at work, except, perhaps, under conditions of extremely high interest rates.

In defined-benefit plans, in contrast, "later retirement" increments are due largely to any higher "final average" salary component in the formula, and to the increased numbers of service years figured into the formula. Defined-benefit plan benefits aren't affected by the mortality factor in the same way defined-contribution plans are because once the full formula "normal age" is reached, the percentage factor in the full formula benefit remains constant.

Options

The number of payout options, particularly those available under a plan like TIAA-CREF, can be practically staggering. Try matching each payout option to your projected situation. The comparisons should help you decide the best option for you. (If you're married when you retire, your right to make some choices may be limited by your spouse's right, under federal pension law, to receive survivor benefits.)

In certain situations, it might be advantageous for the about-to-retire to purchase life insurance to provide for the income needs of survivors instead of electing a joint and survivor annuity option under a pension plan (Martorana 1992). Check it out carefully. *(See options table on next page.)*

Early Retirement Incentives

To help alleviate a pileup of graying personnel, particularly in light of the impending end to mandatory retirement, a number of institutions have developed incentive plans to encourage older faculty and staff to retire. The plans usually make financial arrangements in one of four ways:

- Under a lump-sum plan, you accept a bonus for retiring early, usually some percentage of base pay. Under an increased pension contribution plan, your institution makes up for all or part of the pension deposits you lose in retiring early by upping its contribution over several years prior to retirement.
- A phased retirement plan allows you to reduce your responsibilities to part-time, often without a proportional reduction in salary.
- A bridge plan attempts to replace much of your after-tax income in the period between early and normal retirement, at which age you would begin to collect your normal annuity.

However, those early retirement incentive plans were devised in an era when demographic data suggested campuses could well become saturated with superannuated faculty. More recent analyses suggest quite the opposite may come to pass: that a big cohort of voluntary retirees, coupled with a shortage of qualified replacements, will actually result in a seller's market in academe. So early retirement incentive plans could well be cancelled in favor of strategies designed to keep young-spirited professors on board.

Annuity Options Available Under a Representative Plan

Each of the annuity options produces a different monthly benefit amount because each option has a different guaranteed payment period. The total amount required to fund the benefit is the same no matter which option is selected. The differences simply reflect the varying guarantees. A longer guarantee period provides a higher death benefit than a shorter guarantee period. The higher death benefit is funded by reducing the monthly benefit payable. No "bargain" can be found by "shopping" among the various options; the best option is the one that suits your individual circumstances.

The following table illustrates, for general comparative purposes only, the differences in the amounts that would be payable under the various annuity options. The examples are based on a Straight Life monthly annuity of $100.

	Example A	Example B	Example C
Annuity Age	65	65	62
Beneficiary Age	62	70	65
Annuity Option Type	Mo. Amount	Mo. Amount	Mo. Amount
Straight Life Annuity	$100	$100	$100
Life Annuity - 60 Monthly Payments Guaranteed	99	99	99
Life Annuity - 180 Monthly Payments Guaranteed	90	90	93
*Joint Survivorship Annuity - 75% Continued To One Beneficiary	85	91	91
*Joint Survivorship Annuity - 100% Continued To One Beneficiary	85	91	91
*Joint Survivorship Annuity - Payments Reduced 25% Upon Death of Annuitant or Beneficiary	88	97	95
*Joint Survivorship Annuity - 100% Continued to One Beneficiary Combined with 180 Monthly Payments Guaranteed	80	86	87

* The amounts under the joint survivorship options are based on the age of both the annuitant and the beneficiary. All other options are based solely on the age of the annuitant. Different age combinations produce different results.

Advises one reviewer:

While those early-out offers last, make it a game. How badly do you want out? Sometimes the employing institution wants to reduce the work force, particularly people at the high end of the pay scale. When the deal gets too hard to pass up, GO. For me it was a 'golden handshake' that added two years to my length of service for calculating retirement benefits. Be alert for such incentives.

Even if your institution still offers an early-retirement package, better read the fine print. For example, in fall 1990 the University of California instituted a "Plus Five" voluntary retirement plan for faculty and staff who were at least 50 and who agreed to retire immediately; they were to receive five years extra credit in their pension calculations along with a lump sum payment of three months' salary. **But** the option turned out not to be available to faculty who at any time had received disability benefits, who were gradually reducing their teaching hours through a phased-retirement plan, or who were retiring on or before June 30, 1991.

The estimated $282 million the University will pay out in Plus Five incentives comes from the University of California Retirement Plan fund, money which would otherwise be earning interest, so in a way the Plus Five retirees are being subsdized by their fellow faculty and staff annuitants.

Thus, what for some retirees can be a golden parachute, for others can be a lead balloon (Hinersfeld 1992).

Double-Dipping

It's perfectly possible to draw retirement pay from two or more plans at once.

If you move from a public institution with a state or municipal fund, you may be able to leave your deposits behind to continue to earn interest/dividends, meanwhile joining a different plan, both of which you can draw on in retirement. (Of course, you could also cash out from that public plan.)

If you move to academe from private employment or a government post, again you may be able to draw on both retirement plans in retirement.

If your academic assignment is in the Cooperative Extension Service, you'll be covered by both a federal retirement and an institutional retirement plan. (Of course you'll have to make contributions to both, which may mean scrimping, but it can result in a bigger-than-average combined payout).

Or if you've combined an academic career with extended service in a reserve component of the armed forces, you'll double-dip for sure. Not to mention some inexpensive medical, post exchange, commissary, recreation, club, and theater privileges if you're near an active military base; inexpensive overnight base quarters or campgrounds and space-available worldwide air flights, as a fellow professor/reservist reviewer points out.

And if the rest of you bridle at those military perks; let it be recorded that, quite apart from placing themselves in harm's way, through the loss of cost-of-living adjustments (COLAs) retired military personnel have contributed more than $5 billion toward reducing the federal deficit (Kilcline 1992).

Odds and Ends About Defined-Benefit Plans

Depending on any institutional retirement plan you're in, there may be some ins and outs to it that are so arcane or so rarely applicable that we can't go into any detail on them here. But we'll mention topics you may find valuable to look into:

- Money purchase retirements. As we've explained, under a fixed plan your benefits are usually calculated by use of a formula, which normally yields maximum benefits if you remain in covered employment right up to drawing benefits. On the other hand, under a money purchase option your benefits could be higher if you terminate covered employment several years before applying for benefits.
- Buying creditable service. If you forfeited creditable service during a year or years of leave, if you can document teaching service as a TA before you were vested, or if for some other reason you lost creditable service, you may be able to recapture those credits by buying them back, and thus increase your eventual benefits under a fixed plan. However, to do so might not be as rewarding as investing that money elsewhere.
- Separation benefits. There are a lot of ifs, ands, and buts to this topic. Before you apply, investigate all the angles on taking a separation benefit from a fixed plan.
- Military service credits. You may or may not receive credit for active U.S. military service toward your fixed retirement plan benefits. Check it out.

Pension Plans in Flux

Those of you who've been following the stories in the press know that the world of college and university pension plans is undergoing significant change (Pender 1992, Magner 1992).

For many years, TIAA, the defined-benefit fund with assets of some $56 billion, and CREF, the defined-contribution equity investment fund with assets of some $48 billion, have enjoyed a commanding position, serving some 1,900 institutions of higher education. Until two years ago, moving an individual's grubstake out of TIAA-CREF was harder than getting out of a final exam. Then a watershed agreement with the Securities and Exchange Commission loosened the restrictions, setting off a scramble among investment houses hungry for even a small slice of the huge college retirement pie.

At many institutions the change has resulted in a smorgasbord of investment options. At Stanford University, for example, faculty and salaried employees can now choose from more than 100 mutual funds and annuities offered by six investment managers. One company has even set up a retirement services center in downtown Palo Alto to counsel employees of Stanford and other non-profit organizations in the area.

Spurred by faculty critics of TIAA-CREF's close-to-the-vest policies, institutions from the University of Notre Dame to Rollins College to the University of Nebraska have also begun offering employees a choice of companies to which they can funnel their retirement money. Public institutions in New York, Tennessee, and Washington may follow suit. Other colleges and universities, on the other hand, are either locked into public employee plans or are reluctant to seemingly encourage their employees to "play the market."

Just how volatile that market can be is aptly illustrated by the experience of public employees participating in the state of Wisconsin's retirement system in recent years. In 1990, the system's "fixed" trust fund yielded a 3.6% dividend, while its "variable" fund produced a 14% loss. In 1987, the contrast had been a 6.7% gain versus a 6% loss. On the other hand, in 1991 the variable fund paid an 18% dividend, the fixed fund only 6.3%.

Staff and faculty members young enough to experiment with their pension fund investments may want to investigate the new major players: Prudential, Fidelity, Vanguard, Scudder, Calvert, T. Rowe Price, VALIC (The Variable Annuity Life Insurance Company), Cigna, Twentieth Century Investment, and others. Older employees will more likely stick with what they've got.

Obiter Dictum

We trust you recognize that all this is very much a truncated foxchase through the subject of retirement annuities. So varied are individual circumstances and plans, and the economic conditions under which they both operate, that it's very difficult to generalize. But here goes:

The Commission on College Retirement figures generally that under a representative plan a typical faculty/staff member with 30 years of service will receive benefits equal to 60% of final salary (Ruebhausen 1990).

Fortunately, whatever retirement plan you're in, its central office will likely furnish you with whatever projections you ask for, utilizing whatever assumptions you specify. Indeed, besides a whole library of self-help manuals (*see References at end of chapter*), TIAA-CREF even has a software program for your PC.

While your faculty/staff retirement program will most likely constitute the core of your retirement plan, it can in all likelihood be supplemented by Social Security benefits, spousal earnings, savings such as a TDA, or earnings from other assets. We will discuss these in the balance of this chapter.

MAKING SENSE OUT OF SOCIAL SECURITY

Almost all faculty and academic staff are covered by Social Security. This means they can move from position to position and continue to build up benefits that keep pace with the growth of their earnings — up to a point. After retirement, a progressive benefit formula provides relatively larger benefits to lower-paid persons, and annual COLAs ensure that benefits more or less keep pace with prices, married couples with a single paycheck will receive additional benefits, and surviving spouses will be ensured a continued stream of retirement income. Social Security coverage also offers valuable protection in the event that a breadwinner suffers a long-term disability.

The only exception to the nearly universal coverage among college/university employees are teachers in Maine, Massachusetts, Connecticut, Colorado, Illinois, Louisiana, Nevada, and Ohio public institutions, where pension formulae are calculated to make up for the lack of SS coverage (Ruebhausen 1990), and personnel employed under federal civil service.

Here are answers to frequently posed questions about Social Security:

- *How do you qualify for retirement benefits?* If you work and pay Social Security taxes (Federal Insurance Contributions Act, or FICA), you are earning Social Security credits. You can earn up to four credits a year. If you were born after 1929, you need 40 credits (10 years of work) to get retirement benefits. People born before 1929 need fewer credits (39 if born in 1928, 38 if born in 1927, and so on). If you're like most people, you'll earn many more credits than you need to qualify for Social Security. These extra credits do not increase your Social Security benefit, but the income you earn while working **will** increase your benefit.

Approximate Monthly Benefits if You Retire at Full Retirement Age in 1992 and Had Steady Lifetime Earnings

YOUR EARNINGS IN 1991

Your Age in 1992	Your Family	$30,000	$40,000	$50,000	$55,000 Or More
45	You	$1,159	$1,302	$1,436	$1,491
	You, spouse	1,738	1,953	2,154	2,236
55	You	1,052	1,150	1,231	1,258
	You, spouse	1,578	1,725	1,846	1,887
65	You	977	1,038	1,081	1,088
	You, spouse	1,465	1,557	1,621	1,632

Note: Your spouse is assumed to be the same age as you. Your spouse may qualify for a higher retirement benefit based on his or her own work record. The accuracy of these estimates depends on the pattern of your actual earnings, past and future.

- *How much will your retirement benefit be?* Your benefit is based on your earnings averaged over most of your working career. Higher lifetime earnings result in higher benefits. Your benefit amount also is affected by your age at the time you start receiving benefits. If you start your benefits at age 62 (the earliest age), your benefit will be lower than if you waited until later.

The Social Security Administration's official table, displayed above, shows some approximate benefits for persons with steady incomes (Social Security Administration 1992a).

- *What is meant by "full retirement age"?* The usual retirement age now is 65. Social Security calls this "full retirement age," and the benefit amount that is payable is considered the full retirement benefit. Because of longer life expectancies, the full retirement age will be raised in steps until it reaches 67. This change starts in the year 2000, and it affects people born in 1939 and later. For example, if you were born in 1943-1954, your full retirement age is now 66.
- *Can you take early retirement?* Yes. You can start as early as age 62, but the benefit amount you receive will be less than your full retirement benefit. For example, if your full retirement age is 65, the reduc-

tion is 20% at age 62, 13.5% at age 63, and 6% at age 64. If you're forced to retire early because of ill health, you should consider applying for Social Security disability benefits — the same as a full retirement benefit. If your full retirement age is higher than 65, your reduction will be greater than for people retiring now.

- *Can you take delayed retirement?* Absolutely, until age 70. And if you decide to keep working full-time beyond your full retirement age, you can increase your Social Security benefits in two ways. First, simply by adding a year or years of high earnings to your Social Security record, your higher lifetime earnings will result in higher benefits. Second, your benefit will be increased by a certain percentage for every year you delay retirement up to age 70. For example, if you were born in 1943 or later, Social Security will add an extra 8% to your monthly benefit for each year you delay signing up for benefits between 66 and 70.
- *What about family benefits?* If you're receiving Social Security retirement benefits, some members of your family are also eligible: your spouse age 62 or older, your spouse under age 62 if taking care of your child who's under 16 or disabled, your former spouse age 62, children up to age 18, children age 18-19 if they attend school or if they're disabled. The full benefit for a spouse is one-half of your full benefit. If your spouse is independently eligible for retirement benefits as well as for benefits as a spouse, he or she will get the higher amount.
- *How do you apply?* Very simple. Preferably, you apply in January of the year in which you want your benefits to begin — by phone or at your nearest Social Security office. You'll need your SS number, birth certificate, W-2 forms for last year, family data if members of your family are applying for benefits, and checking or savings account information if you want a direct deposit (which you certainly should).
- *Can you get a personalized benefit estimate?* Certainly. Call 800/772-1213 and ask for a Request for Earnings and Benefit Statement. Fill out the simple form, send it in, and Social Security will mail back your complete earnings history, along with estimates of your benefits for retirement at age 62, full retirement age, or 70.
- *Are SS benefits indexed?* Yes, that's a nice thing about them. Social Security law provides for automatic cost-of-living adjustments (COLAs). Once you start receiving benefits, the amount will go up

automatically, usually annually, if the cost of living rises. For example, the increase as of January 1, 1992, was 3.7%, in each SS benefit.

- *Are SS benefits taxed?* Yes and no, and this gets a little complicated. Three factors govern how much, if any, of your Social Security benefits you must report as taxable income: (a) your adjusted gross income, (b) half of the Social Security benefits you (and, if you're married and filing jointly, your spouse) received during the year, and (c) your base amount, which in 1992 was $25,000 for a single taxpayer and $32,000 for a married couple filing jointly. The amount of Social Security income to be included in your taxable income will be 50% of the amount by which the income plus half of the Social Security benefits exceed the base figure. But no more than half of your Social Security benefits will be taxed under present regulations. (However, Congress could decide that anybody in the higher income brackets drawing Social Security benefits ought to have those benefits fully taxed. If this happens, just be thankful you're in a high enough bracket to qualify for special treatment.)
- *What's this "Retirement Test"?* If you earn more than a certain amount during a year after your Social Security benefits have started, it may reduce the amount of those benefits that year. The test specifies the maximum amount you may earn in salary or self-employment each year and still be entitled to full benefits. The limit that pertains to you depends on your age and also changes from year to year to reflect changes in national average wage scales. For example, if you received Social Security in 1992 and were under age 65, you could earn up to $7,440 without any benefit reduction. After that, for every $2 you earned, you lost $1 in benefits. If you were age 65 to 69 in 1992, you could earn up to $10,200 without loss. After that, for every $3 you earned, you lost $1 in benefits. When you reach age 70, no limit applies. In other words, no amount earned by those age 70 and older will cause their Social Security benefits to drop.
- *Can I keep on working and still draw Social Security?* Yes and no. Because of a combination of tax law and Social Security rules, older persons can end up keeping less than 20 cents of every $1 they earn. Using 1992 figures, it works like this: Persons under 65 lose $1 in Social Security payments for every $2 of earned income above $7,440. Persons age 65 to 69 lose $1 in benefits for every $3 of earned income over $10,200 — an effective tax of 33%. People 70 or older can earn any amount and not lose benefits. Any wages earned in retirement are subject to both Social Security tax and income tax, which often means

an additional tax of 23%. The result: a tax rate of 56%, not counting state and local levies. Once gross income, including tax-free interest and half of one's Social Security benefits, tops $25,000 for a single person or $32,000 on a joint return, the benefits themselves are partly taxed. For someone in the 28% tax bracket, the overall impact could be a tax rate of more than 80% on income earned while drawing Social Security. In every recent year, proposals in Congress have called for removing the cap on earnings for people 65 through 69, but so far the American Association of Retired Persons lobby has been unsuccessful. Given the sad state of the federal budget, you can understand why (Wiener 1992).

- *Is that all there is to it?* Again, yes and no. This final summary ought to give you enough of an outline for planning purposes. But when you get closer to the moment of truth, you'll need more detailed information to make sure you're not some kind of exception that proves a rule. Social Security headquarters issues a surprisingly readable booklet every year, and other excellent explanations are available. (*See References at end of chapter.*)

But there's something more to be said about Social Security. It was never intended to be a total replacement for active-duty income. It's strictly a stopgap. Because Social Security is a regressive benefit, its replacement ratio depends on the level of your salary the year before retirement: the higher your salary, the lower the replacement ratio. For example, if your final salary was $30,000 in 1991, your first-year Social Security income ratio in 1991 would have been 37%; if your final salary was $55,000, your ratio would have been 22%. And it goes down from there.

In other words, our professor planning to retire 10 years from now with an estimated final salary of $85,000 would find his or her Social Security benefit replacing a good deal less than 20% of final base pay. Recalling that a typical institutional retirement plan nets about 60% of final base pay, the two together still leave a gap, particularly when you throw into the equation the effect inflation could have on expenditures and the effect declining interest rates could have on investment years.

How do you fill the gap? One way we talk about shortly.

But first, here are some things you ought to be doing about Social Security all the time — now and later:

From their long experience as consultants in the field, Dale R. Detlefs and Robert J. Myers have drafted this list of **actions everybody should**

take to stay on the right side of the Social Security Administration (SSA):

- When you receive your Earnings and Benefits Estimate Statement, check the earnings information for errors. If you spot any, call the SSA at 800/772-1213.
- Request an Earnings and Benefit Statement from the SSA periodically, particularly if you change campuses.
- Before you file for benefits, get the necessary papers in order. SSA can't use a photocopy of your birth certificate; you'll need a certified copy.
- File your application in January of the year in which you want your retirement benefits to begin (or in October if you're retiring in January-March). Processing takes time, although it usually goes with surprising smoothness. (In fact, a lot of campus registrars could take lessons from the SSA.)
- Any time you think an SSA decision is wrong, you can appeal.
- After you start receiving benefits, if your earnings exceed the earnings limitation, report the information to the SSA office nearest you. Having benefits withheld is less painful than having to pay back benefits that you should not have received. And you will have to pay them back.
- If you lose your card, report the loss to the SSA. They'll send you a new card with the same number. Do not apply for a new number; that would really foul up the works.
- You have to apply for any benefits. The SSA won't come looking for you. They've got enough to do with 40 million people now receiving Social Security benefits each month.
- And give thanks to the Wisconsin economics professor who drafted the Act in the 1930s (Detlefs 1991).

PUTTING FROSTING ON THE CAKE WITH A TDA

If and when you have some disposable income, one excellent way to augment your retirement income stream is through a tax-deferred annuity — a TDA. (They go by various other terms as well. Non-profit organizations typically call them 403(b) plans and for-profits 401(k) plans, after the sections of the federal tax code that created them. TIAA-CREF calls its versions Supplemental Retirement Annuities — SRAs. In general, they're all quite similar.)

In a nutshell, a TDA represents a partnership between the federal government (in the guise of Congress and the IRS), your institution, a financial organization, and you — allowing you to make regular tax-deferred contributions to a designated investment fund, which you then leave untouched, earning interest and/or dividends until you draw it out gradually or in a lump after you retire. In short, you temporarily pay no federal tax on the TDA portion of your pay checks. After 70½ when the government requires that you begin drawing down your TDA, you must pay federal tax on the amounts withdrawn.

More explicitly, contributions to TDAs are handled through your campus payroll system before it issues your paycheck. As a result, you lower your federal taxable salary while providing savings for "bonus" retirement benefits. When the earnings on these contributions, which are also tax-deferred, are also taken into consideration, your dollars squirreled away in a TDA can greatly fatten your retirement kitty. Of course, the sooner you make contributions to a TDA, the larger this nest egg will be.

(If your state uses the federal form in determining your income, your TDA contributions and earnings will be tax-deferred there as well.)

To illustrate, let's say you're again that prof making $50,000 a year, now able to contribute $100 per biweekly paycheck ($2,600 a year) to a TDA. Of that $2,600 contribution, the actual cost to you is only $1,872, because $728 in tax savings comes out of Uncle Sam's pocket instead of yours. Assuming regular contributions and average earnings on them, after 10 years you would have accumulated almost $40,000 from an input of $26,000. A $52,000 input over 20 years would amount to $128,000, and an $87,000 input in 30 years would mean you'd be facing retirement with an extra $322,000 to draw on, not counting any other sources of income, such as self-employment.

TDA Advantages

Depending on the type of TDA vendor and vehicle you select, you can be as aggressive or as conservative as you choose, or you can mix and match or change horses in mid-stream. Likewise, when it comes time for the payoff, you have at least as many options as with most types of investment options.

You own your TDA. If you switch positions, you take your benefits with you, and you can continue contributions at any of nearly 4,600 educational and research institutions offering TDA arrangements — wherever, that is, your particular vendor is available. Some institutions may even add to your contributions. If your particular TDA isn't available with your new employer, you can leave your accumulation in place until you begin receiving benefit payments. Another advantage to a TDA: when you start drawing on it, you may be in a lower tax bracket than when you were still working, so your income taxes will be lower, even counting the income you'll be receiving as you draw out TDA annuities.

There are a couple of drawbacks to TDAs:

- There's a limit on how much you can contribute in any one year (presently in general, $9,500 or 16 and ⅔% of your gross income, whichever is greater — although there are a couple of exceptions to this ceiling you should check out. (For a full and understandable explanation, order TIAA-CREF's free "Tax-Deferred Annuities Worksheet for Computing Your Maximum TDA Contribution," 800/842-2733, ext. 5509.)
- If you touch any or all of your TDA savings before age 59½, you'll pay a stiff penalty.
- You must start drawing it down by April 1 following the year in which you reach 70½, even if you're still working; otherwise you have to pay a substantial penalty on the amount you should have taken out.

How much that is annually is actuarially determined on the basis of your age and/or that of your joint beneficiary.

But it's likely not all of these potential disadvantages need apply to you (Burke 1992).

If you're set up as partially self-employed, drawing income from book royalties, consulting fees, lecture tour stipends, patent royalties, remunerations from articles or other types of public appearances, in addition to your normal duties, you can squirrel away some of that income in a special TDA plan for the self-employed (known as an HR-10 or Keogh). The simplest Keogh (under 1991 regulations) lets you save up to 13% of your self-employment income, with a ceiling of $30,000 a year. A defined-benefit Keogh lets you pick your annual retirement payout — currently as high as $108,963 — and put aside as much tax-deductible savings a year as needed from your self-employment income to provide for that nest egg. (Academics aren't likely to be stymied by that ceiling!)

It would take an unscrupulous financial advisor to recommend not participating in a TDA to anybody eligible, and it takes an impecunious academic indeed not to be able to salt away a little something in a TDA sometime. Again, the sooner the better.

Perpetual Money

When you're building capital rather than living on it, TDA stock funds are particularly attractive. One dollar invested by your grandparent in 1936 would have grown to $517 by the end of 1990, tax-deferred. If taxed annually, however, that same investment would have grown only to $117.

Taking from	*Left after 10 years*	*Left after 15 years*
Guardian Fund	$189,178	$292,980
Partners Fund	195,938	428,692
Selected Sectors	85,452	186,329

A good stock-owning mutual fund can add more money to your nest egg than you take out. The above example assumes an original investment of $100,000. If you withdraw $10,000 every year, you should still wind up with more capital than you started with (Quinn 1991a). All this presupposes, of course, a market displaying reasonable momentum, and not a repeat of 1929 or even 1987.

Interjects one reviewer: "I don't know much about this sort of thing. All I want to do is learn the basics and then find a good advisor."

And another: "Quinn should have included the dates of the original investments in the mutual funds referred to, since stock performance data are end-point sensitive. There may be a question why these particular funds were highlighted, or why they are identified by name."

A Word of Caution

Assuming you have an option about which TDA vendor to choose as the custodian of your funds, any conscientious financial advisor will tell you to check into the solvency of those you are considering, and not simply to pick the one offering the highest rate of return at the moment.

Take, for example, what happened to a venerable $13.8 billion life insurance company in mid-July 1991. It went into receivership, the largest life insurance collapse ever: during a two-month run on its liquid assets, roughly $1 billion flew out the door. (It was only one of more than a dozen expiring that year.)

If that company had been the custodian of your TDA and you were of an age to draw it down, you could collect the monthly payments owed on your annuity, but the savings built up in your annuity would be frozen in place indefinitely, so you couldn't make any lump cash withdrawals. Customers of some other failed financial institutions are in even worse shape; for example, another company is paying annuitants only 70% of the monthly income they're due.

I can protect myself from such a debacle by consulting a national rating service before I sign up, you may think. Guess again. One company boasted an A+ rating by A. M. Best Co. right up until 16 days before it fell. Best knew the company was battling a huge portfolio of bad real estate loans, but it didn't want to make matters any worse, so it let its A+ rating stand while the company worked out its problems. The rest, as they say, is history.

In short, there are honest high ratings and trust-me high ratings. So don't go by just one rating; get second and third opinions from other rating agencies, and sign up only with a company that merits top ratings by multiple agencies (Quinn 1991b). Or, as Will Rogers said (in the 1930s, to be sure, but still true today), "People should worry more about the return *of* their money than about the return *on* their money."

Reading the Ratings

While we're on the subject, we should say a little more about how to read those ratings that independent agencies render on the ability of municipalities, business corporations, insurance companies, and other purveyors of financial instruments to live up to their long-term contractual agreements. The ratings purport to measure "claims-paying ability," "financial strength," or some other codeword, based on an analysis of a company's track record and current condition, as revealed by both public and private data.

None of the five principal rating agencies uses exactly the same scale. For example, the very top ratings differ as follows: Moody's, AAA; Standard & Poor's, AAA; Duff & Phelps, AAA; A. M. Best, A+; Weiss, A. To a professor, those ratings seem appropriate, if a trifle ebullient. But now let's go down the scale to the following ratings by the first four agencies, respectively: C, D, D, C. You might logically think such ratings were at least semi-respectable. On the contrary, they're the absolute bottom ratings. A "B" rating from those four agencies means variously "good" to "average." Only Weiss Research Inc. conforms to an academic scale in which a plain "A" means "excellent," a "C" means fair, and an "F" is a flunk.

So know the scorecards they're using before you jump to conclusions about any rating. What's more, ratings are only a part of a broader analysis a professional money manager would perform (Lincoln National Corporation 1991).

For example, he or she will probably explain a term often associated with 403(b) plans: Guaranteed Investment Contract (GIC). From an investor's viewpoint, a GIC is functionally similar to a bank's Certificate of Deposit in that it promises a definite amount of income for a specified period of time. But there are two significant differences: first, GICs have generally produced higher yields than bank CDs, and second, a GIC is not federally insured, as is a CD. So the "guarantee" is in fact only as good as the financial institution issuing the contract. GICs don't have market risk, but they do have default risk, as investors in those failed insurance companies have discovered to their dismay.

If your TDA account is concentrated in GICs, you might want to diversify into other investments. But if you decide to dump your GICs, watch out for surrender charges, which can be steep. It might be better to direct only new contributions to alternative options. A sound rule of thumb: look twice at any contract offering returns markedly higher than the norm; otherwise your money could be going into junk bonds or blue-sky real estate deals.

COLLECTING COLLATERAL PERKS

According to Donald L. Dudley, medical director of the Washington Institute of Neurosciences in Seattle, "The transition from being a worker to being a retiree is one of the most difficult and major life changes most of us will ever face. ... People become increasingly stressed as they try to adapt to a new situation."

But the flip side of the retirement coin is that you fall heir to a lot of gratuities which can go a long way to relieving any economic stress. As boxing legend Joe Louis was wont to say, "The main use of money is to quiet the nerves" (Dudley 1991).

COLAs

As we've said, under a federal statute, Social Security benefits are "indexed." That is, once a year the government adjusts them to reflect any changes in the country's cost of living, as determined by an arcane analysis of prices for various commodities and services. Hence, COLA — cost-of-living adjustment. Once you're drawing Social Security, you're the happy beneficiary of this policy.

There are a couple of catches. **First**, because your Social Security check is only a portion of your monthly retirement income, and perhaps a small one at that, any SSA COLA will naturally increase only that portion of your income. **Second**, the cost of goods and services used to determine the federal COLA may not be items on your personal shopping list, so the cost of what **you're** buying may actually be escalating faster than the COLA average. **Third**, because everybody who draws Social Security gets a yearly COLA, regardless of his or her other income, some people in a sense are drawing on public resources they may not really need. And who's footing the bill for that government contract? Your children and grandchildren and mine, whose FICA deductions monthly continue to mount. In time this practice may be changed by taxing all our Social Security benefits if we're in a high enough income bracket.

Catches aside, the federal COLA policy is significant. Without it our Social Security benefits could gradually erode under inflationary pressures.

As a retiree you may benefit from other forms of COLAs as well. For example, if you're in a TIAA-type plan, you'll be guaranteed so much a month, and you'll also be eligible for what amounts to an annual COLA in the form of interest and dividends on your annuity, assuming investments produce returns. As a matter of fact, many faculty/staff retirement plans have done better in some years than the COLA percentage raise. Your other investments may be officially or unofficially indexed as well.

(Of course, on the other hand, with some investments you can take a beating in any era of economic ebb. More about that later in this chapter, in the section "Watching Out for Bulls and Bears.")

Cut Rates

Despite growing statistics to the contrary, American society operates on the hoary assumption that most elderly folks are destitute and need discounts on all sorts of goods and services. Most of us could have used these cut rates more when we were in our 20s and 30s, and our children or grandchildren could use them more now. But that's not the pattern. So when you reach retirement age it's easy to go with the flow of gratuities.

As an example of the pile-up of cut rates in the life of a retiree, consider the following events I experienced after being invited to a publishing company to discuss a third edition of a textbook. I'll be reimbursed eventually, but in the meantime:

- Because I've called my friendly travel agent well in advance of departure, she confirms that I am eligible for a 10% discount on a coach ticket with the airline that's made me a member of their "sunset sails" club.

- The hotel chain that I call for a reservation gives me another 10% discount as a member of their "September days" club.
- Stopping in at my neighborhood bank to replenish my billfold, I enter a veritable supply dump of discounts for "senior citizen" customers in good standing — no-charge checking accounts, free photcopies, free financial counsel, special rates on CDs, and wholesale prices on periodic tours, theater productions, concerts, dinner get-togethers, and seminars.
- The credit card I use, issued by my campus credit union, carries no annual fee for retirees, a special interest rate on any balances, and a sticker that says I qualify for a discount on a rental car from a certain agency, provided I don't take a subcompact.
- At the supermarket where I stock up on portable potables and snacks, it's between 10 a.m. and 2 p.m. on a Wednesday, so I get a 5% discount there. (Finally looking my age, I don't even have to show the clerk my driver's license any more.)
- Taking a city bus to campus to talk to a junior colleague, I ride for half fare.
- Loitering on the way at a national fast food emporium, I partake of their "golden oldie" special of the day.
- At the campus men's clothing store where I've shopped for years, I now rate a 10% discount on a traveler's-raincoat-in-an-envelope.
- At the pharmacy where I stop on the way back, I get a 5% discount on prescription drugs.
- Visiting a branch library to check out some competing texts, I know I won't be fined if I don't return them by the deadline.
- Returning to my retirement complex, I enter the domain of still another discount emporium; for instance, a night nurse on call.

And that's just a one-day sample of possible benefits for retirees. Most of us elders could have used those cut rates more when we were in our 20s and 30s, and our offspring and/or replacements can use them more now, but that's not what the culture prescribes. I don't range all over town looking for discounts, yet on that one particular day I saved in the neighborhood of a hundred bucks.

My guess is that the business world will finally figure out that these senior-citizen discounts don't cause any of us to change our buying habits much, and they'll come to a screeching halt. Municipal discounts may disappear, too. In the meantime, take advantage.

Sad to say, there's at least one type of discount you'll lose. If you've been a safe driver, in an approved vehicle, non-smoking, using seat belt and air bag, you've received discounts on your automobile insurance. However, at a certain age, regardless of your driving record, most likely you'll not only lose those discounts but be forced to pay a geriatric premium. Even worse, if you don't pass your periodic driver's test, your insurance company will yank your coverage entirely. (It shouldn't be that way. Drivers in their 60s average only four crashes per million miles. That number rises to 15 per million for those 80 to 84 — but that's still just half the rate of drivers 16 to 19.)

Paid-up Life Insurance

Provided you took out a 20- or 30-year pay policy, sooner or later your life insurance will be paid up. No more monthly deductions from your checking account. What a relief! And if you've let your annual dividends accumulate rather than using them to reduce your premiums, you've sequestered a considerable amount, assuming you've been in good hands. And the pile will keep growing if you leave it in place.

Depending on the practices of your insurance company, you can leave your insurance kitty untouched to enter your estate upon your demise, or you can start drawing it down in monthly, quarterly, or annual installments. In an emergency, you can borrow against it — at the interest rate in effect when you took out the policy (in my case, 4.5%!).

(To tell the truth, if I had it to do all over again, I'd probably take out a big hunk of term insurance at an early age and put into a stock mutual fund the difference in cost between that term policy and more expensive equity-building policies. But in 1950 my economic horizons were limited to the experience of my parents who lost their life savings in the market crash of '29 and salvaged only a Congregational Brotherhood life insurance policy.)

Liquidated Mortgages

Unless you've taken out a second mortgage or an equity loan for some purpose (or unless you're of that minority who never partook of the great American "joy" of home-condo-apartment ownership), sooner or later, too, your residence will be free and clear of debt. Another big monthly check you don't have to write! The only catch: you won't be able to deduct interest payments any more if you've been using a long form.

As a corollary, you'll then be at an age when you'll have to decide whether to maintain your place of residence or turn it into cash for another purpose or venue. (*More about this issue under "Staying Home on the Range?" in Chapter 4.*)

You may have what amounts to other mortgages under the guise of big-ticket loans covered by collateral. Having those finally paid up will be almost as enjoyable as getting out from under a home mortgage.

Disappearing Dependents

Generally, there'll come a period when your offspring are off parental dole. You've put them through whatever level of education they and you have chosen. They're independent, established. You're free at last — at least from tuition, room, board, and textbooks. Enjoy it while you can. For most of the next generation, things are a lot tougher out there than they were for most of us. At a minimum, it's likely you'll have to help on the downpayment on houses. And then you can help with tuition, room, board, and textbook expenses again for grandchildren.

With good fortune, your own parents will have provided well for themselves. Enjoy that while you can: you may have to help meet the astronomical costs of nursing-home care for a mother, father, or both.

Sociologists estimate that more than two million Americans today are or will be of the "sandwich generation" — those persons who care for both offspring and aging parents. For example, of the 120 respondents to a Runzheimer International 1992 survey of relocating professionals, 28% reported they needed help moving their elderly parents.

Fortunately, on average, costs of any dependencies will be considerably less than the small fortune you invested in child-rearing from infancy to 21 or so. You deserve a break today — and tomorrow.

Spousal Income

Assuming you're married and have enjoyed two paychecks, and assuming your spouse has been in "covered" employment — that is, a position in which the employer sponsors a retirement plan, your spouse will sooner or later start drawing retirement benefits, too. During the period of employment, one of your checks may well have gone to help meet major family expenditures. Now that such expenses could well be reduced, spousal annuities may become more discretionary income — another "collateral perk" associated with retirement age (Waldrop 1992).

EXTENDING YOUR CAREER

One of the very best ways to help ensure an adequate flow of income in retirement is to extend your professional career beyond the last monthly paycheck and into entrepreneurship. I say "very best" because entering the realm of proprietorship not only can produce income, but it frequently helps assuage some of that perceived abrupt loss of status that is the bugaboo of many retirees from academe, according to multiple interviews (Milletti 1989).

Loss of status can strike home in big and little ways, and it is often the little ways that bite the most. I can testify from personal experience. Less than two months after retiring, I decided to call my successor just to see how he was doing.

"May I speak to Dean Samson, please?" I asked the office receptionist.

"Who may I say is calling?" she replied.

"This is Clay Schoenfeld," I announced with some authority.

The response: "Would you spell that, please?"

Samson had imported a new office complement that didn't know my name from Adam.

My stress was compounded a month later when I received a call from a coauthor at Ohio State. Not realizing I had retired, he had sent a manuscript for my review to my old address. It came back to him from that office, stamped "UNKNOWN AT THIS ADDRESS."

"Where are you, how are you, and what are you doing?" my colleague wanted to know. I had to give him a quick lesson in some hazards of retirement.

There's scarely a faculty/staff member who isn't an authority on something. That expertise you can continue to turn into money even in retirement, if you're so inclined.

At least half of my retired peers have extended their careers into some form of activity rewarding in more ways than one. **A few examples:**

- a wildlife ecology professor advising a big shooting preserve;
- an animal husbandry technician raising beef cattle;
- an historian revising the umpteenth edition of his junior high civics text;
- a public relations professor practicing the trade;
- a botanist raising, collecting, and selling prairie plant seeds;
- a law professor now executive secretary of a county bar association;
- an urban planning professor translating his books into his native Finnish for a European Community publisher;

- an ed psych professor now a practicing psychologist specializing in geriatric counseling;
- a professional in Russian translating journal articles;
- an ed admin professor conducting workshops around the country for school superintendents;
- a professor of medicine running a clinic at a rural crossroads;
- a speech specialist coaching business executives;
- a business professor serving as a personal finances advisor;
- a physics lab technician manufacturing instrumentation;
- a chemistry professor consultant to a pharmaceutical manufacturer;
- a librarian substituting at a branch.

The list could go on. Some may choose to extend their careers in public service, but the play-for-pay option is there. And the two choices need not be mutually exclusive. For example, that professor of medicine turned country GP carries free at least as many patients as he charges.

For alleviating any retirement ennui and contributing to declining revenues, it's hard to beat extending your career into self-employment. And that carries a bonus. If you designate a discrete element of your abode as workspace, keep precise, documented records of associated costs, and use an IRS Form C, you can deduct all expenses attributable to self-employment income.

One proviso: You've got to stay up on your field. Your verities of yesterday may be dead as a dodo today. On the other hand, you can contribute the priceless perspective of your experience — and keep your name before the public as other than an emeritus.

But if you want to keep the option open, you'd better not wait until you're retired to line up your self-employment ducks. Start planning and negotiating while your name is still an active, marketable commodity.

There is another possibility, of course. Rather than extend your academic career into retirement, you may get more kicks and cash out of an entirely new career. (*More on that option later under "Exploring a Second Career" in Chapter 4.*)

Campus Helping Hands?

Will your college or university help you extend your career? One colleague who thinks it should is Harlan Cleveland, political scientist recently retired as dean of the Hubert H. Humphrey Institute of Public Affairs at the University of Minnesota):

> The thing for a university will be to put to use the experience, wisdom, and capacities for reflective and integrative thinking one will find among those we've heretofore put out to pasture. Reflective, integrative thinking (and teaching) has especially been in short supply in our universities; now, given the demographic transition, we have a chance to see it in long supply.
>
> My suggestion is that universities use this new resource of thinking and teaching to fill sorely neglected gaps in their work. Right now, for example, higher education is far from meeting the world's needs for interdisciplinary and problem-oriented research; it desperately needs to broaden and integrate the knowledge it imparts to undergraduates, and it is far from doing enough to provide remedial education for persons in mid-career to help them recover from the narrow specialization of their postgraduate training and early jobs (Cleveland 1987).
>
> Given half a chance, many academics who, under the old rules, would have been put out to pasture for having another birthday, can do a lot to fill those gaps (1987).

Oncoming crops of new Ph.D.s will argue, of course, that it's now their turn to staff our campuses and that senior people should step willingly aside.

Some institutions are leaning one way, others the other. For example, when the University of California instituted an early retirement plan in 1990, then UC President David Gardner set a tone by anticipating continuing contributions on the part of emeritus professors and pledging the university's resources to their sustained teaching and research. Consequently, a significant percentage of the early retirees under the plan are in fact returning to the California campuses in varying capacities, some more productive than ever.

A Case in Point

Ciro Zoppo, an international relations specialist in the UCLA department of political science, took advantage of the early-retirement plan to retire at age 68 in July 1991.

"I had a terrible backlog on research and publication," he says, "and retiring was one way to catch up before I drop dead."

Freedom from teaching allows Professor Emeritus Zoppo to travel more, a real bonus in his field of European security. "Until now," says Zoppo, "I've had to sneak some of my trips between quarters. You know — rushing to the plane, coming back in time for the first class, and not being able to go away during the quarter. With more freedom, I'm more productive."

Zoppo lost about 9% of his university income, but he's making up the difference consulting. He currently has two contracts with the Department of Defense.

"Being retired doesn't prevent me from getting scholarly grants," he's found. "I've got one now for next year and I'll probably get two more. So I have research assistance when I need it."

Courtesy of his university, Zoppo has a parking place, an office, continuing subscriptions to journals in his field, and access to his department's secretarial services.

"I still take care of students on a personal basis, but I don't have to be on committees," Zoppo says (Hinersfeld 1992).

Don't count, however, on the caliber of treatment that Zoppo enjoyed. Your colleagues are just as likely to suggest your physical presence is no longer appreciated.

Whether you're extending a career or beginning a new one, here's some sapient advice from a reviewer who's done it his way:

> Get something started for you prior to retirement — contract teaching, a business, investing in rental property, consulting, or what have you. It's not only good for your financial future, it's also very good for one's feeling of self-worth: "Well, if the stuff here on campus gets too deep or the dean too oppressive, I can always tell 'em to shove it. I've got something going for me on the outside." Maybe you will never play your presumed hold card, but it feels good to have it.

"A State of Mind"

It's very useful to consider part-time work by stages on the road to full retirement," another emeritus reviewer advises:

> Retirement isn't a given; it's a state of mind: In my mind I didn't really retire, I just quit working for the university. I worked a few years for a retail trade association in the city, and then I went off on my own as a one-man continuing education counselor and had a lot of fun putting on speeches, seminars, courses, and workshops in several states. In the meantime I kept on teaching at the university one course at a time as many terms as I wanted to each year, just to keep my hand in. Now I'm finally getting very lazy these days.

CUTTING THE COST OF LIVING

There are two occasions when you may have to bite the bullet and cut expenses or run the risk of operating in the red: first, when you're still working but struggling to build up equity in a retirement account; and second, when you switch from an escalating salary to stalled benefits.

Here are a dozen practical suggestions for you from an issue of *Parents' Magazine*:

1. Use shopping smarts. Instead of buying staples in dribs and drabs, buy them in big quantities to take advantage of bulk discounts. In the food aisles, buy what's cheaper at the time and eschew gourmet stuff. In the clothing stores, buy fall and winter items when they're on sale in March, and buy spring and summer items when they're on sale in September.
2. Cannibalize some savings to clean up your high-interest "easy payment" debts.
3. Switch to paying the "net" instead of the "gross" on any remaining life insurance pensions. In other words, take any dividends as profit for a time instead of letting them accrue. Even consider switching expensive 20-pay-life policies to term coverage.
4. Cut out or cut down on all expenditures that could be considered luxuries — multiple organization dues, books and tapes you could rent from a public library, expensive entertainment and plush vacations, eating out frequently, and so on. You might even try walking or biking to nearby malls for exercise and economy; as an alternative, organize a car pool among fellow retirees.
5. Learn how to do more things around home. Become a good enough tailor, plumber, carpenter, electrician, and/or motor mechanic to eliminate minor service calls.
6. Tend a garden to provide fresh vegetables in season and to can or freeze. You can do it on 800 square feet or less if you rotate your plantings. If you don't have a back yard, rent an odd lot.
7. Economize on meals. Make budget dishes out of leftovers. Brown bag on a trip to a museum, or whatever. If you eat out, hunt for bargain restaurants. If you entertain, try good, old-fashioned potlucks.
8. Switch from custom doctors to a health maintenance organization.
9. Hunt for cut rates on long-distance phoning — or go back to writing letters.
10. Instead of touring the country, explore vacation spots close to home.
11. If you have a low deductible on your car and/or residence insurance, raise those deductibles to rate a lower premium.
12. If you receive a tax return from the IRS and/or state tax agency each year, reduce your withholding and invest the recaptured income.

(If those ideas sound a little musty, you're right. The magazine issue they appeared in was February 1952. Its author was then a struggling university instructor. Now, 40 years later, he's an economizing retiree. You think he may have been the author of this book? Right again.)

With some adaptations, the advice is still sound today, if you need to pinch pennies. At least that was the tenor of numerous recommendations in the media in the spring of 1992.

For example:

Loren Dunton, president of the National Center for Financial Education in San Francisco and a Depression survivor, was quoted in a Maturity News Service story by Peter Vilbig as saying: "Scrimping is not a word in today's vocabulary. The four words we constantly asked ourselves was, 'Can we afford it?' People today ask themselves, 'Are we maxed out on our credit cards?'"

Steve Davis, editor of *Dick Davis Digest*, was quoted by Marilyn Adams, Knight-Ridder News Service reporter, as offering the following advice: "One fundamental rule is, pay off credit card bills every month. If you remove the interest burden, it's like making 18% or 19% instantly. It's so simple nobody thinks about it."

And financial planner Louise Googins wrote in Credit Union National's *Everybody's Money*: "One consistent factor in people's ability to finance retirement is that they stop financing credit card companies."

Adds a reviewer: "How about keeping your car as long as possible? With good repair, 150-200 thousand miles is entirely possible."

If you were born in 1946 or later, listen to the plaint of a fellow "baby boomer," Duane Freese, a member of *USA Today*'s editorial board and author of *Retirement Planning: The Real Mid-Life Crisis*:

> In the savings department, we baby boomers have been a bust. Our failure to match the savings of our parents and grandparents has cost the economy $250 billion in the last decade.
>
> We must save more. How? It's as simple as one, two, three — making a budget and sticking to it. Just by looking at your spending habits, you may add five percent to your savings without any dramatic change in lifestyle. Put your pennies to work by investing and reinvesting them (Freese 1992).

That there is indeed a difference among generations regarding getting and spending, reviewers of this book provide some anecdotal evidence.

On the margin of this section about "Cutting the Cost of Living," a 73-year-old veteran of the Depression and WWII wrote with a red pen: "Right on!"

A reviewer not yet turned 50, on the other hand, wrote: "Rather than speaking of ways to 'scrimp' and 'cut back,' make the case that retirement is time to break from the shackles of institutional life and to be 'reborn.' Retirement is a second opportunity."

Not in utter nakedness but trailing clouds from our pasts does each of us set attitudes for a new journey.

WATCHING OUT FOR BULLS AND BEARS

Let's say, after taking care of all your other fiscal responsibilities, you still have some venture capital to play with — responsibly, that is. What do you do?

A generation ago at least one magic answer was real estate, either land or buildings or both. For example, in 1961 I bought 59.3 acres of rocks and red oaks in southwestern Wisconsin for $17 an acre. Actually, it wasn't really an investment in the conventional sense: I needed a woodlot full of grouse and deer I could hunt freely in season. It also turned out to be a head start on a boom in recreational property that swept the state.

So, in 1971 I sold off a 9.1 acre corner for $170 an acre, the proceeds going into the beginnings of a cabin which is now a respectable "second home." Last year I selectively cut some mature oaks, netting $4,800 — about six times my initial investment in that parcel. I still have the woodlot and cabin which, according to the township assessor, are worth over $60,000 — besides providing an ideal environment for writing this book.

(Yes, I know you can say had I put that same $1,000-plus into the right growth stock in 1961, I might have a much larger equity today than I do in our woodlot. Granted, but did you ever try holding a family picnic in the middle of Wall Street or hosting a faculty committee in the Merchandise Mart?) But the boom seems to be over in real estate as "growth stock," at least for now in many parts of the country.

Quasi-exceptions could be two market instruments, Real Estate Investment Trusts (REITs) and Government National Mortgage Association (Ginnie Mae) bonds. REITS are essentially mutual funds that buy and sell real estate. While they may lag behind the stock market as a whole, they're generally less volatile than stocks. Ginnie Mae funds invest in government-backed pools of home mortgages. They tend to yield more than Treasury bonds of like maturities, be less sensitive to interest rate changes than longer-term bond funds, and have returns that beat inflation, yet still have that tacit government guarantee (Egan 1991).

So what do you do with any discretionary money?

This seminar cannot offer advice to the investor. Individual, environmental, and calendar conditions are so disparate that even any attempt at generalities is fraught with frustration. But we can offer some broad guidelines — pertinent questions and provisional answers gleaned from avid reading, amateur experience, and professional advisors.

Before you read any further, consider this counsel from a reviewer with expertise in finance: "It's important to stress to your readers not to act on the general advice you provide without consulting a professional advisor who can help on all aspects of the issues raised here."

I couldn't agree more.

Or this from an emeritus professor-entrepreneur reviewer:

> The only thing that really counts is how much income you get out of any accumulation of capital, and how much of it you can keep after taxes; any inheritance as a potential source of resources to sustain life during retirement years; the potential value of frequent and timely consultations with a reputable and ethical stockbroker; the impact on available income stream of taxes (income, intangible, sales, real estate) in the home town versus potential retirement communities elsewhere.

What's Your Objective?

Most people's money-management goals can be narrowed to just three categories: capital appreciation, preservation of capital, and current income. While they're not mutually exclusive, it's impossible to find any single investment instrument that will meet all three objectives equally well.

Your goal for any venture capital will likely depend on a number of factors: how safe or how risky is the use of your group annuity and TDA funds, how old you are, your personal "comfort level," and the state of the economy, for example.

Capital Appreciation

If your objective is to see your money grow, you're unlikely to find any expert who won't advise you to get into the stock market, particularly if your basic retirement funds are secure, you're young enough to withstand short-term market vicissitudes, and you can handle risk without losing sleep. (Of course that's what a broker friend told my dad in the 1920s, whereupon he invested in a Chicago Loop real estate fund; in 1932, out of a job, he settled for a cent-and-a-half on the dollar. On the other hand, every dollar I might have put into stocks in 1950 could be worth over $110 today.)

Particularly when interest rates plunge on investments such as Treasury bills and CDs, or when inflation eats away at your buying power, you'll be glad to have some counter-balancing growth stocks.

For example, over the past four decades, stocks win in a landslide over the competition (Egan 1991):

	Cumulative	**Annualized**
S&P 500 Stocks	$10,968%	12.5%
Corporate bonds	712%	5.4%
Treasury bonds	544%	4.8%
Treasury bills	661%	5.2%
Inflation	434%	4.3%

It's important to realize, however, that in any one decade the scorecard may have looked quite different. For example, in the 1940s small company stocks out-performed Standard & Poor 500 stocks better than 3 to 1, in the 1960s Treasury bills out-performed corporate bonds better than 3 to l, and in the 1930s corporate bonds out-performed large stocks 7 to 0.

If stocks are your choice, what stocks to buy?

One option: the big blue-chippers. There's safety in size, and big companies with stable track records usually deliver at least market returns if not steady gains. Look for companies that control their own destinies, either through size or pricing power or a unique market niche. Pinpoint companies that provide solutions to problems of the era, such as medical care, the environment, and the nation's deteriorating infrastructure.

Even when it comes to income, stocks such as big utilities that pay sizable dividends may be your thing. A utility stock that regularly raises its dividend can produce steadily higher yields over a number of years and will also appreciate in value.

An opposite option: small stocks. They tend to do better in a slower economy because pint-size companies with a well-defined specialty can often render better earnings increases than larger companies that are more closely tied to the economy as a whole. In lush times, however, the reverse may be true. Potential returns may be greater with small stocks, but so are volatility and risk. To cut risk, diversify. A portfolio should consist of a half-dozen small stocks in different industries and geographic locales — a good case for the right stock mutual funds.

A third option: those equity-owning mutual funds that do all the juggling for you and spread your risk. You have your choice — all the way from stock funds that aim for aggressive growth, through balanced-total-growth funds, to funds that deal only in conservative bonds. (Since the late 1970s, balanced funds as a group have had only one losing year.)

By the way, in any discussion of investment strategies, it's important to distinguish between *market* risk (the hazard of capital disappearing) and *interest* risk (the hazard of lowered income with no threat to equity). For instance, the value of a unit in a stock mutual fund can decline without necessarily jeopardizing dividend payments, while the interest yield on a CD can decline without any diminution of the face value of the certificate. Got that straight?

Mutual fund investors may be tempted to base their decisions on one quarter's performance. But a look at the top performer in the first quarter of 1992 shows the danger of such myopia. The fund that posted a remarkable three-month return of 25% is the same fund that trailed the Standard and Poor's 1989 stock index by 28 points. Or take the No. 2 fund: it returned 22% in the first quarter of '92, but in the last decade has posted an average annual return of less than 2% (Kaye 1992).

The best way to get rich in the market, of course, is simply to apply that old maxim, "Buy low, sell high." But that wasn't easy to do in mid-1992, with the the market flirting with record highs as all sorts of people took money out of low-interest money markets and plowed it into stocks, inflating prices.

That behavior made some investment gurus very nervous. "When you hear people saying cash is trash and see them rushing into overpriced securities, that's a sign they're investing with their emotions rather than their brains," said Richard Rand, author of *Contrary Investing in the '90s*. Contrarians like Rand believe in sailing against the current, arguing that what is least popular with the public may be in fact the best place to put your money. And in August 1992 the contrarians said that place was much-despised cash because sometime in the next 12 months the market was going to roll over and head much lower.

Were the contrarians right? Now you know.

According to Jack Egan, one mechanical way to buy low and sell high and produce excellent returns has been described by Michael O'Higgins and John Downes in *Beating the Dow*:

> Out of the 30 blue-chip stocks that make up the Dow Jones industrial average, you identify the 10 highest-yielding stocks, buy the five that have the lowest prices, and hold them for a year. At the end of the year, you readjust. By using yield as your criterion, you are in effect buying the least popular companies in the Dow. That's because a stock's yield

is the annual dividend divided by the stock price; it is highest when the price is lowest (1990).

In 1991 the O'Higgins-Downes system produced a total return of 62%, compared with a 24% gain for the Dow. In the last 10 years the formula has returned 23% a year, the Dow 8.5% (Egan 1992c).

Capital Preservation

Here we're talking mostly bonds — all the way from high-risk corporates to low-risk U.S. Treasuries, with potential yields the opposite of the risk factor. A shifting economic tide doesn't lower or raise all boats; for example, bond prices fall when yields rise. In general, however, if your goal is hanging onto your initial investment without any atrophy, bonds are a surer bet than stocks. What's more, if you're looking for a tax break, you might fare better with Treasury bonds, which are exempt from state and local taxes and offer greater safety than municipal money funds (Sherrid 1991).

Income

The old security stand-bys here are Treasuries and CDs. Up to $100,000 in any one place is government-insured. But when interest rates skid, so does your income. Caught in such a bind, you may perform the celebrated interest-rate shuffle — switching to fixed investments that offer ever higher yields. But the hottest high-interest rate products — no matter how "safe" an adviser may say they are — are inherently risky.

A half-way house can be found in bond issues insured by one of the leading financial guarantee firms. Such firms are unlikely to risk their top credit ratings with dicey investments because their ratings are one of their key marketing features (Quinn 1991a).

One solace: as interest rates go down in an era of declining inflation, and your returns on fixed-income investments go down, the costs of goods also go down or at least escalate slowly, which means real returns on those investments could stabilize at between 4% and 5% — quite good on a historic basis. (For example, the price of a high-end personal computer system, featuring a 90-megabyte hard drive, fell from $2,200 in April 1991 to $1,400 four months later. Unfortunately, some costs don't follow that pattern, like grandchildren's college tuitions.)

When short-term interest rates are unrewarding and long-term bonds somewhat iffy, the safest and most attractive source of income may be the five-year Treasury note. (Remember, you read it here first.)

One reviewer has these critical observations:

> You are 'down' on real property as an investment, and maybe that is

> the correct position now in your part of the country. Aren't there still rewards elsewhere for buying real property (rentals, commercial, acreage, and so on) for investment or for retirement income? All I know is, this worked very well for us.
>
> And you don't mention tangibles as investments. If you are knowledgeable in particular fields, tangibles such as art, antiques, coins, and so on, may well be a good investment choice. But you gotta know what you're doing!

Another reviewer complains that I didn't push tax-free municipal bonds. It's easy to see why she would complain. Not only are municipals virtually the last remaining shelter, but their returns were respectable in 1992 — 6.25% and 6.75% for long-term, investment-grade municipal paper. A taxable investment would have to yield from 8.5% to 9.5% to yield as much income for someone in the 28% federal tax bracket, and current yields on state and local bonds exempt from all three levels of taxes can approach the equivalent of 11%.

There's one big catch: After 10 years, most long-term municipal bonds can be called, or paid down, at the issuer's discretion. Then redemption can pose a problem for investors. For example, on July 1, 1992, from $6 billion to $8 billion in outstanding municipals were redeemed, and over the next few years more than $200 billion worth will be called in. So there really isn't a forever free lunch, but municipal bonds can be fun while they last (Egan 1992b).

What's Your Comfort Level?

"If there is one clear message likely to hold true for investors during these confusing times, it is this: 'Be careful out there!'"

That was the word from Knight-Ridder News Service's banking and finance reporter Marilyn Adams.

Such advice is particularly applicable, regardless of your investment objectives, if you have a low "comfort level," that is, a low level of risk you can tolerate without losing sleep.

Adams' suggestions, stemming from interviews with financial planners from New York to San Francisco:

- Beware of investments promising unusually high interest/dividend returns. On the other hand, nothing is riskier than postponing a secure retirement plan.
- In the same vein, don't take money haphazardly out of CDs to put it into stocks trading at 80 times earnings. A modest 4.5% gain is better than a 20% loss. (For example, *USA Today* reported April 7, 1992, that

"thousands of investors who left bank certificates of deposit for the higher yields of bond mutual funds have gotten a rude shock — most bond funds have lost money this year."

- Use "dollar-cost averaging," in which you commit a set amount monthly that will help smooth out fluctuations in cycles, rather than jump in and out in an attempt to outguess trends.
- Diversify among stocks, bonds, money markets, CDs, terms of investments, sectors, goals — spreading both risk and opportunity during uncertain times.
- Be realistic in your expectations. Recall that inflation increased only an average of 1.3% annually from 1952 to 1965, and never exceeded 3% in any of those years. Interest rates then and later were equally modest. So double-digit inflation/interest rates are an aberration. On the other hand, even if the inflation rate averages only 2% a year for the next 35 years, you would have to double your take-home pay at age 50 to end up even at age 85 — a ripe old age, but not an unusual age (which could include 20 years of retirement).
- If you've ever considered hiring a financial planner to examine your complete financial health and safety, now's a good time. And it might be sound always to get a second opinion.
- Listen to an advisor when he or she introduces you to the concept of relative valuation — a helpful tool for keeping comfortable (Adams 1992).

The idea of relative valuation is simple; it asks that you keep in mind the words "compared to what?" Relative valuation operates at two levels: *within* the equity market, as you compare one stock with another, and *across* markets, as you compare stocks as an asset class with bonds and other investments.

Relative valuation within the stock market involves comparisons of such measures as price/earnings ratios, yields, and changes in analysts' earnings estimates. Results can vary dramatically. For example, the pharmaceutical industry has much lower dividend yields and much higher expected growth rates usually than the utility industry. An investor looking exclusively at yield would opt for utilities, while an investor tilting toward growth would have the opposite bias. Relative valuation analysis within the stock market doesn't depend on the level of the overall market averages.

Relative valuation across investments requires that you estimate the expected return of the entire stock market versus the return on long-term options like bonds, T-bills, and CDs, versus short-term interest rates. Then you have to set your relative valuations against associated levels of risk (Lazzara 1992).

Contrary to conventional wisdom, you don't necessarily have to go for the most gut-wrenching ride to get the highest returns. A study by two professors, Eugene Fama and Kenneth French of the University of Chicago business school (Egan 1992a) challenges the widely held assumption that the most *volatile* investments do the best over time. They cite two other risk factors — small size and low price — as important determinants of return. When you choose well, they say, the payoff is greater with small companies because it's like betting on long shots. Small-company shares, while they didn't do better than stocks of large firms during the 1980s, have out-performed them by about 4% over a longer time, Fama and French point out.

The Fama and French study also contends that "value" stocks, whose price is low relative to per-share net worth, should do better over the long run than growth stocks, whose price is based on the rate of company earnings (Egan 1992c).

If all this is so confusing that your comfort level is off the chart, don't hesitate to perform a relative valuation of your safety deposit box or your mattress.

How Do You Protect Your Securities?

If you're exchanging securities in the financial markets, you have a number of options for protecting yourself.

The Securities Investor Protection Corporation is a non-profit entity created by Congress in 1970. The SIPC insures each brokerage account for up to $500,000 (cash is covered only to $100,000). In the event of a brokerage house failure, the SIPC either attempts to replace your securities or pays cash to settle the account. Some brokerages provide additional insurance coverage as well.

On average over the past decade, seven securities firms have foundered each year, requiring SIPC assistance. Whenever possible, the accounts of the failing firm are transferred by a court-appointed trustee to another broker, a process that takes about a week. If that avenue isn't open, you may have to wait a few months for your money. If you've signed a hypothecation agreement permitting your broker to lend your securities for trading purposes, that can lead to some pretty complicated paper trails if the firm fails.

As an alternative, you could register all securities in your own name and deny the privilege of a broker lending or borrowing against your securities. In that case, in the event the broker fails, your fully owned nontransferable securities will be delivered to you by the SIPC. In the meantime, of course, exchanging any of those securities will require specific communications.

Or you can take physical possession of your securities, keeping them in a home safe or a bank safety deposit box. However, this can make portfolio management inconvenient, and routine investment chores may not be handled expeditiously, costing you money.

Another option is a custodial or agency account with your bank. The bank safeguards the securities, collects and reinvests income, will buy or sell securities to order, and will provide account records for investment management and tax return purposes. Securities in such accounts aren't assets of the bank and can't be reached by the bank's creditors in event of a bank failure.

NOTE: We're talking here about protecting yourself from the collapse of a securities custodian. None of these devices protects you and your securities from a fall in the securities market. There you're on your own.

What About Your Abode?

So you bought a home (house, condo, or apartment) a good while ago and are counting on converting that cash-and-sweat equity into retirement income. Until recently you were indeed riding a real-estate wave. The price of a median house nationwide outpaced inflation by 27% in the 1950s, 6% in the 1960s, and 26% in the 1970s. But increases in home values actually fell slightly behind the 4.7% annual inflation rate of the 1980s, so you may have lost a significant hunk of equity in your abode, depending to an extent on your location. In the 1990s, without rapid population growth or speculative investment to spur demand, home prices may barely keep up with inflation.

Softening mortgage rates may prompt you to consider refinancing, but refinancing fees could easily wipe out any short-term gains in reduced interest rates, and a bank appraisal might reveal that your abode is worth less today than last year, hurting both your pocketbook and your pride (Hage *et al.* 1991).

In self-defense you may want to consider trading down to smaller accommodations long before retirement, and putting the profit into less volatile investments. Since there may be substantial tax considerations in such a move, it's wise to consult a knowledgeable accountant (Freese 1991).

(You'll find a lot more discussion about the retiree housing issue in "Staying Home on the Range?" in Chapter 4.)

RECOGNIZING THAT TAXES SHALL ALWAYS BE WITH YOU

Like you know what, income taxes shall always be with you in retirement. And in retirement your income-producing sources will no longer necessarily take care of your burden through "withholding." The monkey is now on your back.

As Uncle Sam will tell you in an annual package of materials:

> In most cases you must make estimated tax payments if you expect to owe, after subtracting your withholding and credits, at least $500 in tax for the year, and you expect your withholding and credits to be less than the **smaller** of (a) 90% of the tax shown on your current tax return, or (b) 100% of the tax shown on your tax return for the previous year (the return must cover all 12 months).

In other words, you need to make estimated tax payments to cover income that is not subject to withholding; for example, earnings from self-employment, interests, dividends, rents, alimony, capital gains, and so on.

In the package (Form 1040-ES or OCR) will be a worksheet to help you figure everything out, a set of coupons to accompany your checks, and handy return envelopes. You have the option of paying by the quarter, starting by April 15, or paying for the year, again by April 15.

Some people prefer to pay annually, getting the whole business over with in a lump. Others say there's no point letting the government collect interest on money that could be earning for you. Whatever, there's a substantial penalty for failure to declare and pay a sufficient portion of the total tax you believe you'll owe in any year. In addition to the Feds, some states exact an estimated income tax return as well as the feds.

There is, of course, the conventional wisdom that your income taxes will be lower in retirement. That may indeed be true. But don't be shocked if changes in tax codes, the disappearance of some deductions, a combination of incomes, or some other factors produce an April surprise.

How to Trigger an Audit

Starting in 1992, the Internal Revenue Service, following orders from Congress to better police us taxpayers, began to watch with added zeal a number of practices,

- Anybody with an income over $100,000. (Don't you wish?)

- IRA deposits by anybody covered by an employer's retirement plan (most people in academe).
- People who claim more in home office expenses than they earn through self-employment. (Watch it!)
- People who cash in a retirement plan (like a TDA) and keep the funds rather than roll them over into another plan, but then neglect to pay the tax or an early-withdrawal penalty.
- Self-employed people who fail to document the depreciation write-offs they claim on business equipment (as any tax accountant will advise you).
- People who put more into TDAs, Keoghs, and the like than they're allowed. (Ignorance of the law is no excuse.)
- Generous gifts of property to charities (or even to your institution's foundation).
- Large travel and other business bills that smell like personal expenses (such as conventions in Las Vegas and the Bahamas).

As long as you reasonably believe that something may be deductible, claim it — but be prepared for an audit (Wiener 1992).

TAKING CARE OF KITH AND KIN

Depending on individual circumstances and predilections, any consideration of ensuring an adequate income stream in retirement could include providing for your immediate or extended family both throughout your life and after.

A parent or parents in desperate straits, a spouse in failing health, indigent offspring, deserving grandchildren, even an aging aunt or uncle could warrant following your Good Samaritan instincts.

While you're of sound mind and body, you'll probably want to face such issues yourself. But what if you're not in the picture?

To answer that question, you might start by asking yourself such questions as these:

- How much income will my family need when I'm gone? How much estate and inheritance tax will my estate incur? How can I avoid challenges to my estate plans? Do my provisions for my spouse qualify for any marital deduction? Will my death interrupt my family's financial protection? What is the most tax-effective way to provide something for grandchildren?

- Should spouses enter into a marital property agreement? Should they own property jointly? Should they have living wills or health care powers of attorney? Should they give durable powers of attorney to each or others?
- What if my spouse hasn't the patience, the ability, or the time to cope with administering our assets, or would prefer to be free to visit family members at will? What if age or illness someday rob my spouse of the energy and alertness needed to deal with even the most routine financial matters? What if an ex-spouse of an offspring beneficiary could lay claim to a substantial sum of your estate? What if aged parents are in no position to handle money you bequeath in a will?
- Speaking of a will, nobody smart enough to be in academe will fail to observe these simple rules: make it promptly, give it careful thought, make sure it's proper, deposit in a safe yet accessible place, and name an experienced and permanent executor/trustee/personal representative.

Comments one reviewer: "You can't stress enough the importance of executing a will. Among the issues discussed in this section, that's priority No. 1."

But a will may not be enough to provide satisfactory answers to crucial questions. In that case, consider setting up a trust. "A trust?" you ask. Yes. A trust isn't just for the wealthy. It's a way to protect your heirs for all you're worth. In fact, it's the next best thing to eternal life.

Trusts Once Over Lightly

A trust is a form of asset management in which you place your assets in the hands of a trustee (trusted manager), either as an individual in whom you have confidence both to outlive you and to follow your directions, or the trust department of your bank. Under typical conditions, you deposit cash, securities, or real estate in a trust. You provide instructions in a trust agreement, which tells the trustee how to manage and/or disperse your assets. The trustee must act only in accordance with your instructions, as broad or as specific as they may be, and act only for you and those persons you wish to benefit. You can give your trustee the authority to use his or her judgment in certain situations. For example, you may want your trustee to decide how much to pay for a grandchild's education, how much to pay for improvements on a beneficiary spouse's home, how much capital to advance for starting a son-in-law's business, or how to manage investments.

Aso-called **testamentary trust** is established in your will and becomes effective only after you die. In case you envisage a time when you might want to be free of decisions, you can create a **living trust**, designating yourself or others as the trustee and beneficiary. Ordinarily, as the grantor of the trust you maintain complete control over the assets. You may reserve the right to deposit and withdraw your property at all times. Investment recommendations made by the trustee you can accept or reject.

You may reserve the right to terminate the trust at any time, or to in effect turn over to your trustee the management of your assets in case you lose the time, skill, or faculties (and we use the last word loosely, as you can recognize). In short, setting up a trust is sort of like delegating to a dean the functions of a department chair.

Lawyers and Legacies

A trust costs money, of course, depending on the size and complexity of your assets and the extent to which you delegate responsibility. But it may be well worth the investment in terms of enhancing your comfort level and escaping some of the tedium and costs of probating your will.

Needless to say, in any consideration of wills and trusts, the counsel of a qualified attorney, one in whom you place utter faith and confidence, is a wise choice, although not required in many states.

If you really have a flair for it and propose to go it alone in estate planning, at least avail yourself of one of the excellent guides in print, making sure it's updated to conform to the latest tax changes and covers the laws of your specific state (Brosterman and Adams 1991).

And while we're talking about legacies, don't forget to at least consider remembering the source(s) of your benefactions, your alma mater and/or your present source of livelihood, which could be one and the same, or one or two of many "thousand points of light" options (Pentera 1989).

A reviewer adds:

> When it comes to charitable contributions, remember that donating property or other resources to a non-profit agency upon your or your spouse's demise can involve an arrangement whereby you buy in effect a lifetime annuity. Some retirement complexes offer lifetime residence for both parties and medical care in return for such bequests. But rising health care costs may up the ante.

Another reviewer concurs:

> You ought to stress the benefits of planned giving in providing for one's heirs. Examples abound that demonstrate one can leave more to the heirs by establishing charitable remainder trusts and the like. A certified financial planner is conversant with this issue.

Done.

Estate Planning

Proper estate planning can help you achieve many of your personal, family, and financial goals, which might include the following:

- Maintaining an adequate income stream or lifestyle for your spouse, children, or other beneficiaries.
- Ensuring that your assets are distributed and perhaps even managed according to your wishes.
- Minimizing total death taxes and transfer cost, so as to leave as much of your estate as possible for the next generation.

Without proper planning, there can be unexpected and unintended results. Such is particularly true with respect to state marital property laws. A thorough job of estate planning can give you that peace of mind that comes from knowing exactly what will happen to your estate upon your death (Thornton 1991).

But, as one reviewer suggests, complete estate planning rightfully includes exercise and healthy living habits: "That can do more to control future expenditures than any other scheme." We devote a good deal of the next chapter to the subject.)

SIFTING AND WINNOWING ADVICE

> With each passing day, new signs emerge that an economic rebound is underway. — *U.S. News & World Report*, July 15, 1991.

> Plummeting car sales, weak retail activity, and rising unemployment claims provide the freshest evidence that America may be slipping back into recession — *U.S. News & World Report*, Nov. 25, 1991.

By now you know which of those two predictions was the more accurate. They can be used to illustrate the dilemma most of us face in sifting and winnowing the wheat of sound financial advice from the chaff of off-the-cuff tips.

From that same *U.S. News & World Report*, for Oct. 21, 1991, here's some counsel from Jack Egan that seems to ring true for any academics out of their element:

> As the preoccupation with retirement intensifies in the '90s, ... anxious whether they can save enough and lacking in market expertise, many people make the process of investing far more complicated than it needs to be and often wind up with not enough to show for the effort. They shift with market tides, invest in the fad of the moment, search out the hot mutual fund, or impulsively act on the advice of the latest guest on Louis Rukeyser's "Wall Street Week" (on PBS).

> Everyone knows you won't make money without picking good investments. But many fail to appreciate the even greater power of discipline over two, three, or four decades and a simple, consistent system that focuses on the long haul. "Sticking with a strategy, almost any strategy, will work better for most people than constantly shifting from one investment to another," notes John Matkese, director of research for the American Association of Individual Investors.
>
> There are a number of good ways to make retirement investing both simpler and more rewarding. When used together, they can help you methodically put money to work [and] ... meet your long-term objectives with a minimum of fiddling (Egan 1991).

To make it all easy on yourself, to show that the simpler your investment plan, the more likely it will work, Egan has these suggestions:

- When you can't touch it, you won't spend it. Set up some kind of automatic transfer to the vehicle(s) of your choice (which is just what you're doing with your retirement annuity now and perhaps with a TDA).
- Use dollar cost averaging. Trying to buy low and sell high sounds smart, but in practice it usually means acting on a hunch. By setting aside a certain amount each month, you forget about attempting to time the market. Your vendor will buy some shares cheap and some shares on the high side, but the average price should be favorable.
- Go for growth stocks, particularly if you have a span of time before retirement in which to let the market smooth out any bumps and grinds. While as a retiree you will naturally stress current income and safety, you probably should leave an anchor to windward in growth stocks because you might be drawing on your nest egg for a long time.
- Consider dividend stocks for income. The Standard & Poor's *Outlook* in 1992 recommended four regional telephone companies and six metropolitan utilities.
- Diversify, but don't overdo it. To be adequately protected, you probably need only a handful of funds invested in different kinds of assets that don't all rise and fall at the same time. Keeping money in a score of accounts with different institutions is a bookkeeping nightmare.
- Tax-deferred variable annuities could become the soundest retirement savings vehicle of the '90s (as if you didn't know that already).

After the turn of the year, in the Jan. 13, 1992, *U.S. News & World Report*, Anne Kates Smith joined with Egan to add this counsel for the uninitiated:

- With inflation at 3%, one-year CD investors earn a not-so-unusual 1.4% real rate, and if they want to preserve capital they'll wait out those basement-level rates rather than jump from CDs into something they don't understand.
- But anyone facing a stack of simultaneously maturing CDs should switch to "laddering" by staggering the maturity dates of deposits: a typical ladder might divide $10,000 into four $2,500 CDs maturing six months apart. Every six months, when a deposit matures, buy another two-year CD so all your money isn't tied up at the market's low.

That seems like reasonable advice, as long as you remember the date and at least until you know your way around, whereupon you will have sifted and winnowed out your own favorite grains of wheat from the chaff.

The End of Illusion?

Whatever advice you seek or get bestowed upon you, you'll have to put it into the context of what media commentators are saying.

An Associated Press roundup article in Sunday newspapers across the country Nov. 24, 1991, spoke of "a new American frugality in the waning years of this century."

The story went on like this:

> Profound changes are occurring in consumer confidence and business strategy. ... People are worrying abut the well-being of future generations, not just another tough year ahead. ... It's really more than economics, it's a social psychological change. ... We have to go back 100 years to the Industrial Revolution to see the types of fundamental changes we're seeing now. ... Businesses are keeping leaner inventories and laying off thousands. ... Consumers are downsizing their expectations and spending. ... Many experts expect the worst of the suffering to be temporary; others don't see an immediate end to the new frugality. ...
>
> Professor Benjamin Friedman, chair of Harvard University's economics department, blames government policies of heavy spending and borrowing for creating 'A false prosperity' during the 1980s, one that has been copied by corporations and individuals alike. ...
>
> 'Those live-for-today policies,' Friedman says, 'violate basic moral principles that have bound each generation of Americans to the next: That men and women should work and eat, earn and spend, both privately and collectively, so that their children and their children's children would inherit a better world.'

Reporter Vivian Marino concluded her report with the assessment that "millions of Americans are wondering if the old formulae have gone stale."

Much the same tone was set by *Newsweek*'s premier economics reporter, Robert J. Samuelson:

> What's been lost is the psychology of plenty. ... The pleasure of the early postwar decades was that people spent beyond their expectations (because) there was more of everything, from housing to medical care, than people had expected. ... Now the reverse is true. Our needs constantly outrun our incomes. ...
>
> Something else also hurts our prospects. Curiously, we have become less devoted to economic growth.

Samuelson ends on a somewhat upbeat note:

> Whether we can regain our confidence depends on how well we cope with changes. It would help if we kept our perspective; to remember that, despite our problems, we have achieved remarkable progress. The record is something to improve, not to discard. What we have going for us is our innate optimism and tradition (March 2, 1992).

Or this from Rudigar Dornbushch, Massachusetts Institute of Technology professor of economics, speaking to the American Economics Association in New Orleans early in 1992:

> Consumers feel in their bones that they are worse off than 10 years ago. They don't have a lot more income, they have a lot more debt, and they are far more vulnerable. Before, they were willing to believe that everything was going to be all right as long as taxes did not increase. ...
>
> They also understand that massive bank failures and falling real estate prices are not symptoms of prosperity but more nearly the collapse of a house of cards, and above all, an indication that trust in government's wisdom and prudence is altogether misplaced.
>
> However, the loss of confidence has been overdone. The country is not bankrupt, there will not be another 1930s, and the average American will not be paying rent to a Japanese landlord. But a deflation of optimism is not inappropriate if it helps improve policies.

Just how our economic/social/psychological climate will play out, only time —and sifted and winnowed experience — can tell you.

That Grain of Salt

Whatever predictions you attend to in your sifting and winnowing of advice, take all of them with the proverbial grain of salt.

- For instance, here was the assessment of a British politician rendered on Oct. 25, 1911, by the respected editor of the *London Spectator*:

"We cannot detect in his career any principles or even any constant outlook on public affairs; his ear is always to the ground; he is the true demagogue. ..."

The person referred to: Winston Churchill.

- This from the British Chancellor of Exchequer, David Lloyd George, on July 23, 1914, the very eve of WWI:

  I cannot help thinking that civilization, which is able to deal with disputes among individuals and small communities at home, and is able to regulate these by means of some sane and well-ordered arbitrament, should be able to extend its operations to the larger sphere of disputes among states.

- Consider the classic words of a University of Wisconsin-Madison professor of economics, describing the cataclysmic stock debacle of 1929 as "merely a technical adjustment of the market."

You needn't go far back into history to find bum predictions. Remember the Soviet premier who was going to bury us, the U.S. four-star general who saw light at the end of the Vietnam tunnel, the lips we read in the 1988 presidential campaign?

When it comes to soothsayers, it can be a puzzlement. Take your pick — and hold onto your hat, as the saying goes.

SOME BENEDICTORY STRATEGIES

Because I've known him for 50-plus years and admire and trust his fiscal acumen, I'm turning over a finale of this chapter to Professor Emeritus Doug Osterheld:

Pre-Retirement Do's

1. If you don't have a tax-deferred annuity (TDA), open one at once for the maximum amount you can through the campus office designated to handle your benefits.
2. Immediately begin to deposit the legal maximum amount in an individual retirement account (IRA). Contributions can be made only from earned income; annuities, dividends, interest, and so on don't count. If your current cash flow won't allow you to contribute the maximum allowable, consider borrowing money to do so in the last few years prior to retirement.
3. If you have independent or self-employment earnings, establish a Keogh plan.
4. If you have plenty of time before retirement, you can opt for some

risk in any investments. But if you have only a few years, investment safety should be your primary concern.

5. Develop a 10-year income plan, identifying amounts, rate of return, maturity dates, level of security, and other considerations.
6. Review carefully the income tax implications of both your present and future planning. While paying the least tax legally permitted is an acceptable motivation, don't make investments solely to achieve "tax savings"; if you lose your money, you've gained nothing.
7. Build into any financial planning an estimated inflation factor. In trying to determine the effect of inflation on the amount of income you'll need in a given year, use the "Rule of 72," which holds that if you divide 72 by the rate of inflation you estimate will occur over a given period of years, you'll find the target year by which you'll have to have doubled your income to offset the assumed inflation rate. For example, for an estimated inflation rate of 4%, divide 72 by 4 to get 18 — which means you'll have to double your income within 18 years to enjoy the lifestyle you currently maintain.

Post-Retirement Do's

1. If your TDAs and/or IRAs aren't performing up to par, consider rolling them over into other instruments, either for current use or for the future.
2. Since it's improbable that the precise time at which such funds might become available will be the most favorable time in the investment marketplace, maintain some money-market-type fund that you can draw on to make promising lump sum investments over time.
3. Establish an "acceptable" rate of return as a guide to when to invest and in what.
4. Don't invest everything at once, and never all in the same place. Diversify to protect yourself from instrument idiosyncracies. Achieve a balance among short- and long-term investments. The financial world calls the desirable programming of maturity dates "laddering."

All-the-Time Do's

1. Avoid procrastination. Putting off until tomorrow what should have been done yesterday is simply financial suicide on the installment plan.
2. Establish definite financial objectives and implement a plan for reaching your goals. Spend at least as much time planning your financial future as you do planning a vacation.

3. Appreciate the rabbit-like multiplier effect of money invested at compounded interest/dividends.
4. Recognize the impact of inflation.
5. Understand tax laws and implement strategies to take advantage of legal breaks and shelters.
6. Diversify your investments and take no unnecessary risks.
7. Protect yourself against unforeseen exigencies.
8. Bring family spending under control.
9. Avoid unrealistic expectations. In the financial world, as in most areas of life, there aren't any free lunches.
10. Seek professional advice, or at least that of knowledgable peers (Osterheld 1992).

A FINAL LECTURE NOTE

Before you undertake today's "Quickie Quiz," for this section, let's review some key points covered in this class session:

Inflation

Any increases in living costs can erode your purchasing power and your standard of living in retirement. To offset inflation, your income must rise each year. Provided you don't go back to work, this income must come from a pool of assets that's also growing, or from a pool that's large enough initially to meet your needs without being depleted too soon.

Retired individuals, or those nearing retirement, are understandably inclined to reduce their investment risk by placing more emphasis on income and principal stability than on capital appreciation. It's important to realize, however, that relying principally or solely on conservative investments could expose your nest egg to erosion, as indeed has happened recently with the significant decline in interest rates. Rising taxes could also take a toll.

Just as during your working years, you'll want to diversify to meet your needs both for safety and liquidity and for capital growth. How much you allocate to each objective will depend on your individual needs and other sources of income. Common stocks represent more short-term risk than other financial assets, but have provided higher long-run returns and a greater margin over inflation or declining interest rates than other investments. But here again diversification could be the better strategy — meaning stock mutual funds rather than individual stocks.

Health Care Contingencies

Health and custodial care costs are among the most pressing retirement expenses. By the end of the current decade, the average American family's outlays for health care are expected to jump from $4,269 a year, or one-eighth of current family income, to $9,397, or 16.4%, according to a recent study (Rich 1991).

Don't expect Medicare to save the day. Medicare typically covers less than half of participants' routine health care costs, and practically none of the costs of lengthy nursing home stays or home care. And the coverage offered by your institution's insurance plan may erode under the pressure of escalating medical costs. The alternative? Specialized/specialty catastrophic insurance policies you'll have to pay for. (*More about all this in Chapter 3.*)

Retirement Plan Distributions

Since a share of your retirement income may come from your IRAs or TDAs or other individual retirement programs, you'll need to be familiar with the rules and tax considerations concerning withdrawals, especially if you expect to receive any lump-sum distributions. Rules address the amount and timing of your withdrawals, and many are based on your life expectancy. Lump-sum distributions present a range of choices with significant tax implications. It may be wise to consult a professional.

Social Security

Social Security replaces only a portion of your pre-retirement income, so you need to be familiar with the various benefit levels and tax regulations affecting them. Full benefits reflect how long you've worked, how much you've earned, and your age at retirement. Benefits rise with inflation, but are partly taxable.

Getting Started

Getting started on a retirement financial plan is the hard part. Most of us are more practiced in the art of procrastination. That's the whole point of the following "Quickie Quiz." Gather all the pieces of the puzzle, including information on your investments, sources of income, health insurance situation, major expenses, and so on. Then see if your income on ahead will meet your long-term objectives during retirement.

Quickie Quiz

1. Using your sharpest pencil and your best crystal ball, fill out this budget for retirement living:

Estimated Monthly Family Income

	Present	At Retirement	After 10 Years
College/ university salary			
Retirement/ pension plan			
Social Security			
Annuities (TDAs, Keoghs, etc.)			
Royalties, honoraria			
Savings, CD, etc., interest			
Loan interest			
Stock and bond interest			
Stock dividends			
Income from rental property			
Profits on sale of any equities			
Self-employment			
Other			
Totals			

Estimated Cost of Living

Housing (mortgage, rent)			
Home maintenance			
Furnishings			
Auto/transportation			
Food			
Health care			
Personal			
Clothing			
Recreation			
Travel			
Retirement program(s)			
Taxes, insurance, interest			
Savings, investments, TDAs			
Family support (including alimony)			
Other			
Totals			

2. Using the data you've just assembled, analyze as frankly and honestly as possible how you'll stand financially when you retire, and figure out (a) what you're going to do with any surplus money, or (b) how you're going to make up any shortfall.

3. Answering the following questions will help you review, on a somewhat equal basis, various investments you may be considering:

1. Does it have a tax deferral or shelter feature?

2. Is that feature before or after taxable income?

3. Does the feature include only accumulation of earnings?

4. What is the rate of interest?

5. For how long is the rate guaranteed?

6. Is there a maximum amount that can be invested? How much?

7. Is there a minimum amount to be invested? How much?

8. Is there a minimum period that the investment must be in effect without penalty?

9. What are the fees for implementing or maintaining the investment? Front-end load or commission? Annual maintenance fee? Management fee? Rear-end load or surrender charge? How long do the fees run?

10. Is the investment insured? If so, by what agency? To what limit?

11. If the investment is not insured, what backing does it have?

12. Will the plan allow you to make changes without charge as your investment goals change?

13. Whom have you consulted about what you propose to do?

14. Will your cash flow accommodate the investment?

15. Are you prepared to assume any losses? What are your plans for any windfalls?

References

Adams, Marilyn, 1992, Knight Ridder News Service, Feb. 9.

Brosterman, Robert, and Kathleen Adams, 1991. *The Complete Estate Planning Guide* (New York: Mentor).

Burke, Francis D., Jr., 1992. "Financial Planning," *Journal of the American Society of CLU & ChFC*, January, pp. 15-17.

Cleveland, Harlan, 1987. "The Abolition of Retirement," *Change*, Nov./Dec., pp. 8-10.

Detlefs, Dale R., and Robert J. Myers, 1991. *Guide to Social Security and Medicare* (Louisville, KY: William M. Mercer).

Dudley, Donald L., 1991. "Coping with Retirement: Stress and Life Change," *Journal of the College and University Personnel Association*, Summer, pp. 1-4.

Egan, Jack, 1991. "Money Guide," *U.S. News & World Report*, July 15, pp. 50-80.

Egan, Jack, 1992a. "How You Can Afford to Retire," *U.S. News & World Report*, May 25, pp. 67-70.

Egan, Jack, 1992b. "No More Munificent Municipals," *U.S. News & World Report*, June 22, p. 85.

Egan, Jack, 1992c. "1992 Money Guide," *U.S. News & World Report*, Aug. 10, pp. 46-51.

Freese, Duane D., 1992. "Boomers a Bust When It Comes to Saving," *USA Today*, Tuesday, April 7, p. 11a.

Freese, Duane D., 1991. "How to Win the Retirement Game," *Bottom Line Personal*, Sept. 30, pp. 5-6.

Hage, David, *et al.*, 1991. "Living with Less Inflation," *U.S. News & World Report*, Oct. 7, pp. 55-64.

Hinersfeld, Daniel, 1992. "Golden Parachute or Lead Balloon?" *Lingua Franca*, April/May, pp 43-47.

Jaffe, Jacob H., 1992. "Report on First CORF Survey/Evaluation of Benefits and Perks for Retirees," *AEJMC News*, March, p. 1.

Kaye, Steven, *et al.*, 1992. "Mutual Fund Miscues," *U.S. News & World Report*, April 13, p. 75.

Kilcline, Vadm T. J., 1992. "TROA's Stance on COLAs," *The Retired Officer Magazine*, July, p. 10.

Lazzara, Craig L., 1992. "The Stock Market: How High Is Up?" *LNC Multifund Newsletter*, Spring, pp. 3-4.

Lazzara, Craig L. 1991. "Money Management: Skill and Luck," *LNC Multifund Newsletter*, Fall, pp. 1,4.

Lincoln National Corporation, 1991. "Independent Ratings: Just What Do They Mean?" *LNC Multifund Newsletter*, Fall, pp. 2-3.

Magner, Denise K., 1992. "A Growing Number of Colleges Offer Options for Retirement Investment," *The Chronicle of Higher Education*, May 13, pp. A17, 19-20.

Martorana, R. George, 1992. *Your Pension and Your Spouse — The Joint Survivor Dilemma* (Brookfield, WI: International Foundation of Employee Benefit Plans).

Milletti, Mario A, 1989. *Voices of Experience: 1500 Retired People Talk About Retirement* (New York: TIAA-CREF).

Osterheld, Doug, C., 1992. Personal correspondence in author's files, Feb. 14.

Osterheld, Doug C., 1984. *Financial Planning for Retirement* (Madison, WI: University of Wisconsin System).

Pender, Kathleen, 1992. "College Retirement Pie Draws Investment Firms," *San Francisco Chronicle*, April 6, pp. C1, 6.

Pentera, Joseph 1989. *A Guide to Creative Planned Giving Arrangements* (Indianapolis: Lincoln National Life).

Quinn, Jane Bryant, 1991a. "Is Your Insurance Company Safe?" *Newsweek*, July 29, pp. 38-39.

Quinn, Jane Bryant, 1991b. "Golden Years, Gold Included," *Newsweek*, Sept. 9, pp. 60-61.

Rich, Spencer, 1991. "Start Saving Right Now for Health Care," *Washington Post National Weekly Edition*, Dec. 29, p. 37.

Ruebhausen, Oscar M., Ed., 1990. *Pension and Retirement Policies in Colleges and Universities* (San Francisco: Jossey-Bass).

Sherrid, Pamela, 1991. "Investing," *U.S. News & World Report*, October 7, p. 94.

Sunberg, Alfred D. 1989. "Tax Changes, Retirement and Pensions," in Holden and Hansen, *The End of Mandatory Retirement*, (San Francisco: Jossey-Bass).

Social Security Administration, 1992b. *Retirement* (Baltimore: Social Security Administration).

Social Security Administration, 1992a. *Understanding Social Security* (Baltimore: Social Security Administration).

Thornton, Grant, Accountants and Management Consultants, 1991. Personal correspondence in author's files, Aug. 27.

TIAA-CREF, 1991. *Guiding Your Retirement Savings* (New York: TIAA-CREF).

TIAA-CREF, 1991. *Looking Ahead to Retirement* (New York: TIAA-CREF).

TIAA-CREF, 1991. *Estimating Your Retirement Income* (New York: TIAA-CREF).

TIAA-CREF, 1991. *Comparing Income Options* (New York: TIAA-CREF).

TIAA-CREF, 1991. *Taxes and Your Retirement Annuities* (New York: TIAA-CREF).

Waldrop, Judith, 1992. "Old Money," *American Demographics*, April, pp. 24-32.

Wiener, Leonard, 1992. "News You Can Use," *U.S. News & World Report*, March 9, pp. 68-72.

Wiener, Leonard, 1991. "How You Can Afford to Retire," *U.S. News & World Report*, Oct. 21, pp. 86-94.

3

Providing for Affordable Health Care

Mastering the Mysteries of Medical Insurance

Medicare, Medigap, short-term care, paying up, and long-term care.

Performing First-Echelon Maintenance

Facts of life, self-help programs and taking charge of your health — you're only as old as you feel.

Switching Horses in Mid-Stream

Selecting a new doctor, and making out advance directives.

Health Care Reforms on the Horizon?

Two approaches under consideration.

Quickie Quiz

References

Right up there with ensuring an adequate income stream in the lexicon of academic retirees is providing for affordable health care. And the two essentials are symbiotic. An adequate income stream makes possible a range of health care options, and affordable health care buttresses any income stream.

So individually and institutionally idiosyncratic are the ins and outs of health care that any complete treatment of the subject would take on the dimensions of a Ph.D. dissertation. Therefore, to keep this chapter within reasonable bounds, we're going to adopt three devices:

First, we build the discussion around our prototype 55-year-old professor planning to retire at 65, and merely indicate that there are exceptions to every rule applying to such a person.

Second, we urge you to obtain and read the following three guides, which are readily available and excellent sources on just about every detail of the subject:

1. *Guide to Social Security and Medicare*, published annually by William M. Mercer, Inc., 1500 Medinger Tower, Louisville, KY 40202; 502/561-4541. Price: $4.
2. *Medicare Handbook*, published annually by the federal Department of Health and Human Services, available free at *any* Social Security Administration (SSA) office.
3. *Planning for Health Coverage in Retirement*, published periodically by TIAA-CREF; 800/842-2733, ext. 5509, also free.

(Not to consult the latest editions of these manuals would be like failing to cram before a crucial final exam. They're listed alphabetically, not in any order of preference.)

Third, in this discussion, we offer valuable clues about what to look for in those three invaluable manuals, supplemented by practical tips gleaned from personal research and experience and that of knowledgeable retired colleagues.

MASTERING THE MYSTERIES OF MEDICAL INSURANCE

Everybody's heard of Medicare (not to be confused with Medicaid), the health insurance program provided by the federal government for people age 65 and over. Although Medicare benefits are excellent, they fall short in various ways, so you'll need additional insurance during your retirement to make up for at least some of those shortfalls. Helping you identify those gaps and selecting supplementary insurance is the mission of this section.

(Please recall that we'll be talking about a person who's retiring at 65. If you retire earlier or later, various permutations obtain, each of them covered in the three references.)

Medicare

The Medicare program actually has two parts: Part A, Hospital Insurance, and Part B, Medical Insurance. The reason for the distinction is that the two programs are financed in completely different ways. Part A you've been prepaying through your FICA payroll taxes based on your work covered by Social Security. In other words, once you stop paying monthly FICA "dues," Part A Hospital Insurance is yours at no further cost. Part B Medical Insurance you pay for in part by monthly premiums deducted from your Social Security allotment (in 1992, $31.80 a month; it could go up). The rest of the cost the federal government picks up from general revenues.

Hospital Insurance (Part A)

Part A protects you against much of the costs of hospitalization, certain related outpatient care, and certain home health services. When you secure your entitlement to Social Security benefits, your Medicare Part A coverage kicks in automatically at age 65, fully retired or not.

Part A pays only for what are variously called "recognized," "covered," "reasonable" services as determined by the SSA (not by your physician(s) or the hospital). The benefit payment amounts change each year in reflection of changing hospitalization costs.

Standard Hospital Care

For each hospital "benefit period," you must come up with a portion of the cost yourself. (In 1992, the hospital deductible is $652; it's been going up each year.) A benefit period expires 60 days after your discharge, so if you're readmitted within 60 days, you pay no "deductible," but if you're readmitted after that benefit period ends, for whatever reason, you have to pay another deductible, and so on. Once you've met a deductible, Medicare A pays for up to 60 days of reimbursible (according to the SSA) charges. After that you must contribute a "co-payment" (in 1992 from $163 to $326 a day, depending on the length of your stay). Another benefit period expires 60 days after another discharge, and so on again *throughout your life* (not in any calendar year).

Covered services include a semi-private room, meals, regular nursing attention, and routine supplies. Part A does not pay for personal-convenience items like a private room, private nurse, or TV. For some strange reason it doesn't pay for the first three pints of blood. (You may think that's a fitting gesture on the part of the feds.) Nor does Part A pay for the services of doctors — that's the business of Part B.

Special Facilities Care

Psychiatric hospital care, post-hospital care in a skilled nursing home, home health care, hospice care, care in Christian Science sanatoriums, care in non-participating hospitals —all are covered to some extent in certain circumstances by Medicare Part A. The permutations are varied and lengthy. For example, Part A will pay for certain post-hospital "skilled" nursing care, but not for "intermediate" or "custodial" care. Consult the recommended reading list at the end of the chapter for more details.

Medical Insurance (Part B)

When you enroll in Part A of Medicare, you also automatically enroll in Part B, unless you tell the SSA specifically that you don't want it — an unlikely event.

Part B Medical Insurance helps cover services you receive from a doctor and certain other related services, such as ambulance transportation, home dialysis equipment, outpatient physical therapy, and radiation treatments.

You are responsible for the first $100 of any expenses under Part B each calendar year. After that, Part B allows 80% of all the SSA terms "reasonable" charges, and you co-pay the other 20% (except for psychiatric services, for which Part B allows only 50%).

That term "reasonable" is the catch. To the SSA, "reasonable" means the part of a physician's or supplier's charges that it will approve. Many physicians "accept assignment"; that is, they will accept as full payment whatever Medicare will approve, even though their own fees may actually be higher, so you only have to co-pay the 20%. Other physicians do not accept assignment and thus will not settle for what Medicare approves, which means you have to pay the entire difference — on top of the Part B deductible and 20% of the "reasonable" (as determined by the SSA) charges.

What's more, there's quite a list of medical expenses Part B doesn't cover at all — for example, routine physical exams, glasses, foot care, prescription drugs taken at home (which can be a big-ticket item). For a complete list of items covered and not covered, consult the recommended guides.

Family Coverage

Under many circumstances, your spouse, ex-spouse, widow or widower, or a dependent parent may be eligible for Part A hospital insurance when he or she turns 65, based on your work record. Almost anyone who is 65 or older can enroll in Part B medical insurance by paying a monthly premium. You don't need any Social Security work credits to get this part of Medicare, but if you don't have work credits you'll have to pay a premium.

Medigap

As you can see, Medicare provides basic health care coverage, but it doesn't pay all of your medical expenses, and it doesn't pay for much long-term care, as in a nursing home.

For that reason, many private insurance companies sell insurance to fill in the gaps in Medicare coverage — "Medigap" insurance.

There are a number of different kinds of insurance you can buy to cover some or all of the medical costs that Medicare doesn't cover, or even to pay for health services that aren't included under Medicare at all.

The true Medigap policy is "supplementary" to, or "integrated" with, Medicare. A 1990 federal law directed insurance regulators in the states to devise by mid-1991 uniform national models for all policies claiming to be Medigaps. At a minimum they must cover Part A deductibles and co-payments, Part B co-payments, and the "blood deductible" — and be guaranteed renewable. Good Medigap policies do a lot better than that, picking up, for example, medical costs beyond Medicare's accepted schedule.

Plan/Policy Options

Most colleges and universities let retirees remain in the group health plans they sponsor for active employees. Although some institutions already paying the full cost may keep on doing so, most either split it with you or ask you to assume it altogether. Increasingly, institutions are likely to divert more costs to retirees. You're dependent, of course, on your past employer's continuing to make wise decisions in providing good coverage through reliable companies.

Public institutions of higher education in some states have an ingenious, invaluable "fringe benefit" method of helping retirees meet their health insurance costs — from an accumulated sick leave escrow account. In essence it works like this:

Each employee is entitled to "X" days of paid sick leave a year. For each day of sick leave you don't actually take, your salary for that day is sequestered in a special account. What's more, if a sick instructor's duties are assumed by colleagues, the absent person isn't required to count sick leave until the end of a semester. Hence, in a period of 30 or 35 years of active duty, it's possible to pile up a substantial amount of money in your accumulated sick leave account, which the institution then uses to pay health insurance premiums until the account is depleted.

(For example, when I retired in 1985, my Wisconsin Teachers' Retirement System sick leave escrow was calculated to foot all my Medigap premiums for some 20 years, depending, of course, on how sharply those premiums rise.)

Even if you have to pay the entire premium yourself, it's usually your best bet to stay with your employer's group plan. Group health rates are usually markedly lower than individual rates, and you're likely to get more benefit bang for your premium buck than you would from insurance you bought on your own. And usually whatever coverage those plans provide for you they also provide for your spouse and dependents.

Besides the lower cost and more comprehensive coverage, an employer's Medigap plan is to your advantage in at least two other ways. First, individual policies usually don't cover the treatment of pre-existing conditions — health problems that you had before you bought the policy — until a waiting period expires, a period that can range from six months to two years; in the meantime you're exposed to the risk of large out-of-pocket expenses that you could have been avoided had you stayed with your present group policy. Second, to purchase a new policy, you may have to prove "insurability." If you don't make the grade, you'll be rejected or at least you'll have to pay a substantial premium.

If for some reason you don't want to continue under your group plan, the recommended guides offer excellent suggestions on how to evaluate alternate policies. If your group plan Medigap options are severely truncated, it's just possible a private plan would be better, even though more expensive. Or, if you enjoy taking risks, you always have the choice of insuring yourself by setting aside "X" amount a month in a personal health care account. Increasingly, some institutions are requiring employees to form just such reserves (Cutler 1992).

Service/Coverage Options

Assuming you stay with your college/university health insurance program, you may have some choices among types of hospital/medical plans. There are three broad types: Standard (fee-for-service), HMO (health maintenance organization), and POS (point-of-service) — each with its advantages and disadvantages, depending on your personal preferences. If your preferences change, you may be able to change plans at a specified "it's your choice" time annually.

(For example, at our second home near Spring Green, WI, under our UW-Madison group, we have a choice among a half-dozen Medigap vendors, ranging in 1992 from a $394.57-a-month standard option to a $259.98-a-month HMO (both being family plans with one Medicare person involved.)

Standard Fee-for-Service. This is the good, old-fashioned American system of medical care married to Medicare. You're free to go to any doctor(s) you choose, wherever you or they are. Particularly if you're traveling, or occupying two seasonal residences far apart, that aspect is very important. So is the privilege of consulting the GP or specialist(s) you're used to and who know(s) your medical history. But any such traditional loose network of health care providers may be less efficient and probably more expensive than a so-called "managed care" system.

HMO. Enter health maintenance organizations. In return for a flat monthly premium, HMOs provide almost everything from complex surgery to routine consultations — generally for no or minimal extra charges. When you're enrolled in Medicare Part B, you can sign up with any HMO that has a contract with Medicare and serves the area in which you live. But you have to use the services of a health care provider who's a member of that HMO. If you consult a doctor who doesn't belong, you're on your own. The same goes for care received outside the HMO's service area, except in the case of a real emergency.

POS. Point-of-service is a hybrid, a cross between a standard plan and an HMO, in which, in effect, you sign up for an HMO, but if you want to go to a non-HMO physician you pay something extra. In a related version, the preferred provider organization (PPO), you get all or most of your care from affiliated doctors who charge the insurer according to a negotiated rate schedule (Kritz 1991).

POSs and PPOs are not universally available. Other arrangements may surface as health professionals, insurers, and society struggle to contain health costs. Were anything like a national health insurance program to emerge, everything we're saying in this section could go out the window. (Don't hold your breath.)

NOTE: Our generalities about comparative costs among types of medical service/coverage are just that, generalities, subject to significant variations. For example, a nationwide survey showed in 1992 that on average, HMOs cost $3,046 per employee, 14.7% less than standard insurance. Newer types of managed care saved less. But the savings varied widely. Chicago clients saved 16.4% over standard insurance with HMOs and 25.3% with PPOs. But in Seattle, HMOs cost only 1.3% less and PPOs cost 18.4% more. In Houston, HMOs cost 3.6% more than standard coverage, PPOs 13.4% more. The key problem, according to surveyer Foster Higgins, is that the quality of managed-care operators varies widely. "Well-run plans save money; poorly run plans do not," says Higgins (Anderson 1992).

Specialized/Specialty Short-Term-Care Insurance

The health care profession classifies the woes that can afflict us into two major types: *Acute* medical problems, such as a heart attack or a broken wrist, which usually call for short-term treatment with recovery as the goal; and *chronic* medical conditions, like Alzheimer's disease, which need long-term care with the goal of maintaining function.

Long-term care questions we treat in a later section. Here we'll talk about a variety of short-term though acute medical situations for which there are a variety of Medicare-coordinated insurance options you can consider, and which may or may not be available through a group plan via your college/university.

Major Medical/Catastrophic

Such policies cover the high cost of major illness, injury, or dental work over and above health services covered by Medicare and your Medigap policy. They usually have a large deductible and hence are relatively inexpensive — yet when dovetailed with Medicare and Medigap are invaluable at times.

Specified Disease Coverage

These policies provide benefits only if you become ill because of a particular disease, such as cancer or Parkinson's. The vendors usually limit the benefits to a certain dollar amount, which time can erode. To the extent that they frequently duplicate Medicare, Medigap, and Major Medical/Catastrophic, they usually aren't worth the money.

Hospital Confinement Indemnity Coverage

Such policies pay a fixed amount for each day you're in a hospital, up to a specified number of days. Unnecessarily duplicative if you've got comprehensive coverage under another policy or policies.

Dental

Medicare doesn't cover dental care other than certain surgical interventions, so if your Medigap policy doesn't either, a special dental care policy might be a good bet. But better evaluate it very carefully in consultation with a medical insurance specialist.

Travel

Remember that Medicare does not usually pay for hospital or other medical expenses outside the U.S. (exceptions include Canadian facilities if nearest to your home or while traveling to and from Alaska). Many Medigap policies don't cover you outside the U.S. either. If you plan to travel abroad, check your Medigap coverage. If you're not thus covered, investigate private short-term travel insurance. Shipboard illness coverage is problematic. Check it out with the line and your Medigap vendor.

Words to the Wise

Choosing health care insurance within or outside any group coverage can be an intimidating experience — many different kinds of insurance, many different vendors, many things to consider.

Here are some useful tips:

- Seek advice from your state insurance commissioner, your campus personnel office, and/or from a professional "insurance consultant" listed under that title in the Yellow Pages.
- Shop carefully. Contact several different companies and compare cost and coverage.
- Understand what you're buying. Don't take a salesperson's word for anything. Go over the fine print carefully.
- Don't buy more insurance than you need. Overlapping or duplicate policies may sound good, but more and more policies have clauses under which the companies don't pay for services paid for by another company.
- Avoid policies that pay a set dollar amount rather than a percentage of cost, lest inflation erode your coverage.
- Avoid policies that provide benefits only for a certain length of time rather than for life (except travel policies, of course).
- Watch out for "waiting periods" and "pre-existing condition" exclusions.
- Prefer a policy that protects your right to renew automatically.

- Prefer a policy that pays for that big-ticket item — prescription drugs used at home.
- Beware of scams. Don't believe any insurance salesperson claiming to be from the government. Medigap policies are not sold by the Medicare program or by any other state or federal agency.
- Take your time. Don't let a salesperson pressure you, and never pay the agent cash. Allow yourself to make an informed decision, just as if you were evaluating a graduate student's thesis or weighing a major purchase order.
- When your policy arrives, read it to make sure it provides the coverage you ordered.

The Paying-Up Rigmarole

Any trauma associated with choosing health care insurance can be as nothing compared with the turmoil connected with sorting out and paying the bills that come your way from any hospital stay or medical service. And you won't find anything on this topic in those recommended guides.

First of all, when you become eligible for Medicare benefits, you'll get a card containing your claim number — your Social Security number and the letter A. Safeguard this card because no claim will be paid without it. The card is the best evidence that you're covered.

(If your spouse has Medicare benefits under your work record, his or her card will have your claim number and the letter B. If his or her Medicare benefits are based on his or her own work record, the card will have his or her own SS number and the letter A.)

You'll likely have a Medigap card, too, and perhaps major medical, dental, and other cards as well, for your varied coverages. Place them all flat on the platen of a copy machine and run off a dozen sheets. Submit a copy to a hospital or clinic registration desk so you don't have to paw through your purse or billfold to establish your *bona fides*. (I learned this technique the hard way when I was turned upside down on an emergency room gurney while an aide struggled to get at my hip pocket; meanwhile I was literally suffering a heart attack.)

Medicare claims don't go to the government. They're processed by an insurance company or other organization under contract with the federal government. Part A may be handled by one company, Part B by another. For example, in my state, Blue Cross-Blue Shield is the Part A agent, Wisconsin Physicians Service (WPS) the Part B agent. So when you get envelopes in the mail bearing the names of such companies, don't ignore them; they're your pipeline to Uncle Sam. Your contract agents can change from time to time if they're underbid for the business.

Those hospital charges to be paid by Medicare Part A, any hospital under Medicare contract will submit directly to the agent organization. At the same time, the hospital may very well send a copy to you, somewhere stamped, "This is not a bill" or "This claim has been submitted to your insurance company(ies)." The bottom line may choke a horse, but just ignore it. Help is on the way.

Medicare will pay the hospital directly. If Medicare payments don't cover the hospital bill, if you have Medigap and other insurance, and if the hospital has a "Good Samaritan" code of conduct, the hospital will file the additional claims with the Medigap and supplementary insurance companies for you. So it's perfectly possible to run up a big hospital bill and never process any paper or write any check yourself. If the hospital doesn't do any Medigap/supplementary filing and sends you the balance of the bill, you'll have to submit the necessary claims yourself, get the reimbursement checks, and endorse them over to the hospital — provided the hospital hasn't been howling for its money in the meantime, in which case you'll have to pay up and wait for your insurance check(s).

If after six months the hospital still sends you plaintive or threatening demands to pay up an extraneous bill or two, it's safe to assume that your insurance didn't pay for some uncovered expenses — and to write out a final check. (For example, after the usual post-60 prostate protocol last year, I waited out the hospital until I got a "Please attend to this account" bill — for $2.37, a meal my wife had partaken in my company.)

Now let's turn to Medicare Part B billing. Doctors and other suppliers of covered medical services may submit charges directly to the Medicare agent organization by "taking an assignment," as we've said, which means they accept the amount recognized by Medicare. But that still leaves you with a 20% bill. If that doctor and supplier are courteous, they'll submit other bills to your Medigap and supplementary insurance companies, and if your policies are so constituted, you won't wind up with any paperwork or check-writing at all.

Even if your doctor does not take assignment, under federal law he or she must send a claim to Medicare for you. Again, if your doctor and supplier are courteous, after they've received payment from Medicare, they'll submit a bill to your Medigap and supplementary companies for the balance, and if your policies are so constituted, you again won't wind up with any paperwork or check-writing at all.

But suppose your doctor and supplier don't process all your possible claims? First, you get a notice from the Medicare agent stating how much the agency has paid the doctor/supplier and how much you owe. Second, you have to submit that statement (sometimes together with a company form and a copy of the original bill or bills) to your Medigap insurer with the tacit request that the insurer fork up the balance. Whereupon, the fates willing, you'll get a Medigap check, which you then endorse over to the doctor/supplier. In the event that the two payments don't satisfy the doctor/supplier, you'll get a bill for any balance, which you then submit to your supplementary company. If your policy covers you in this situation, you'll get another check, which you also endorse over to the doctor/supplier, or the insurance company may pay the doctor/supplier directly. If the third payment doesn't satisfy the doctor/supplier, you'll get a bill for any final balance, which you have no recourse but to pay (after a suitable lag in which you wait to make sure all possible appropriate transactions have indeed taken place, since some doctor/supplier computers seem to spew out monthly bills regardless of what's going on).

In between these varied transactions, you'll probably get statements telling you what each agency has done, but which don't mean you have to do anything for the moment but file the pieces of paper for future reference. (You may also get premature bills pressing you for payment; file them for the now.)

At any stage, there are appeal procedures in case you believe you've been underpaid by Medicare, Medigap, a supplementary policy or policies, or any of the above.

A Representative Paperchase

Now if all this sounds complicated, it can be. So let's try to simplify the process with a "for instance":

- When you check in at the hospital registration desk, display your coverage-card sheet to make sure the hospital bookkeepers have up-to-date information on your insurance.
- Check to see whether the hospital will file your Medigap insurance claims for you or whether you'll have to do that yourself. (By law the hospital has to file your basic Part A claim with the Medicare agent.)
- Take along as well a list of any prescription drug names and numbers so the attending physician knows what regimen you're on, and what he might tell the hospital pharmacy to make up for you. Ordinarily, you can't bring along and use your own prescriptions.

- Unless your Medigap policy is generous or your doctor specifies otherwise, don't ask for or accept any services that aren't normally covered by Medicare plus and Medigap policy(ies).
- From each attending physician/specialist/service, determine who will file your supplemental insurance claims for you and who will leave it up to you. (They each have to file your Medicare Part B forms.)
- As you leave, you may or may not have to sign a statement acknowledging receipt of services. (Unless you're a really perverse person familiar with medical hieroglyphics, you won't risk delaying your departure indefinitely by quibbling over any non-covered charges; besides, you can always appeal later.)
- Once home, the first epistle you'll probably get is an enormously detailed statement from the hospital for your information, stamped "A claim has been filed with your insurer." File the statement as a souvenir.
- In time you'll get a Medicare statement announcing how much Medicare has paid the hospital under Part A. File it, in case the hospital doesn't follow through by filing your supplemental insurance claims.
- In the likely event that the hospital will do that filing for you, you'll receive Medigap and major medical statements indicating that your supplemental coverage has clicked in. File them for reference.
- In the unlikely event that the hospital hasn't filed any Medigap insurance claims in your behalf, you'll have to do it yourself. Send a copy of the Medicare Part A statement to your Medigap company together with your policy number. (Some Medigap companies may even insist that you fill out a special form and attach the original complete hospital bill as well as your statement of Medicare coverage.)
- In case your Medigap doesn't cover all the hospital bill balance, repeat the process with your major medical insurer, if you have one.
- From the company or companies, you'll get a statement indicating how much they've paid the hospital, or a check made out to you to be endorsed over to the hospital.
- Now for the moment of truth: If you hear no more, you're homefree. If you get a final statement from the hospital, indicating who's paid what as well as any remaining balance, let a decent amount of time pass to allow for any bookkeeping errors along the line. (They can happen.) Then pay the remaining hospital bill out of petty cash.

- Meanwhile you'll be getting statements from Medicare indicating which individual medical service providers they've paid under Part B, or Part B Medicare checks made out to you to use in settling up with those providers. Save the statements. (They may come all together or in a series, depending on when the claims were filed.) Send in any checks, properly endorsed.
- In case any medical service provider doesn't file your supplemental-insurance claims for you, then you have to do it yourself. Again, start with your Medigap company and continue if necessary with your major medical insurer.
- The company or companies will either pay your providers directly or send you a check for you to endorse over, accompanied by a statement indicating what they have and haven't covered.
- Finally, another moment of truth. Final bills from your doctors/specialists that you have to pay out of pocket (unless you have a valid protest of some sort). In any case, wait another decent interval before paying up, because even the finest surgeons can have business offices that make a habit of sending out "final" bills before they received all insurance payments.

A couple of final cautions:

- If your Medicare agent and your Medigap company are one and the same, don't compound the confusion by not reading each piece of mail carefully to distinguish what's going on.
- If your doctor/clinic are associated with the hospital, again discern carefully which element is communicating with you.
- While HMOs normally facilitate all this paperchase a good deal, HMOs have been known to go bankrupt, leaving customers to seek other regress.
- As you can see, remember that any hospital paperwork associated with Part A doesn't include the bills associated with Part B attending physicians and services. (For example, that prostatechtomy bout of mine included a Part B internist, proctologist, anesthesiologist, blood bank, and other medical service bills, each of which had a different protocol for submitting claims. Sorting them out was almost worse than the surgery.)
- If the medical care provided you at any particular time isn't associated with in-patient care, naturally you can skip the Part A stuff in this narrative and go past "Go" to the Part B drill.

My retiree colleagues and I talk a lot about these paperchases that can drive you up the wall. Our facetious solution: Don't do anything until a sheriff knocks on your door.

Actually, there are ways out. Engage a consort — a geriatric services office associated with a hospital, clinic, or some other organization that will help you with all the paperwork for free, or a bank trust officer who'll do it for a fee. Another option: look in the Yellow Pages under "Insurance Claims Processing Services" — commercial specialists who again will handle the whole thing for a modest sum. Or just relax and enjoy the hassle, reminding yourself it's nothing more than you experienced years ago as a sophomore trying to register for classes, pay your fees, and buy your textbooks all on the same day, or the travail in an armed forces induction line. (But wouldn't you think technology would have come up with a solution by now?)

But you don't have to take my word for it about the paying-up rigmarole. In a June 14, 1992, *Washington Post National Weekly Edition* story headlined, "If Your Illness Doesn't Kill You, the Paperwork Might," staff writer Spencer Rich quotes Irwin W. Kues, senior vice president for finance of the Johns Hopkins Health System in Baltimore: "The billing situation is a nightmare!"

Yet be of good cheer. Those same medical care minions who are complicating your life may be saving it. Besides, retirees have lots of spare time in which to try to lick the system, don't they?

Long-Term Care Insurance (LTCI)

My retired colleagues and I jawbone a lot, too, about the issue of long-term health care insurance — whether to take it out and, if so, what type of policy to buy.

One fact is clear: neither Medicare nor Medigap cover long-term care except to extents sharply limited by type, place, and duration.

Another fact is clear: long-term care can get very expensive — in a professional nursing home, a 1992 average of $30,000 a year in real money; at home with volunteer help, a severe physical and mental strain on the family provider(s).

One fact is not so clear: What are your odds of needing long-term care? You can find responsible data to the effect that "about seven in 10 married couples turning 65 can expect that one spouse will need nursing-home care sometime before death." On the other hand, you can find equally responsible data to the effect that while the previous data may be true, "a typical nursing-home stay is less than six months."

So the odds are against your staying in a nursing home six months or longer. But if you do, you may be in for a very long spell indeed — and a very expensive one.

Whether you'll need long-term care will depend on the degree to which you'll need help in performing the "activities of daily living." This phrase usually signifies six distinct tasks — called "the ADLs" for short: bathing, dressing, using the toilet, transferring from bed to chair and vice versa, eating, and controlling bowels and bladder.

Some of my colleagues say, "So what if long-term care eats away at my retirement income and my assets; all that means is that my beneficiaries won't inherit as much. So all long-term care insurance really does is protect my next of kin."

Other colleagues say, "If long-term care insurance can help sequester my income and assets for me and my beneficiaries, I'm all for it."

(For an excellent extended treatment of the issue, see a new free TIAA-CREF booklet, *Long-Term Care: A Guide for the Educational Community*, 800/842-2733, 5509. Or go to your nearest SSA office and pick up another new, free *Guide to Choosing a Nursing Home*, complete with a checklist to help you compare one facility with another.)

Shopping for Nursing Home Insurance

If you decide to take out a long-term care policy, the sooner the better, because rates rise precipitously with your age, and most policies have an age limit beyond which nobody is eligible — typically 75 to 79.

The LTCI market is very fluid at present. You ought to start shopping by getting from your state insurance commissioner a list of those companies approved to operate in your state, and by talking to peers who've already been down the LTCI road.

Armond Budish, a Cleveland attorney specializing in geriatric law, has a list of 13 questions you ought to ask of any potential policy before you sign on the dotted line:

1. **Can the company raise the premium?** If you can't renew the policy each year at the same rates, you might be forced to give it up.
2. **When do the benefits start?** The longer the waiting period, the less expensive the policy; on the other hand, the longer you pick up nursing home expenses yourself.
3. **What types of nursing home expenses are covered?** A policy that doesn't cover custodial and intermediate as well as skilled care is of limited utility. So is a policy that restricts you to a particular type of facility.

4. **Does the policy cover home care?** Try to get one that does, to include household assistants as well as licensed aides, and one that covers day care away from home as well.
5. **Does the policy cover only "medically necessary" care? Who decides what is "medically necessary," your physician or the insurance company?** This is a crucial consideration, because if care is no longer necessary for rehabilitation or improvement, it becomes intermediate or custodial care — not covered under a "medically necessary only" policy. Prefer a policy that covers intermediate/custodial care as well as skilled-nurse care.
6. **Does the plan offer an inflation-protection option?** You might not need your insurance for 10 years, whereupon today's benefits will have been drowned in rising costs. This option is well worth any small added premium.
7. **Does the policy provide benefits for necessary care while you're traveling or staying in another state?** Important if you're apt to be on the move.
8. **What if the policy is canceled?** Let's say you pay premiums for 10 years and then opt out. Are you left with nothing or a small equity?
9. **Does the policy contain a premium-waiver option?** Some policies say that after you start receiving benefits for a period, you don't have to continue to pay premiums and the policy will remain in force. A valuable provision.
10. **Can the policy be upgraded?** As LTCI improvements are made, can you latch on to any?
11. **How does the policy treat existing medical conditions?** Some policies either exclude coverage on them or impose a waiting period before coverage goes into effect for those conditions. Other insurance carriers will require a strict physical.

    Make sure any pre-existing condition coverage includes such long-term diseases as Alzheimer's and Parkinson's.
12. **Does the policy restrict coverage by requiring a hospital stay prior to nursing home admission?** Most states have outlawed this type of barrier.
13. **How secure is the company?** A lot of fly-by-night outfits have gotten into the LTCI game. Your security could depend on the financial health of the insurer. Double-check with your insurance commissioner and with a couple of rating services. Everything being

equal, go with a big-time, diversified insurance company with a name to protect.

14. **Is the amount of coverage you're purchasing realistic, given lengthening lifespans and inflation?** What did I do? At age 70 I took out an LTCI policy from the "don't leave home without one" people, costing $1,042 a year — on the chance that someday I'll need almost that much a week for nursing home care (Budish 1991).

If you have a life insurance policy already in force that permits you to tack on a rider covering LTC, that's another alternative. TIAA-CREF has a new, highly rated "Teachers LongTerm Care" insurance policy, but to be eligible you have to be employed by or retired from a "TIAA-CREF-eligible" institution, meaning a non-profit educational or research entity, and aged 40 to 84. Spouses, parents, and parents-in-law are also eligible. If your institution is a participant and you're still on active duty, you may be able to arrange to have your premiums deducted from your salary check or, if you're retired and a TIAA-CREF annuitant, deducted from your monthly benefit.

The Medicaid Method

Truth to tell, you have another option in regard to long-term care — the Medicaid method.

Some people may think that Medicare and Medicaid are two different names for two different aspects of the same program, but they're not; they are separate and distinct in organization and funding. Medicaid is a state-run program (with federal assistance) designed primarily to help pay the health bills of poor Americans, regardless of age. Each state has its own rules about who is eligible and what is covered under Medicaid. You might qualify for both Medicare and Medicaid. If you'd like to know more about the Medicaid program in your state, contact your local social services or welfare office. Here, all we can do is generalize.

In most states, you can get at least part of a long-term-care free ride in a participating nursing home or at home if you qualify for Medicaid by being at or below a requisite level of assets and income.

Most states set the Medicaid poverty line for a single person at $2,000 to $4,000 in assets (aside from a home and a car) and a meager monthly allowance of $300-$500.

It's highly unlikely that any retired academic will be at that level in the normal course of things, so to qualify for Medicaid you would have to engage in divestment, or "spending down." For example, you could give away all your assets to your children or other beneficiaries or place them in an irrevocable trust (Budish 1990).

There's one catch: you have to have completed all spending down to the poverty level 30 months before you apply for Medicaid. In other words, you can't wait until you're confined to a nursing home and then propose to divest. That's illegal, and states can severely limit strategies by which one spouse may shelter assets under the name of the other or of another relative.

As a matter of fact, that 30-month proviso is the federal embargo, and the law allows states to extend the period. Some have done so — up to four years.

A recent federal law has set up safeguards against poverty for your spouse in the event you spend down to qualify for Medicaid. Since 1990 a spouse could keep a home and a car, plus a minimum of $12,516 in jointly owned assets, and a minimum joint monthly income of $856. Although they can go higher, most states stick to those minimums.

My colleagues and I argue about this Medicaid method of qualifying for a nursing-home dole. Some see it as a cop-out, an immoral way of going on welfare, shifting to society (read, your children and mine) the costs you rightfully should bear.

A nursing home administrator in Virginia agrees. She's often overheard relatives bragging about beating the system.

"It's an immoral process," she says (Baker 1992).

Others among my colleagues say, "My taxes have supported the program, and if an accidental or deliberate change in my fortunes entitles me to public assistance, I have as much right to it as anyone else."

A Virginia lawyer specializing in advising elderly clients agrees: "The law allows it. It's difficult for me as an attorney not to explain to clients what the law allows, any more than a tax attorney would fail to advise his clients of legitimate tax-dodging alternatives" (Baker 1992).

How to resolve the controversy would make a good essay question for a final exam in a course on ethics.

If you opt for considering divestment, don't do anything until you've checked in detail with the regulations applying in your state — regulations that have a habit of changing annually with economic tides. And the best way to do the checking is to consult a lawyer experienced in divestment.

He or she is apt to tell you something like this:

> To be legal, divestment must be irrevocable and unconditional. That is, a gift of property to your children cannot have strings attached. Other-

wise it isn't a completed gift. In order to qualify as a divestment, your children must be free to do anything they want with gifted assets.

You should also realize you'll be disqualified from receiving Medicaid for that "penalty period" following divestment (normally 30 months). So if you decide to divest yourself of your assets, you should be sure to retain sufficient funds to cover the costs of nursing home care during the penalty period, should that become necessary (Langer and Roberson 1992).

Don't be surprised if states, hamstrung by skyrocketing Medicaid costs, blow the whistle on many forms of spending down.

There are practical problems with putting yourself on welfare: The Medicaid program is being squeezed, so the quality of your care could drop. The loopholes used by the middle class will eventually be closed, so you may have planned for naught. Even if you qualify, Medicaid patients may get poorer treatment, in poorer facilities, than those who can afford to pay. You may even have trouble getting a bed.

Then there's that question of morality again. The huge loopholes in the Medicaid law, exploited by well-to-do seniors, are creating a legion of false poor, collecting public money they don't deserve, says *Newsweek* columnist Jane Bryant Quinn: "You saved all your life to buy yourself red-carpet treatment in your old age. Why get greedy and throw it away?" (1992).

There's a real flaw in our national health care policy that sometimes results in true unfairness, however.

For example, there are two 70-year-old men with similar assets. One has a stroke and the other a heart attack. The one with the stroke winds up in a nursing home for six years at a cost of $216,000, only a pittance of which is covered by Medicare. The heart attack victim undergoes bypass surgery in a hospital at a cost of $250,000, of which Medicare covers all but $3,000 (Baker 1992).

No wonder C. Everett Koop, former U.S. surgeon general, calls our present national health care system "a shell game and a national disgrace."

PERFORMING FIRST-ECHELON HEALTH MAINTENANCE

When I was an infantry platoon leader, the Army assigned responsibility for vehicular maintenance by unit or echelon. For instance, first-echelon maintenance was the responsibility of the driver, second-echelon that of the company motor pool, third-echelon that of regimental engineers, and so on, back to LOGCOM port overhaul.

With all the backup available, you might think the Army would go easy on an errant lieutenant. No way. I was once severely reprimanded for an unacceptable record of first-echelon maintenance. (The fact that most of my jeep-repair problems were the result of German artillery fire meant nothing to the rear-echelon record keepers.)

The same principle holds in health care. Each of us as individuals is responsible for first-echelon maintenance. A faithful regimen can save trips to an infirmary or even to a MASH.

Facts of Life

How you feel about your own health and what you feel able to do about your physical condition are the keys to your wellness as a retiree.

The good news is that people aged 50 to 70 perceive themselves as healthier and feel relatively younger than do those under 25. The image of the feeble older person has in point of fact been replaced in many cases by the sun-tanned golfing retiree.

The bad news is that the latter stereotype doesn't apply to a lot of people. In reality, many older people suffer from chronic illnesses, such as arthritis, cancer, high blood pressure, or diabetes. So some elderly people with serious health problems may be deluding themselves. A Duke University study, for example, found that 44% of the aged who were actually in poor health rated themselves as in good or excellent condition.

Your perception of your health, then, may be at least as critical as the actuality in taking remedial action.

Very important to you as well is the fact that many of the diseases experienced by older people tend to be "life style" illnesses; that is, they can be prevented or improved by medical technology and most definitely if you take a more responsible role in changing unhealthy habits.

Why can feelings of good health and health itself improve with age? According to an exhaustive *Psychology Today* survey: Older people seem to care for themselves better than young people. They take more preventive measures, such as getting regular checkups, eating breakfast, and getting enough sleep. People over 60 exercise more than those in their 40s and 50s, eat to excess less often, and seem to be less self-conscious and neurotic than younger people.

What's more, of those people 65 and older, those with higher levels of education tend to rate their health more favorably than those with less education, and those staying active physically and mentally rate their health status more accurately than other older people.

Overall, the majority of Americans of all ages agree that retirees are healthier today than a decade ago. (However, we shouldn't overlook another reality about health and wellness. As former U.S. Secretary of Health, Education, and Welfare Wilbur Cohen liked to point out, "While it's true we're a healthier, more able population, that doesn't mean everyone.")

How can you go about trying to control your health? The respondents to that *Psychology Today* survey said that "diet, exercise, and positive thinking are very important." Through a planned, systematic health-and-wellness program you can gain greater ongoing health, a feeling of physical capability more of the time, a prolonged life with fewer bouts of illness, and the good nature that flows from self-mastery and personal achievement (Shea 1991).

Self-Help Programs

Most first-echelon (you) health maintenance (wellness) programs are based on these premises:

- Wellness is our natural state and can be preserved through alertness, healthy habits, and early attention to developing illness or health problems.
- A health risk profile is the starting point — filling out a detailed questionnaire on lifestyle, mental outlook, and medical and family history, and taking a thorough physical exam can lead to a profile that not only identifies your personal health risks but suggests how your "risk-age" can be reduced if you change or adopt behaviors. See your doctor.
- Lifestyle — that is, habits you engage in every day (smoking, drinking, and eating propensities, for example) have a major impact on the likelihood of illness and the length of your life. (Although genetics can play a part, too.)
- Change for the better in personal (even family) habits you can achieve through professional advice, personal training, and peer support.
- Stress management — determined relaxation, avoiding excessive behavior, giving up self-destructive habits, coping effectively with external stressors that you can't eliminate, avoiding being drawn into negative interpersonal transactions, satisfying pastimes — can usually help sustain your health dramatically *(See Chapter 4)*.
- Discipline — managing your stress, giving up deleterious habits, engaging in an exercise program, and so on — comes from your gut and has little to do with chronological age. (In the retirement complex in

which I live, for example, the most vigorous, dedicated exercisers are two 97-year-old women who walk at least a mile a day no matter the weather, and take a fishing vacation in the northwoods every summer.)

- Support systems can be of signal assistance: group exercise therapy, drug or alcohol counseling, dietary home cookin' or cafeteria menus, and so on.
- Regular medical exams constitute the hard core of a support system. (I wouldn't be writing this book today were it not for a semi-annual exam that spotted prostate cancer in an early enough stage to respond totally to surgery.)
- Peer support is invaluable, maybe even irreplaceable for some: an absence of negative messages from peers, organizational support, support at home, plenty of opportunity to practice salutary behavior, a network of similarly inclined people. Your campus may offer such services.
- A comprehensive, long-term program is what we're talking about, not an assortment of short-term "fad" efforts.
- A "normative subculture" — in other words, what sociologists term an optimum environment in which to grow old gracefully. It might be worth a move to experience one (Shea 1991).

  Says a doctor/reviewer:

> The points you make about diet, exercise, and prevention are correct and well said. Another idea on maintaining health which you don't mention but you exemplify is to maintain an active intellectual pursuit and productive capacity. For some this might include volunteering, or offering expertise, such as you're doing, to others starting out in academic life.

The bottom line in a wellness program is you — not your physician, your kin, your spouse, or your support group(s). **You** have the greater responsibility for your own health. (But don't carry this dictum to the extreme of not seeking professional or peer help when you really need it.)

Taking Charge of Your Health

Writing in a special "The Pursuit of Health" supplement to late-1991 issues of *U.S. News & World Report*, Robert Barnett (editor of *The American Health Food Book*, a cookbook with over 250 kitchen-tested low-fat, low-sodium recipes and a comprehensive guide to food and nutrition) offers one of the best summaries we've seen on how to give ourselves more healthy days, regardless of age:

- If you don't smoke and you give yourself good food, pure water, proper exercise, and the skills to manage stress, you'll increase the chance that your last years will be free of disability, heart disease, or cancer.
- Good eating habits reduce the risks of coronary heart disease, stroke, diabetes, obesity, certain cancers, and osteoporosis.
- Regular exercise — both aerobic and strength training — similarly reduces your risk of developing heart disease, stroke, and diabetes.

"There's no doubt that individuals who are more physically active throughout life have larger skeletons and greater bone mass, and, with increasing age, a lower risk of fractures," says William Haskill, a professor of medicine at Stanford. Exercise and diet can lead to permanent weight control.

Studies show that people who exercise and diet greatly improve their chance of losing weight and keeping it off, says Haskill. Diet alone can result in weight loss, but usually once the diet stops, the weight returns.

The right program can also reduce fatigue, increase your endurance, and even lift your mood. Eating right can give you more energy to develop strength, flexibility, and endurance. Strengthening exercises help us stay lean and strong. Flexibility enables us to move confidently, fluidly, and with less chance of injury.

"A short brisk walk is one of the most reliable mood elevators I've ever encountered," says California State University's Robert Thayer. In his studies, a short walk far surpasses a snack as a way to counter mid-afternoon fatigue: "A 10-minute walk, rapid but not exhausting, enhances energy, often reduces tension, and tends to increase the optimism with which people view their personal problems."

No matter what your age, there's no better time than the present for starting to take charge of your health. The longer you procrastinate, the more untractable some unfortunate habits may become. So idiosyncratic are wellness programs that you're well-advised not to do too much reading, talking about, or trying one until you seek professional counsel, Barnett concluded (Barnett 1991).

(My regimen? A professionally prescribed very low salt/fairly low cholesterol diet, a daily hike or stationary-bike ride, golf in summer, hunting in fall — and that regular physical exam.)

References — Printed and Interpersonal

A retired executive secretary of a state medical society, who critiqued this chapter, told me:

Clay, you've left out two very important points.

First, it's an excellent idea to keep at home a ready reference on health and your body. One of the very best is the American Medical Association's *Family Medical Guide* (Pleasantville, NY: Reader's Digest Press). It's particularly useful for boning up before seeing a doctor.

Second, some senior citizen groups sponsor exercise sessions and health seminars, and have or know of resource documents on such matters as advance directives.

Questions You May Ask

Q. I want to live long **only** if I can feel and look good and be mentally sharp. Can I?

A. Yes, if you take care of yourself.

Q. My habits weren't always healthy. Does this mean I'll be sick when I'm old?

A. It's never too late to change.

Q. Smoking, drinking, fooling around? How bad can they really be?

A. Pretty bad.

Q. Heart attacks run in my family — so what good could it possibly do to change my life-style?

A. Plenty.

Q. I hear a lot about "silent diseases." How do I find out if I've got one?

A. There are many kinds of tests to detect many kinds of diseases.

Q. Sometimes elderly people can't seem to think or remember. Can I avoid that?

A. Stimulation by learning maintains and adds to your brain power.

Q. When I'm old, I don't want to be cranky and set in my ways? How can I not be that way?

A. Seek companionship (Ubell 1992).

Good-Medicine Cabinet

Taking charge of your health ought to include always making sure you have a well-kept medicine cabinet. Cheryl Ray, a hospital outpatient pharmacy clinical staff pharmacist, recommends 10 items "that are the most common to provide needed comfort":

- Analgesic (aspirin or its counterpart)
- Antacid
- Antidiarrheal

- Antiseptic and bandages
- Antibacterial ointment
- Antihistamine
- Decongestant
- Emetic
- Laxative or stool softener
- Thermometer

Ray has these added tips:

- These products may all be purchased by brand name, but may be cheaper if you buy them in generic form.
- Look for label warnings about use for particular disease states or with other prescription drugs, and also check dosage.
- On a periodic basis, check the expiration date on your medications and discard anything that's expired.
- Keep an up-to-date list of any prescription drugs in your billfold or purse, with the telephone number of your pharmacist.
- If any of your ailments aren't relieved by taking over-the-counter medication, seek medical advice or attention.
- Feel free to contact your physician or pharmacist with any questions you may have about over-the-counter drugs.
- Secure your medicine cabinet from grandchildren's little hands (Ray 1992).

"You're Only as Old as You Feel"

People in their early 60s tend to visit the doctor more and feel more frail than people older than that, and the reason may be largely psychological, according to Paul Kerschner, a gerontologist and senior vice president of the National Council on Aging:

> The problem is that people in their 60s are nearing the transition to retirement, and they begin to feel age 'creeping up on them.' There seems to be something of a barrier that you cross — a period of time when you begin to worry about oncoming aging. This occurs for men especially around ages 62 or 63, a little later for women.

Statistics collected among 2,000 seniors by the ICR Research Group for Marriott Senior Living Services show that people aged 60 to 64 report more problems walking, dressing, and preparing meals, and more visits to doctors than do people 65 to 69.

Dr. Kerschner comments:

- In many cases, people beginning to think about aging start visiting doctors to reassure themselves. If they forget something, they think it's a problem of aging.
- Another part of the problem may be people around them. Many people in their early 60s tend to view themselves as frail compared to younger friends and colleagues that they frequently come in contact with. People over 65 tend to spend more time with those their own age and become comfortable with their new age group.
- Perception also plays a role. A 60-year-old person may get up in the morning and decide he or she feels weak because of age, while someone older may get up, feel the same way, but conclude he or she feels pretty good for their age.
- Some of the problem is whether society considers you old. For example, if a 30-year-old politician were to become ill on a trip and vomit at an embassy dinner, people would think little of it. But let the same illness strike a 67-year-old, and people wonder if something serious is wrong (Schmid 1992).

Yes, indeed, there may be something to the old saying, "You're only as old as you feel."

SWITCHING HORSES IN MIDSTREAM

When you get ready to retire, it's likely that your primary physician will be retiring, too, not to mention any retinue of medical specialists with whom you may have become familiar.

But to reduce the number of changes in your life attendant to retiring, you may want to consider changing doctors well beforehand. On the other hand, you may prefer to play out the string as long as possible.

Whenever, changing your general practitioner or internist of long standing can be traumatic. He or she can know you intimately, and vice versa. He or she may not make house calls, but you know there's always a friendly voice on the end of the line when you phone in with an emergency or routine question. And you know where your complete medical dossier is.

If for purposes of economizing on medical costs you've switched from a standard insurance plan to a form of managed care, then you've already surmounted the change from your individual doctor to a platoon in an HMO-type clinic.

Selecting a New Doctor

But suppose you haven't. How do you go about selecting a new physician or physicians?

One logical way is to ask your old physician for recommendations. Yet that doesn't always work. At least it didn't in my case. The names my doctor gave me were of his long-time colleagues, who turned out to be either retiring or not taking on any new patients.

If your doctor is in a clinic of associated private physicians and surgeons, you can simply move from one office to another, provided you feel you'll be compatible with a younger member of the firm.

Seeking advice from campus colleagues or from other trusted friends is an acceptable option, although be prepared to be appalled at your perception of the bedside manner of someone recommended to you highly by a peer.

The county medical society will give you a list of conveniently located, board-certified MDs, but it's unlikely the executive secretary will go beyond that with any pointed suggestions other than to run down an alphabetical list.

Whatever route you take, here are some criteria to consider in making your final selection of a new primary doctor:

- Whether you prefer a blunt approach, a hand-holding manner, or something in between, make this criterion a measurable one in consideration of your peace of mind over a long haul.
- Remember the whole point of the exercise and pick someone manifestly younger than you so you won't have to go through the whole process again before your death certificate is signed.
- Looking ahead to when you may be less mobile, choose somebody in a location convenient to wherever you expect to be at the time of your retirement.
- If you can determine, pick somebody who isn't known to be in Aspen or in the Bahamas those months of the year when older folks fall prey to the most diseases.
- If you have a choice among persons with comparable medical track records, pick somebody with whom you share backgrounds or lifestyles so the odds are better that you'll be simpatico. For instance, if you're a poker-playing Knights of Columbus Rotarian from New England, let your proclivities play a role.

- Again if you have a choice, pick somebody whose talents lie in the direction of treating any medical condition you're known to have.
- On the question of whether or not your spouse and you should go to the same GP, let the doctor decide. Some prefer such an arrangement; others reject it. But it's a good idea that your doctor meet your spouse.
- How does he or she handle access on off-hour legitimate medical emergencies or concerns? Is he or she available then, or will you be advised to take your troubles to a hospital emergency room? If you're likely to be referred to medical colleagues when your primary's away, try to get to meet those people ahead of time.
- Don't hesitate to shop around. You're not likely to buy a new car without taking a test drive; why do anything less in selecting somebody so crucial as a doctor?
- A not-so-minor consideration to throw into the hopper is whether or not the doctor will file your supplementary insurance claims for you or rather delegate such chores to patients.

Whatever, be of good cheer. You may be shocked at first at how young and inexperienced a new doctor can look and seem, but just remember that his or her medical knowledge is hot off the grill. After all, when you and your department go looking for a new assistant professor, you go by credentials, not by age; in fact, your policy may well be "the younger the better." Well, don't hesitate to apply the same principle in your search for a new health care provider.

When my long-time dentist departed for Sun City suddenly, in a broken-bridge emergency I went to the nearest clinic, where the only available professional was someone who looked young enough to be my oldest granddaughter. She turned out to be the best dentist I've ever had. When she moved to an associated clinic on the far side of town, I followed.

Just as your doctor retires, so sooner or later will your lawyer, broker, trust officer, member of the cloth, butcher, baker, candlestick maker. So you're apt to switch more than one horse in midstream. The procedures we've suggested for replacing a physician apply in principle to replacing other providers of services. It all may not be pleasant to contemplate, but it's doable — just one of those things that goes with the territory of growing older.

Making Out Advance Directives

Something else that goes along with growing older is making out advance directives — the legal documents that convey your wishes about your health care. They may also name a relative or friend to make decisions if you become unable to do so. Advance directives, which usually take the form of a living will and/or a durable power of attorney for health care, you write while of sound mind and before you become seriously ill.

(*You'll find more detail on this subject under "Folding the Tent" in Chapter 5.*)

HEALTH CARE REFORMS ON THE HORIZON?

It's hard to pick up a newspaper or newsmagazine or watch a TV newscast these days without reading about country-wide health care problems and/or impending reforms. As we've said, were any or all of the 20-some bills pending before Congress in spring 1992 to become translated into federal statutes, some or much of this chapter could become obsolete.

In general, there are two broad, basic approaches to health care reform under consideration:

One is a completely or largely government-regulated and operated program that would establish minimum nationwide health care standards with everybody having access. It would wrap Medicare and Medicaid into a single-payer payment system with funding and other guarantees. Means testing — the more you can afford, the more you pay — would probably be a stipulation. The program would be strictly managed by a government agency and health care providers tightly regulated.

Another approach would leave in place the private-sector health care provider and insurance industries, with the government defining benefit plans and setting performance standards. A public-sector program would ensure that the poor and destitute had comprehensive health coverage, to include prevention and wellness services. All others would have to insure themselves through private insurance or employer-provided plans.

Given the country's normal incremental approach to reforms, what's likely to emerge is some combination of the above. In any case, we're all probably facing some accommodations. For example, to provide adequate care for every person in an environment that includes the most advanced technologies available, some controls seem inevitable on how, when, where, and how much care each of us rates. Courts could become more realistic in balancing malpractice and liability claims against providers while protecting patient rights (Kilcline 1992).

Given the diverse economic, social, and political requirements of a diverse population, the whole process won't be easy, swift, or sure. But health care costs, now more than $700 billion a year and mounting at more than twice the overall inflation rate, would seem to demand some form of remedial action.

Such action won't come easily because the issues are as much moral as fiscal — how, when, where, and for whom to ration health care.

Medicare costs in 1992 were $118 billion, up 270% from 1990, four times the rate of inflation. The program grew so rapidly because there are more post-65 people in the population and because health care costs rose substantially faster than other costs in society.

So to "freeze" Medicare spending really means deciding who's not going to receive care under the program — or how much less health care to provide everyone eligible.

And there's a further catch that illustrates the moral dilemma facing federal budgeteers:

Almost 40% of Medicare funds are spent on the elderly in the last 30 days of their lives, just over 50% for care in the last 60 days of people's lives, and nearly 60% on the elderly in the last 90 days of their lives.

If we retirees thought we were home free from major issues of public policy, we ain't seen nothin' yet.

QUICKIE QUIZ

Part I. *You are interested in several medical insurance plans. To compare their relative benefits and costs, submit each option to the following battery of questions:*

1. How much is the monthly premium?

2. How much is any annual deductible?

3. How much is any contract maximum?

4. How much co-payment is required for prescription drugs? ambulance? medical supplies? physical/speech/occupational therapy?

5. Are physicians with the following specialties affiliated with the plan, and are they "Board Certified" in that speciality: surgery? orthopedics? mental health? gynecology? eye care? internal medicine? geriatrics? other?

6. If you require the services of a specialist not affiliated with the plan, will the plan refer you to that specialist?

7. If one plan under consideration is an HMO, can you select your personal primary physician within the HMO? Can you change your HMO primary physician if you are dissatisfied? How frequently?

8. Do you need your primary physician's referral to see a specialist within the HMO?

9. What is the total number of doctors affiliated with the plan?

10. Where are the providers located: hospital? doctors' offices? care outside office hours? pharmacy? skilled nursing facility? specialists?

11. Who will see you for routine office calls: nurse practitioner? physician's assistant? doctor?

12. What coverage is provided for: dental care? vision exams? glasses or contact lenses? outpatient mental health? alcohol/drug abuse treatment? blood transfusions? wellness programs? other?

13. What coverage is provided for emergency care: out-of-area life-threatening emergencies? out-of-area urgent care? out-of-area routine care?

14. If you have a dispute with the plan, are appeal procedures satisfactory?

15. Do the physicians and other care providers treat you with courtesy and deal with you honestly?

16. Are doctors accessible when necessary?

17. If you need urgent care, are you able to schedule an appointment promptly?

18. Is the waiting period for routine checkups reasonable?

19. Is it reasonably easy to call to make an appointment or ask a question?

20. Can you call the plan doctor when you have questions about your care?

21. Is the plan striving to improve the quality of medical care it provides? If so, how?

22. Will the provider(s) process Medigap and specialty insurance claims or is that the responsibility of the patient?

23. Is the plan striving to improve the quality of medical care it provides, and if so, how?

24. By what percentage have the plan's rates been going up annually?

25. Would you recommend membership in this plan to others?

26. Are colleagues who are members of the plan recommending it to you?

27. Are you and your spouse in agreement on a plan?

28. Are prescription drug dispensers widely available under the plan?

29. Is a primary physician of your choice about to retire?

30. Must you pass a physical exam before becoming eligible?

31. Is there a waiting period before coverage becomes effective?

32. Are pre-existing conditions covered?

33. Are plan headquarters personnel forthcoming in answering questions?
34. Are you sure that what appears to be a less expensive plan actually provides you with adequate coverage?

35. How crucial to you is the absence of a particular type of coverage in a plan? For example, out-of-area urgent care?

36. How crucial to you is the presence of a particular type of coverage in a plan? For example, dental care? eye care?

37. Are dependents fully covered under the plan? under what conditions?

38. Will your campus personnel office give you a confidential rating of the plans?

39. Is there a "health fair" you can attend for additional information?

40. How often and how easy will it be to change plans if you wish to do so?

Part II. *If and when you're faced with deciding for yourself or a loved one on a long-term care facility, answer the following questions posed by the United Seniors Health Cooperative, a Washington, DC, cooperative organization:*

1. Are neatness and good maintenance evident?

2. Is the atmosphere cheerful, with plenty of human contact?

3. Is the staff well-trained, stable?

4. Does a professional staffer encourage residents to participate in a well-organized activities program?

5. Can residents have some of their own furniture to give their rooms a homey feeling?

6. Is the food appetizing, prepared under the supervision of a credentialed dietician?

7. Do residents have a choice between eating in a dining room or in their rooms?

8. If a resident has to go to a hospital, will the room be held for him or her?

9. Does the home have a residents' council where grievances and new ideas can be aired?

10. Is an ombudsman on the premises on a weekly basis?

References

Anderson, Kevin, 1992. "Survey: Savings on Health Care Vary," *USA Today*, April 7, p. 1B.

American Medical Association, 1991. *Family Medical Guide* (Pleasantville, NY: Readers Digest Press).

Baker, Donald P., 1992. "Squeezing Through the Loophole in the Medicaid Law," *The Washington Post National Weekly Edition*, March 28, p. 34.

Barnett, Robert, 1991. The American Health Food Book (New York: Dutton).

Budish, Armond D., 1991. "Shopping for Nursing Home Insurance," *The Retired Officer Magazine*, October, pp. 49-51.

Budish, Armond D., 1990. *Avoiding the Medicaid Trap* (New York: Henry Holt and Co.).

Cutler, Neal E., 1992. "Financial Gerontology," *Journal of the American Society of CLU & ChFC*, January, pp. 26-28.

Kilcline, Vadm T. J., 1992. "In Pursuit of National Health Care," *The Retired Officer Magazine*, February, p. 4.

Kritz, Francesca Lunzer, 1991. "Picking a Medical Plan," *U.S. News & World Report*, Nov. 4, pp. 77-80.

Langer, Richard J., and Linda Roberson, 1992. "Your Legal Advisor," *Mature Lifestyles*, Jan., p. 9.

Quinn, Jane Bryant, 1992. "Policies for Old-Age Care," *Newsweek*, April 30, p. 61.

Ray, Cheryl, 1992. "Basic Medications Every Family Should Have in the Medicine Cabinet," *U-Care Newsletter*, March, p. 4.

Rich, Spencer, 1992. "If Your Illness Doesn't Kill You, the Paperwork Might," *Washington Post National Weekly*, June 14.

Schmid, Randolph E., 1992. "People in Early 60s Feel Frail, Study Says," *Naples* (FL) *Daily News*, March 12, p. 6F.

Shea, Gordon F., 1991. "Successful Health and Wellness Programs," *Managing Older Employees* (San Francisco: Jossey-Bass).

Ubell, Earl, 1992. "Health: Take Charge!" *Parade Magazine*, April 26, pp. 6-8.

4

Developing Activities for Self-Fulfillment

Rudy Schafer, thoughtful retiree from California's academe who had some pithy things to say at the beginning of this book, now writes again:

> I've been thinking further about that idea of the two factors that are important in enjoying retirement — control of your life and a reasonably wide range of options to be exercised. It occurs to me now that either of these is not really operable in the absence of some kind of philosophy of life — some deeply satisfying tastes, interests, and overall goals. In effect I described an automobile without any steering mechanism.
>
> A potential retiree probably should begin by making some sort of inventory of his or her life thus far, and on that basis start planning the rest of the trip, so to speak.
>
> For example, you might contemplate your present employment. What do I like about it? What don't I like? How can I continue the "likes" and eliminate or minimize the "don't likes"?
>
> Then list the things you've always wanted to do and never have — learn to play an instrument, take flying lessons, go scuba diving, investigate a phenomenon, curl up and read, and so on. Arrange them in priority order as a basis for a retirement plan. Some of us are like caged birds. The cage door is suddenly open, yet we're afraid to fly out.
>
> You might also want to contemplate what you'd like to leave the world when you depart — some great discovery, invention, work of art, book for posterity, a scholarship fund, all your remaining relatives well cared for, or what have you. Usually we don't think about such things until it's too late to do anything about them.
>
> As Dr. Johnson once observed, nothing sharpens the mind like facing an imminent hanging.

A fitting introduction indeed to this crucial chapter.

Adequate income stream, affordable health care, activities for self-fulfillment — and the greatest of these may well be activities for self-fulfillment, or, as the national Commission on College Retirement terms the third essential, "the retiree's sense of identity and self-worth" (Ruebhausen 1990).

Another colleague puts it this way:

> The good life in retirement isn't just monthly income enough to lead a reasonably comfortable existence, or even good health added. Half of it — 50/50 or 40/60 or whatever — is just plain your state of mind.

You can't read more than a couple of pages into Milletti's *Voices of Experience: 1500 Retired People Talk About Retirement* (New York: TIAA-CREF, 1989) before you get to a quote like this from a 71-year-old dean:

> The day before you retire you are somebody, you have power and respect. The day after you are a has-been. This leads to a psychological shock from which some retired persons never recover. They must be kept professionally busy.

This, from a 76-year-old librarian:

> I truly liked my work and devoted my time and thought to it almost exclusively. ... I think I carried it to extremes. Now I can't find the impetus to enrich my life with other interests.

Or one more, from a 69-year-old professor:

> I did have a problem adjusting, but with a wide selection of hobbies and activities it was quickly and satisfactorily resolved.

In this mini-essay, a 78-year-old professional/technical person says it all:

> I didn't think I would have difficulty adjusting but I guess I did. I suggest doing something, especially something new and different, as soon as possible after retiring, ...
>
> I can't see why any live person should be bored. I hope your report can urge others to get busy and do something. The greatest advantage of retirement is the freedom to do what one wants to do, and the related freedom not to do what one does not want to do (Milletti 1989).

In keeping with that retiree's recommendation, this chapter we devote to the adage, "Don't just stand there, **do** something!" — by talking about a dozen-plus options that are just about everybody's for the taking, from the fanciful to the purposeful, all calculated to help keep the wolf of ennui from the door.

No reader, however, should assume that the broad self-fulfillment options we discuss here — 15, to be exact — are necessarily all there are. They just happen to be those that show up most frequently in the literature, in interviews, in reviewer comments, and in experiences. You may very well discover an entirely different diversion or two. In that case, follow your own lead. (And, if you're so inclined, let us hear about it.)

As that great American philosopher, Yogi Berra, propounded: "When you come to the fork in the road, take it."

NOTE: The Milletti book is the only one that TIAA-CREF doesn't offer free, but it costs only $3 postpaid, and it's well worth it and then some. Call 800/842-2733, extension 5509, and they'll send you a copy with an invoice. It's been reprinted four times since it first appeared in 1984 — a testimony to its utility for everybody contemplating retirement from academe.

WALKING TO THE NEAREST CAMPUS EXIT

> I would have liked the opportunity to take a leave of three to six months to try out retirement before actually doing so. The real experience of being retired cannot be understood fully unless one is able to undergo some sampling of it: a person's real feelings of being severed from the academic marketplace would then become more clear. If institutions could devise ways of making it possible to take pre-retirement tryout leaves before making a final decision, it would be a boon to the individuals concerned, especially those who are ambivalent about retirement.

So wrote a former college administrator in Milletti's survey.

In other words, walk — don't run — to the nearest campus exit.

And there is a way to do it: retire officially but continue to work part-time for your college or university. If you're in a TIAA-CREF retirement plan, when you reach the retirement age of your choice, TIAA-CREF will send you your monthly check, whether you continue to work or not. If you're in a state, municipal, or parochial retirement system, chances are the regulations will permit you to work up to 49% of the time without forfeiting your retirement annuity, although the income can affect your SS benefits.

What's more, around the year 2000 and beyond, institutions of higher education may discover they're facing a shortage of qualified Ph.D. candidates for the plethora of positions left open by a massive cohort of retirees (Bowen and Rudenstine 1992). So the chances are good your institution will welcome an opportunity to extend your academic career indefinitely at half-speed.

Let's review the opportunities the National Commission on College Retirement recommends that colleges and universities extend to senior faculty and staff to help preserve their sense of status and capture their beneficial contributions:

- Continue part-time in a department or office
- Perform in a different yet appropriate area
- Present non-credit or retiree courses and seminars
- Participate in ongoing research programs
- Teach summer classes or workshops
- Act as a consultant to a campus unit
- Serve as a campus spokesperson to campus constituencies
- Work with student groups (Ruebhausen 1990)

Your part-time work/involvement doesn't need to be on your present campus. You may find a refreshing assignment at a sister institution across town or down the road.

Although it may not be possible or propitious for you to retain your campus office, much less your parking stall, working in a bull-pen of grad assistants can be stimulating. And then there are those other perks that could continue: free or cut-rate tickets to athletic and theatrical events, economical cafeteria fares, discounts on books and other logistical supplies, access to libraries and wellness facilities, and so on — depending on institution policy.

Depending on campus policy, too, even as a part-timer you may enjoy some measure of secretarial support — invaluable if you've never learned to use your own PC or word processor.

Milletti writes:

> The bridge between full-time work and full-time retirement, retirees suggest, should be part-time work — or is part-time retirement a better phrase? A 66-year-old academic, for example, tells how "the two days a week I continue to spend in my profession on campus is making my retirement more rewarding, since it permits me to retain my job skills and my professional contacts as well as allowing me to grow in my profession and even branch out into related fields. I would strongly recommend to any future retiree that he or she continue work part-time rather than retire totally." A former department chair, now 79, wishes she had followed such a strategy. "I would like to have had an interval of part-time teaching or research and more travel in the earlier years," she says. "Retiring abruptly at a fixed age is a shock that should be avoided." Adds another former educator, age 87: "I believe continuing part-time after retirement is an advantage. It allows for gradual adjustment from a full schedule to a limited and then non-remunerative schedule" (Milletti 1989).

If your institution doesn't encourage, or even prohibits, part-time work on the part of a retiree, why not get yourself appointed to a campus commission — either before or after your retirement — that will foment action on these recommendations by the National Commission on College Retirement?

Every college and university should:

- Establish an office of retirement services.
- Help retired faculty members retain their institutional identity — maintenance of library, computer, and parking privileges and continued access to other facilities and activities, particularly athletic facilities,

fitness programs, libraries, labs, lectures, sports, theater events, and faculty dining rooms.

- Develop plans for phased retirement via part-time employment.
- Provide assistance to researchers who want to continue their work.
- Implement programs using retired faculty to serve the mission of the institution.
- Make better use of retirees as a resource for other institutions.
- Develop a variety of vehicles for continued intellectual activity.
- Encourage and facilitate volunteer and paid employment opportunities for retirees; in particular, explore the possibilities of cooperating with local businesses and government agencies in establishing coordination programs for retirees.

Says the Commission:

> The prospect of the change in way of life that retirement represents is frightening to many faculty and academic staff approaching retirement. Just as important, the loss of retired faculty talent is something that institutions and society at large can ill afford. Our series of recommendations is directed at those complementary concerns.

Why don't you take it from there?

(**A reminder about a catch:** There's a limit to what you can earn in wages or self-employment and remain entitled to full Social Security benefits. *Look back into Chapter 2.*)

A suggestion about another catch: If you stick around in some capacity, don't make a nuisance of yourself by "pulling rank."

W.E.B. Griffin narrates what happened in the U.S. Navy in a somewhat similar circumstance at the beginning of World War II:

> A whole flock of commanders and captains and even flag officers had been called back from retirement. They had come back willingly, even eagerly, and their experience was welcome. But at times ... [there were] disputes over Naval protocol between the retreads, who were exquisitely sensitive to the prerogatives of rank. ... Even when there was no question of seniority, a good many of the retreads seemed to have an uncontrollable urge to question orders they had been given (Griffin 1991).

Get the picture?

The New Hampshire Experience

In fall 1990, the University of New Hampshire faced severe state funding cuts that left its advising center with a requirement to cut 30% of its staff. The situation forced the university to face the question: "How can we continue to offer quality advising for 2,500 undecided students with fewer qualified advisors?" The answer: Why not supplement the staff with volunteer emeritus faculty?

UNH's advising center handles only undeclared students. Once students declare a major, the respective departments assume responsibility. So Center advisors must be broadly familiar with UNH programs.

The vice president for academic affairs generated a list of emeriti prospects and sought departmental approval for each one. Four were ultimately selected and put through a refresher course reviewing policies and procedures before being assigned regular weekly advising appointments at the center. They were also encouraged to design special workshops.

One retired Pulitzer-prize winning retired journalism professor created two workshops: "A Writer Talks About Writing" and "What I Wish I Had Known Before I Went to College." The workshops garnered such a positive response he was persuaded to repeat them during orientation week.

For the University, the employment of the emeritus faculty has been a win-win proposition all around, says Marcia Rollison, center assistant director:

> The emeritus faculty bring knowledge and maturity to advising sessions that you don't always get with new faculty or professional advisors. And because they're volunteers, you get faculty who enjoy advising rather than those who are doing it for merit reasons. The staff benefits by being able to go to the emeriti when they have discipline-specific questions, and the emeriti allow us to target areas that we can't always provide expertise in. The emeriti who are generalists are comfortable taking the time to talk to fully undecided students who have no idea what they want to major in or how to go about selecting one.

UNH doesn't see the emeriti program as a stopgap measure any more. Even if the purse strings loosen up to allow hiring more professional advisors, "I definitely think we'll want to continue using volunteer emeriti," says Rollison.

Meanwhile, the volunteer emeriti faculty themselves are enjoying walking, rather than running, to the nearest campus exit (Santovec 1992).

The Nebraska Experience

At the University of Nebraska-Lincoln, a dedicated, imaginative alumna and retired administrative assistant, Clarice Orr, coordinates Retirees of the University of Nebraska (RUN), which links needs of specific university departments with the skills of retirees, the better to enhance student services, enliven the whole campus community, and challenge retirees.

"The concept behind this is that UNL retirees have such a wealth of knowledge, experience, and wisdom," Orr says. "They're such a valuable resource I believe the University should take advantage of them. The University and the retirees both get something out of the program."

Orr developed the idea 10 years ago, but not until 1992 were funding and office space made available. Now Orr is contemplating a "dorm grandparents" program for "students who need a stable person in their lives — someone who doesn't have any axes to grind and who can accept them" (Rowell 1992).

The Wisconsin Experience

A campus Employee Assistance Office at the University of Wisconsin-Madison was operating with a bare-bones staff until some 75 volunteer retirees showed up to help with consultation and referral services for employees experiencing medical, personal, behavioral, or work-related problems.

"The experience and energy the volunteers bring to the program is a big plus — for us and for them," says the EAO director. "They bring all kinds of ideas, and they look forward to helping solve problems."

Also, at UW-Madison, an Office of Inter-College Programs publishes an annual list of staff and faculty retiree volunteers and their areas of expertise, and distributes it to middle and high schools around the state as a "bank" of assembly speakers, classroom adjuncts, or parent-teacher consultants.

"There's scarcely a current event to which one retiree or another can't contribute background and insight," says the program's director, "and the volunteers get great satisfaction serving as campus ambassadors" (Bjerke 1992).

An Experience in Illinois

An Associated Press story the last week of May 1992 told daily newspaper readers around the country about the tentative results of a study tracking high school valedictorians and salutatorians 10 years after their commencements. The honor students, it seems, don't wind up being any more successful than their less scholarly classmates.

In the fine print at the end of the story you found the co-investigator was an Emeritus University of Illinois professor of education, Terry

Denny, who told reporters, "We're going to follow these subjects for at least another five years."

Professor Emeritus Denny is representative of a growing cadre of retirees from academe who are walking, not running, into scholarly inactivity.

TURNING YOUR BACK AND FACING BREAST FORWARD

Working part-time after retirement for your institution or any other in academe may not be your thing. It can have its flip side.

As one of Milletti's correspondents wrote:

> I still have a few grad students, but they tend to be marginal compared to the mainstream when I was teaching full-time. Unfortunately, your colleagues may exercise their bureaucratic clout and give you the marginal course nobody wants. And unfortunately, too, the students become aware of the lack of bureaucratic clout a part-time retired professor has and they scramble for the most secure base they can find.

Another Milletti retiree from a different perspective:

> My job at the university involved responsibility for an extensive building program — dealing with the faculty, the deans, the business department, the chancellor, the board of trustees, the city planning commission, state agencies, members of the legislature, federal agencies, and a private donor.

In his prime he says he found it all "a fascinating task," so he stayed on part-time, only to discover that the fizz had gone, that he was "just plain tired."

And another: "I was out of the mainstream of research. Others made the decisions, undertook the planning, directed the endeavor. I probably had the attitude of the old draft horse who doesn't know how to relax and hand over the torch."

A former engineer, age 72, offered this specific alternate plan for a phased-in retirement: "I believe everyone should have to retire mandatorily at age 45, assume a secondary role until 55, then retire permanently. The good life comes too late in life."

There is indeed something to be said for, in Robert Browning's words, turning your back and facing breast forward. It's probably particularly important in the case of a campus administrator. Nothing can be so disconcerting for a new provost or dean as to have his or her predecessor looking over their shoulder all the time, or worse — offering unsolicited advice about "how we did it before."

I learned this invaluable lesson by brilliant example from the outstanding leader I succeeded as commandant of a United States Army Reserve command and general staff college.

"Colonel," I said after the ceremony, "I'd appreciate it if you'd stop in here at the armory every so often and be on tap for an occasional phone call." Came the precise reply, "Clay, this is now **your** command. Don't call me, I'll call you. And you'll only see me socially out of uniform from now on."

Retirement benefits and personal savings may decline in the future, with individuals taking more responsibility for their own economic security in old age. The likely result will be increasing flexibility in employment options for retirees and pensioners, including part-time work.
— Christine Day, "Education and Politics in Our Aging Society," *Planning for Higher Education*, Summer 1992, pp. 34-41

Had he hung around or come up with recommendations, he would indeed have clouded my ability to establish my own regimen and make my own decisions. I followed that example when I stepped down as dean of inter-college programs — and my successor more than once remarked how much my absence was salutary, although he did invite me back once to give a lecture — to a group of retirees returning to the campus as special students.

I've seen at least two cases when former academic leaders looked over the shoulders of their successors so persistently that unit cohesion was seriously jeopardized. Tom Clancy may have said it best in his 1991 novel, *The Sum of All Fears* (New York: Putnam), describing a Navy captain rotating out of conning a submarine into a Pentagon staff job:

> He'd be able to ride the boats, of course, ... but henceforth he'd be a tolerated visitor, never really welcome aboard. Most uncomfortable of all, he'd have to avoid visiting his former command, lest the crew compare his style to that of their new CO — possibly undermining the new man's authority.

Turning your back isn't for everyone, of course; it's an option that applies particularly to former department chairs, college deans, and higher administrators. I know a number of retired professors, for instance, who have made it a practice to check in with their former colleagues every week or so, and one retired registrar's office staff member who's welcomed back practically daily for the expertise she's acquired over long years of student counseling.

One reviewer remonstrates:

> It seems to me the solution to problems regarding part-time professional status or the need to give a new administrator a free hand could also be addressed by planning one's contributions. One need not necessarily just walk away from a job. One could search for alternative work in other departments or offices. The key is not just the situation, it's the retiree's desires and motivations.

Absolutely. Indeed, as a Milletti respondent recalls, if you turn your back you may miss "the stimulation of professional meetings, faculty contacts, the social aspects of academia, such as having lunch with colleagues and the congenial association with many of my colleagues during the working day, the intellectual energizing of work with eager students." On the other hand, he goes on, "you may not miss having to cater to your superiors."

To think that stimulation can only be found on a campus is, of course, a patronizing attitude. And to think that life in retirement will be barren of catering to powers that be is, of course, naive.

Even Gen. Norman Schwarzkopf of Desert Storm fame had this to say shortly after retiring: "It isn't quite what I had expected. I can't even get a plumber to come to the house."

Yet breaking away from the campus — except for occasional visits — may be just what you'll respond to. As Milletti titles one of his chapters, **"I'm free! free! free!"**

Alvin Toffler calls it "exchanging a Bureaucracy for your own Adhocracy."

Uncomplicating Your Life

So sharp can be the break from campus routine for retirees from academia that some of us wallow around indefinitely before we begin to get on track in our new venue.

Fortunately, there are steps we can take to smooth the adjustment to a less complicated life.

A professional "organizer," Stephanie Culp, author of *Streamlining Your Life: A Five-Point Plan for Uncomplicated Living*, has this to say for our benefit:

- **Make a commitment to change**. Let go people, habits, and possessions that are no longer so relevant to your life.
- **Take control of any problems rather than let them control you**. Put energy into solving problems instead of worrying about them. Resolve to be productive. Ask others for advice. Move on from problems that aren't within your own power to solve.

- **Control that old academic perfectionism**. You aren't in direct competition with anybody any more. The best can be the enemy of the good.
- **Don't slip into procrastination**. If you wait for "the right time," it will never come.
- **Identify the mission of your new life, your goals, your priorities**. What's really important to you and yours?
- **Prioritize the people in your life**. You no longer have to spend time with people you don't care about.
- **Re-evaluate your possessions**. Get rid of things you don't use or that no longer suit your new lifestyle. Separate need from want.
- **Maintain some kind of a system**. For ongoing serenity, devise a routine for handling the mail, keys, eyeglasses, shopping, cooking, filing, laundry, bills, and so on (Culp 1992).

It's all not as difficult as it may sound.

FINDING PASTIMES FOR FUN AND PROFIT

"The only trouble with retirement," says a retiree friend of mine, "is that you don't get any days off!" There indeed can be sheer joy in a busy retirement — doing everything you've wanted to do all your life but didn't have enough time to do. Options are manifold.

For example, here is the range of activities enjoyed by the indicated percentage of retired faculty and staff in Milletti's survey:

Reading, 92%
Socializing with friends on a regular basis, 75%
Gardening, home improvement, 71%
Recreational travel, 66%
Hobbies, crafts, 61%
Writing, painting, and other creative pursuits, 43%
Religious and church activity, 37%
Community service, political activity, 35%
Sports or physical fitness program, 33%
Professional or other job-related organizations, 32%
Civic, fraternal, or other formal group, 31%
Educational programs, 28%
Retiree club or organization, 23%

Most of these activities and others we discuss in more detail in later sections of this chapter.

Here let's savor more directly the kaleidoscopic nature of pastimes Milletti's retirees are practicing — by listening to some of their recorded remarks. Several are using their new-found freedom to explore the world:

"Nature walks and field trips" ... "I'm in England now that April's there" ... "49 states, 42 countries" ... "Explore back roads" ... "We took a long, long trip to remove my husband from any temptation to check up on his successor — the winter months in New Zealand and Australia" ... "Have visited every continent, including ten times to Europe."

Others are investing their time in interests that didn't easily fit into their lives before retirement:

"I signed up for a sculpture class at a local museum school, and now I calculate and construct mathematical objects" ... "My prime interest for a long time has been woodworking" ... "I took up painting after retiring and have become an ardent enthusiast" ... "I have a well-equipped pottery studio in my home and turn out handsome and useful pieces" ... "I've had a portable loom for many years" ... "Coin collecting" ... "Tinkering with mechanical things" ... "Sewing clothes for grandchildren" ... "I bought an electronic organ" ... "Composing and playing music" ... "Managing the real estate I invested in over the years" ... "Playing the stock market" ... "Write articles on photography and sometimes a newspaper column" ... "I'm learning to play the piano" ... "Crossword puzzles" ... "Jigsaw puzzles" ... "My Model-T Ford hobby."

Many are taking advantage of their retirement from academia to expand the horizons of their minds:

"I've had a five-year appointment as an educational consultant in Southeast Asia" ... "Library curator emeritus" ... "Formal consultations and other professional activities with the National Academy of Science" ..."Time to read a lot, time to write a little" ... "Writing at my own pace, without the necessity of impressing colleagues and peers and administration" ... "Cooking classes and real estate courses" ... "Consultations have come quickly — and now I can say exactly what I believe is best without worrying how it reflects on my university. Also I don't worry if my recommendations aren't accepted" ... "Read fiction and other literature in addition to professional material" ... "Writing a book about my specialty, anesthesiology" ... "Developing electronic and computer circuits" ... "I'm pursuing my interest in traditional Chinese thought."

A number have become more involved in activities of the soul:

"We are Christian Quakers and make each step of our lives a matter of prayer" ... "I had a chance to return to the ministry" ... "Solitude and contemplation" ... "I was my religious denomination's official observer at Vatican Council II" ... "Quiet reflection and remembrance" ... "Thinking about the philosophical, psychological, and political problems of life."

Still, other retirees find satisfaction through involvement in the community:

"I do community plays and act in a new theater in town" ... "Coach Pony League baseball teams" ... "Chair of a retired men's club" ... "United Way" ... "A driving desire to complete tracing our genealogy" ... "Aid church-sponsored potluck suppers."

Many remain forever young in body:

"I'm a tennis pro as well as string rackets" ... "I get outside in the spring to build stone walls, lay a stone terrace, get a garden started" ... "I try to swim at least a quarter of a mile five days a week" ... "Improving the 100-year-old family woodlands" ... "Fishing" ... "Saw, chop, and rack firewood for our wood-burning Franklin stove" ... "I spend time on a 22-foot sailboat with a galley, head, and berths for five" ... "I've built two houses with my own hands" ... "Square dancing" ... "Archaeological excavations."

Now if that list of pastimes doesn't give you any ideas, that probably means you're already practicing a favorite pastime or have one or two all picked out for retirement time.

For example, one reviewer writes:

> Music is so important to me that I think your readers might also find it equally fulfilling. Even if they've never had a lesson in their life, even if they don't know how to play anything, it's never too late to learn. I guess this would apply to any artistic endeavor, but retired people certainly have the time to practice long enough and often enough to achieve real proficiency, from which derives satisfaction. As Orsino says in *Twelfth Night*, 'If music be the food of love, play on!'

While it's perfectly possible to work into a pastime after retiring, it's helpful if you can simply escalate the amount of time you devote to an activity of some standing.

As this 81-year-old fellow retiree puts it:

> Don't wait until retirement approaches to prepare for the change. Lead a broad enough life so that you can develop and keep activities and interests outside your main job to carry over into retirement.

My prime pastime? You guessed it. Writing for fun and profit — four books, two scholarly papers, five semi-popular articles, three speeches, a year's worth of a national newsletter for deans and department chairs — in six years of retirement.

Should your prime pastime be starting up a small business, you can draw on a special type of help. Retired business people will share their expertise with you through the Service Corps of Retired Executives (SCORE) in the federal Small Business Administration. They'll give free advice on cash flow, expansions, inventory, financing, and other demons that can plague small business. Information is available at 800/827-5722.

Managing Money

A very special kind of activity for fun and — you hope — profit is money management — your money.

Let's let Emeritus Professor Doug Osterheld expound:

> If the fascination of financial planning has heretofore eluded you, give the subject a chance to capture a part of your time and interest, as it has the real potential for improving your income stream as well as providing a stimulating outlet for your intellectual energies.
>
> If, on the other hand, you've already engaged in some financial planning, you may think that, once planned, you can forget about it. But it's highly unlikely in this era of sweeping economic, social, and cultural changes that you can be sanguine about stopping the planning process, even if you've worked out a master plan.
>
> One of the joys of retirement, in fact, can be a more thorough and constant supervision of your resources, no matter how modest they may be. It can be an intriguing and rewarding enterprise. Whether you invest in the stock market, bonds, CDs, the money market, real estate, government securities, gold or silver, tax shelters, life insurance, annuities, commodity futures, art objects, stamps, or any of the mutual fund variations of the above, there should be continual scrutiny of the instrument or instruments you select and of any master plan of which each is an element.
>
> A proper investment strategy is this: Make sure you've investigated thoroughly all the possibilities of all the instruments available. You may find it productive to make use of some of the many resources available to you: weekly and monthly financial magazines at your library, registered representatives of security houses, banks, S&Ls, newspapers, TV programs (Osterheld 1984).

But you don't have to be a semi-professional money manager to get your kicks out of investing. A member of my over-the-hill gang, a former professor of musicology, regales us on the tee with tales of his buying

Treasury bills through the mail from a Federal Reserve Bank. And another, a former professional/technical lab manager, even attends stockholder meetings of a nearby direct mail giant.

Your community may abound in seminars for amateur money managers which become sort of social events. Just be sure you obey that TIAA-CREF injunction: "Don't play poker with your eatin' money!"

For information on how you can form an investors club, you can write to the National Association of Investors, 1515 East Eleven Mile Road, Royal Oak, MI 48067, or call 313/543-0612.

SERVING SOCIETY

Many faculty/academic staff retirees find great satisfaction in doing voluntary community-service work — as one puts it, "paying a little rent for your place in the world."

The philanthropic activities members of Milletti's 1,500-member cohort engage in look like this, in descending order of frequency:

- Community/civic activities, such as United Way, Boy Scouts
- Educational/cultural services, such as Head Start, museums, libraries
- Church, synagogue, or related activities, such as Sunday school teacher, choir director
- Hospital or health services
- Assistance to older people, such as Meals on Wheels driver, aide at a senior citizens center
- Other, such as government and private social agencies, election polls, counseling services

This 68-year-old woman is fully involved, and then some:

> It's pleasant to be able to plan and participate in volunteer and civic activities — hospital board, blood bank, planning for elderly housing, programs for school children, president of the country club, class chair for college, consultant to a company, church, fund drives, garden club.

Which brings up a couple of hazards:

You may feel so disenchanted with no longer being employed in a worthwhile endeavor or so driven by a desire to serve that you load up on volunteer activities to the detriment of your health and your leisure.

You may fall victim to the stereotype that retirees have so much free time they can be depended on for all manner of activities, organizations, and responsibilities.

Or you may find yourself in a situation that misses by a mile your own high standards of administrative efficiency, and wind up thoroughly frustrated.

On balance, however, the retirees I know all have at least one favorite charity and derive a good deal of pleasure out of continuing to help make the world go round.

Examples:

- Donating services to a former academic department — mentoring new hires and helping graduates find jobs.
- Working in the mollusk department of a university's zoological museum.
- Serving as hospital receptionist/guide
- Taking deaf and/or blind persons for walks
- Organizing for League of Women Voters
- Interpreting for South American patients in a cancer clinic
- Library-work substituting
- Serving church suppers
- Hospice volunteering
- Bible club ministering
- Rehabilitating homes for low-income persons

Two former administrators have found a particular métier as capitol lobbyists for their state retired teachers' association — blocking an attempt by the governor to raid teachers' retirement system funds.

At loose ends, William McCandless has helped form Reachout '56, a Princeton alumni project that channels class members into public-service work as their professional careers wind down. McCandless mentors second graders in a Trenton, N.J., school; other Reachout members transport inner city kids to museums or coach sandlot sports. McCandless says that for many former executives retirement offers an opportunity to pay attention to the world around them: "We rode oak-paneled trains into walnut-paneled offices. We never see the ironbound sections until they crumble around us" (Beck *et al.* 1992).

My contribution? You might have guessed this one, too. Combining a background as a preacher's kid and in the military with public relations skills to serve on a county Salvation Army board as fund drive media consultant.

Influencing Public Affairs

Activists offer these tips for influencing public affairs through grass roots organization:

- Band together with like-minded retirees.
- Decide what you want to accomplish and whom you must influence.
- Make a list of things you need to know.
- Do library research, and then more library research.
- Find appropriate professional colleagues who will volunteer their services — lawyers, public relations persons, scientists, and so on.
- Study which tactics make the most sense — letters, phone calls, leafleting, petitions, meetings, picketing, public service broadcasts, news releases, electioneering, and so on.
- Collect a modest "war chest" to cover necessary expenses.
- Identify public records that contain information you need.
- Learn how to use the federal Freedom of Information Act and state information laws.
- Identify government agencies with relevant jurisdiction.
- Identify local sister organizations sympathetic to your cause.
- Seek help from national organizations that deal with the issues you're addressing.
- Get to know news media editors and reporters who deal with your community or the issues you're concerned about, and keep them informed.
- Keep your organization together by keeping members active with regular meetings and specific work assignments.
- Hold your meetings at sites readily accessible to retirees, and keep the meetings short and to the point.

Don't let age be a factor. Melissa Poe is a Nashville, Tennessee, 12-year-old head of a 30,000-member environmental organization that distributes two million newsletters every other month and inspires numerous save-the-environment activities (Price 1992).

Any 72-year-old could have the same right stuff in her or him.

The Asheville Experience

Possibly the ultimate in retiree/community collaboration is taking place in Asheville, NC, where retirees can attend a seven-week Leadership Asheville Seniors course in which political, educational, and philanthropic leaders teach the participants about the community's needs — drug addiction, dropouts, the usual litany of city problems. Then the retiree-graduates fan out to contribute their varied talents to alleviating distress.

Examples:

- Mel Hetland, ex-professor of education, works at Randolph Elementary School in a downtrodden section of Asheville. Once a week he teaches reading to first- and third-graders and devises science demonstrations for fifth-graders. "The big reward," he says, "is that I'm helping some teachers develop techniques for relating to students — techniques that I had a lot of experience with in my own career."
- In a laboratory at the University of North Carolina at Asheville, part-time Professor John Stevens is doing research on the Mossbauer effect, a nuclear technique that physicists use to study the structure of matter. He's begun grouping his regular undergraduate and graduate students with retirees coming back to school. "It's been one of the most fruitful semesters I've had in 20 years," he says.
- Bob Etter, a retired scientist, and Terri Spangler, a UNC-Asheville student, have begun an interesting partnership. Working as a team, they run painstaking analyses on specialized equipment, which they learn about as they work together. At first apprehensive at having a senior citizen looking over her shoulder, now Spangler pays the program the ultimate compliment: "It's the kind of thing I'd like to do when I retire."
- Carolyn Rosenthal, ex-librarian from New York City and Washington, DC, runs a reading discussion group for adults in rural communities around Asheville. "At first," she recalls, "I had to convince them they could be members of a reading group. Now a lot of those people are candidates for courses at the College for Seniors."

The Leadership Asheville Seniors course and the College for Seniors are both part of an Asheville Center for Creative Retirement, along with a Senior Academy for Intergenerational Learning — one of the reasons, along with climate and scenery, that's making Asheville a Mecca for retirees, thanks to the sponsoring UNC-Asheville (Ryan 1991).

EXPLORING A NEW CAREER

You'll recall that in Chapter 2 we took a look at the option of extending your academic career into "civilian" life, so to speak, for both morale and money rewards. Here we'll discuss a quite different option — diving off the pier into a new job totally or largely unrelated to your professional career.

There are drawbacks to considering this possibility:

- The level of risk-taking that goes with this territory may not be your cup of tea.
- Although discrimination is illegal, you may find doors subtly closed to anybody old enough to be retired.
- Or you may be expected to perform professional duties for peon pay because you're drawing retirement benefits.
- And then there's that Social Security ceiling on incomes for annuitants under age 70.

But such barriers won't block you if you're determined to soar into the wild blue yonder for satisfaction and cash. It's being done every day by former professors, administrators, and technical people.

Here are some examples with which I'm familiar:

- a former mechanical engineer in the business of restoring old cars
- a classics professor turned professional landscape architect
- a nursing administrator became a salesperson for a home products company
- a veterinary lab technician turned toxicology consultant
- a consumer sciences professor manufacturing ethnic dolls
- a medical doctor become a real estate salesperson
- a sociologist elected mayor
- a buildings-and-grounds superintendent become district representative for a Congressman
- an English professor/fly-tier named to a state natural resources board
- an economist administering a social welfare agency
- a placement director operating a fast-food franchise
- a composition/literature professor serving as a State Department consultant
- a geography professor recruiting for the CIA
- a dormitory chef presiding over a fast-food restaurant
- a physical therapist turned merchandise buyer
- an oncologist writing entries for an encyclopedia

- an ed psych professor in the travel business
- a journalism professor turned actor in commercials
- a chemistry lab technician become a police detective

I guess you could say, you name it and there's a former denizen of academia out there doing his or her thing in exciting, novel ways.

Robert Legrand may speak for all of them: "The money wasn't worth it. I hated it. I didn't like being at someone else's command, or being in an office."

Holder of two University of Chicago degrees in business administration, Bob Legrand was a campus auditor before starting a new life — as a masseur (West 1992).

Don't let the culture shock of unemployment get you down. Henry M. Wallfesh tells this story to *Newsweek* reporters:

> I didn't shave for six days. At cocktail parties, people would ask how I spent my time. Depending on how flippant I felt, I'd say, "I pull the wings off butterflies." As much as I hated commuting from my home in Stanford, CT, to New York City, I found I missed the train ride. It was like living in Elba. Then, after a mourning period, I assessed what I really liked to do, what I'd never do again, and created a new job for myself. I advise corporations, write articles, and give speeches on all aspects of retirement through my own fledgling firm, Whale Communications. Only now I work at home in T-shirts and start most of my talks with "And then it happened to me. ..." (Beck *et al.* 1992).

A reviewer declares:

> A second career is the best means of providing for one's economic future and subsequent happiness, and if money is not a primary concern, this second career can appropriately include public service and volunteerism.

Retiree Advantages

In a growing number of instances, retirees may actually have an advantage over younger people.

For example, Days Inns, one of the country's largest hotel chains, goes looking for older job applicants, particularly for its national reservation centers, because, as senior vice president Richard Smith says, "They're good workers, they tend to be more conscientious than the average younger worker, adapt well to change, and have low absenteeism" (Rice 1992).

A more unusual situation finds residents in United Jewish Federation nursing homes hired as panel members to taste-test dishes prepared in the

Federation's commissary, part of a program to improve geriatric diets in the New York City area (*NonProfit News* 1992).

Career-Change Guides

There are plenty of career guides out there, including some specifically for academics embarking on career changes.

Expanding Faculty Options: Career Development Projects at Colleges and Universities, Roger Baldwin, Louis Brakeman, Russel Edgerton, Janet Hagberg, and Thomas Mahar, 1981 (Washington, DC: American Association for Higher Education).

The Three Boxes of Life and How to Get Out of Them: An Introduction to Life/Work Planning, Richard N. Bolles, 1981 (Berkeley CA: Ten Speed Press).

What Color Is Your Parachute?, Richard N. Bolles, 1989 (Berkeley, CA: Ten Speed Press).

Reshaping Faculty Careers, Todd W. Furniss, 1989 (Washington, DC: American Council on Education).

Joyce Lain Kennedy's Career Book, Joyce Lain Kennedy, and Darryl Laramore, 1988 (Lincolnwood, IL: National Textbook).

Teaching and Beyond: Nonacademic Programs for Ph.D.s, K. P. Reilly, and S.S. Murdich (Albany: State University of New York Press).

You may even get some valuable advice and assistance from the career placement center on your campus. Take tests to determine your abilities and interests; you may be surprised at what you learn about yourself. Consult with "headhunters."

Pursue your education. Take courses in areas tangential or totally apart from your areas of specialization. Try workshops and short courses at a community college. Use your network of contacts: talk with colleagues, friends, relatives, and neighbors to explore possibilities. Be alert to ideas and interests that might develop into career opportunities (Schoenfeld and Magnan 1992).

Hot Tracks in 20 Professions

If you're really serious about exploring a second career, why not go with the flow by harnessing your latent talents to where the big openings — and big bucks — are, at least according to U.S. News & World Report's Oct. 26, 1992, feature, "1993 Career Guide Best Jobs for the Future." The magazine drew on interviews with business analysts across the country to stick its neck out on signal career opportunities in the years at hand:

Accounting— *environmental accountant*, evaluates the bottom-line impact of environmental issues, threats, and regulation, and advises law firms, companies, and government.

Computers— *network administrator*, defines computer needs, buys equipment, and maintains "local area networks" (LANs).

Consulting— *outplacement consultant*, provides corporations with professional development programs for severed employees and survivors.

Education— *special education teacher*, serves school district programs for pupils with learning disabilities.

Engineering— *civil engineer*, guides repair and replacement of nation's infrastructure.

Environment— *toxicologist*, educates firms and the public about health risks and their mitigation.

Finance— *investment professional*, analyzes and/or manages investment opportunities and portfolios.

Food science— *restaurant site selector*, scours hill and dale for places to open new businesses.

Health care— *nurse practitioner*, treats many patients without a doctor's supervision.

Human resources— *training manager*, supervises a broad range of in-house educational/technical programs for workers.

Insurance— *actuary*, forecasts the probability of accidents, illness, and death, and predicts the magnitude of their costs.

Law— *intellectual property lawyer*, specializes in patent, trademark, and copyright protection.

Manufacturing— *chief information officer*, rides herd on all of a firm's disparate computer groups.

Marketing— *product management*, explores how best to market each new entry.

Medicine— *family physician*, shuns specialization and engages in general practice (GP).

Nonprofits— *member services director*, arranges educational programs and issues publications.

Office administration — *technical administrative assistant*, trains and supervises clerical staff.

Publishing— *electronic publishing specialist*, produces books entirely on computers and creates electronic products such as software.

Retailing— *merchandising manager*, knows what customers want, how to buy at good prices, and how and when to dump stale goods.

Telecommunications — *wireless specialist*, works for manufacturers that build the high-tech machinery for cellular transmissions.

Anything there sound interesting? Practical?

(You'll notice, by the way, that this list may seem short on opportunities for retirees from the liberal arts. But, as we've seen, who's to say an ex-sociology professor can't become an actuary, or that an ex-comp lit professor can't manage bonds?)

Entrepreneurial Opportunities

In another *U.S. News & World Report* article, Lisa Moore and Richard Newman list the following areas as offering particularly promising opportunities for retirees preferring to operate as independent entrepreneurs rather than as employees:

- Home health care
- Temporary-employment agencies
- Geriatric services
- Business consulting
- Information brokers
- Alternative dispute resolution
- Environmental cleanup

"Seniors can best assure success by targeting such areas that promise to be the powerhouses of the '90s and then carving out a niche that capitalizes on their expertise," Moore and Newman advise. "One way to reduce risk is to buy a franchise, which offers the security of an established name, weeks of intensive training, and national advertising" (Moore and Newman 1992).

Even if you have no particular thought of exploring a second career, a hobby may turn into one. One of the most contented retirees I know is a law professor who got so good at training his own hunting dogs, he now owns and operates a kennel for the purpose. And a former professor of nursing has turned her computer programming hobby into developing/designing software for pharmacists.

But don't feel useless if you're not into an extended or second career. Retirement needn't be tiring. Just don't squander time, because, as Ben Franklin wrote, "time is the stuff life is made of."

Books for the Job Hunt

If you zero in on a promising new career, then comes the classic chore of job hunting — something most expatriates from academe haven't done for a long time. You won't lack for guidebooks. For example, Denver's largest book emporium has an inventory of some 30 books on interviewing, 45 resumé cookbooks, and 875 general job-search and career-development books.

Out of the scores of books on the market, the classics and the newcomers that follow are the likeliest to give job hunters a boost, says Amy Saltzman (1992):

What Color Is Your Parachute?, Richard Nelson Bolles, 1989 (Berkeley, CA: Ten Speed Press), $12.95.

Careering and Re-Careering for the 1990s, Ronald Krannich, 1991 (Woodbridge, VA: Impact Publications), $13.95.

Not Just Another Job, Tom Jackson, 1992 (NY: Times Books), $12.

In Transition, Mary Lindley Burton and Richard Wedemeyer, 1991 (New York: HarperBusiness), $20.

Surviving the Cut, Kevin Murphy, 1991, two audiocassettes (New York: Bantam), $10.

Shifting Gears, Carol Hyatt, 1992 (New York: Simon & Schuster), $10.

Résumés That Knock 'Em Dead, Martin John Yate, 1988 (Boston: Bob Adams), $7.95.

The Smart Woman's Guide to Resumés and Job Hunting, Julie Adair King and Betsy Sheldon, 1991 (Hawthorne, NJ: Career Press), $8.95.

Sweaty Palms, H. Anthony Medley, 1984 (Berkeley, CA: Ten Speed Press), $9.95.

Books to avoid, says Saltzman, are those that propose to reduce job hunting to a "logical" formula, do little more than direct readers to think about what they do best, or make overt sales pitches for ancillary software or videos.

PRESERVING DOMESTIC TRANQUILITY

This is a very sensitive subject, so up to a point the less said about it the better, lest we mislead more than assist.

But the topic can't be avoided entirely because it is so ubiquitous; in a recent six-week span, Ann Landers, Sally Jessie Raphael, Oprah Winfrey, and Phil Donahue all devoted space or time to the threat retirement can pose to love and marriage.

A worst-case scenario apparently can go something like this:

During the many years in which one spouse was away at work and/or traveling, out of self-preservation the stay-at-home spouse had developed activities and routines. With retirement, the picture can change suddenly. The retired spouse is constantly underfoot, doing little annoying things like adjusting the thermostat or switching channels on the TV, asking, "What should we do today?" of a spouse to whom if it's Tuesday it must be grocery shopping.

Togetherness, in short, ain't always what it's cracked up to be.

Writes one Milletti correspondent, a 65-year-old woman:

> Retirement was an adjustment difficult to make for us both for about six months. ... Ideally, I applaud constant sharing, but it isn't always possible. Awareness of the need for such sharing ought to be taught in a pre-retirement course to eliminate: "I don't know where anything is kept!" "Just show me how!" "Why won't you let me do anything?" "I just like to help." "What can I do next?" To a woman [used to doing everything for herself], these questions and statements make her feel like she suddenly had one more child tugging at her skirt.

The situation can be exacerbated if two working spouses don't retire at the same time. One is ready to travel to the four winds, the other wants to culminate a career with one more contribution.

On the other hand, retirement can offer a golden opportunity for many husbands and wives to discover anew their friends and family — and themselves.

Witness this cheery Christmas letter I got this year from a pair of recently retired collegial friends of mine at another institution:

> *Webster's Dictionary* definition of retired is "to withdraw to a secluded place, to give up one's work, no longer working, etc." DON'T YOU BELIEVE IT!!! For those of you who have already reached retirement status, you know better. And for those looking forward to it, rest up before you get there.
>
> Jim is still very much in demand as an ag econ marketing consultant, and I have a steady round of domestic, social, and civic activities.
>
> In April we packed up and moved to our bayshore cottage until October. Jim hauled his computer down to help him keep up with his work — when we weren't fishing. We did things to the cottage that we didn't know we knew how to do. We have made so many lovely friends and we have enjoyed spending more time with Jim's family. We missed our campus friends, but we did manage to have several of them down to fish, beach, and share sunsets. Of course some of them didn't realize the invitation included hammer and saw.

Obviously this isn't a couple that's bugging each other about how to squeeze the toothpaste. Their retirement is more like a second honeymoon. Apparently, the secret's a familiar one, both well before and during retirement — communication — considerate, continuous communication, at low decibels.

But effective communication doesn't have to mean utter togetherness. Preserving each partner's personal space has a lot to do with ensuring compatibility.

As one reviewer/couple notes:

> It's imperative for each spouse to have large blocks of time spent outside the home, or in separate areas of the home.
>
> Also, it's important for the spouse formerly more fully employed to pick up a commensurate proportion of chores — shopping, for instance.

Another reviewer adds:

> Although no one likes to contemplate it, there's this advantage to not becoming too intertwined, too interdependent, to maintaining some individual pursuits. If your spouse dies, as did mine, it's tough enough without having been inseparable.

And still another:

> I think you're avoiding something. Sometimes changes in life circumstances can — and should — result in spousal divorce. You shouldn't avoid mentioning it out of squeamishness.

(We told you this was a sensitive section.)

To end on a brighter note, conflict can be a key to connubial bliss. At least that's the conclusion of a University of Wisconsin-Madison professor of child and family studies, after analyzing the relationships of nearly 400 married couples in the Detroit area beginning in 1986.

Susan Crohan says that her findings belie the romantic notion that couples should regard fights the way sheep regard wolves — as a threat to marital survival. Quite the contrary, one of the surest predictors of marital stability is a couple's ability to deal constructively with conflict. In other words, the couple that argues together constructively stays together.

"Constructive conflict means engaging, not avoiding, each other," Crohan counsels. "It's then important to clearly state your feelings, but not blame. Conflict avoidance avoids nothing. If both spouses are avoiders, that's a short-term fix and a long-term disaster" (Crohan 1992).

Now you know.

CEMENTING FAMILY TIES

Since I live in a retirement complex, I may have a ringside seat on what motivates retirees, and I can testify that the most common topic of conversation around our dining-room tables is "family" — spouses, alive or deceased; siblings; grown children and their present or ex-spouses; grandchildren and their families; great-grandchildren; and — at least in two cases — great-great-grandchildren.

Is this a retirement-complex aberration? Not according to some recent polls, writes Kenneth Walsh:

> One survey finds the country, propelled by aging baby boomers, heading toward a broad renaissance of cultural moderation that emphasizes *family* — whatever its configuration — as a fundamental source of personal contentment and stability. Even those boomers once enamored of countercultural experimentation are returning to devotion to spouses, children, and parents.
>
> "With all the pessimism and economic drift," says sociology Professor David Popenoe of Rutgers, "people are looking around and seeing what after all is most important in their lives — relationships."
>
> Reinforced by a growing body of survey research, public mood analysts agree that the model for this trend is the 1950s. They say that, since the 1970s, Americans are gradually rediscovering the importance of family ties. The percentage of Americans who say a good family life is "very important" has risen from 82% in 1981 to 93% in 1991, according to a Gallup Poll. And the increase is particularly strong among young people (Walsh 1991).

What was vouchsafed in those 1991 reports seemed to show no signs of abating in 1992, according to Thomas Palmer in the *The Boston Globe*:

> Today one of the most potent messages of commercial advertising, business, politics, sports, entertainment, media — it may even be printed on the shopping bag you take home — is "family."
>
> "We can say with greater certainty that the new economic scarcity of the '90s does cause people to place a greater premium on family ties," acknowledges University of Massachusetts sociology professor Ralph Whitehead, Jr.

On the other hand, some of such optimism about a return to family ties may be misplaced, says Larry Bumpass, a University of Wisconsin-Madison sociology professor and demographer:

> Reports in the 1980s that surging divorce rates had finally begun to decline may not mean what they seem to. A 10% downturn in divorce, followed by a long plateau, is more a statistical illusion than evidence of change. In fact, social forces that have been shredding marriages

> since the mid-1960s are alive and may be gathering steam.
>
> Today's politicians frequently call for "a return to family values," but it's all smoke and mirrors. A lot of conservatives are good at articulating these views, so it might appear to be happening, but it's not. The high divorce rate is a long-term trend.
>
> Nothing resembling a return to family values is happening. It would be foolish to jump to the conclusion that a brief deviation in the divorce rate means a return to more stable family life. (Bumpass 1992)

A more comprehensive yet just as gloomy a scenario was put together by four reporters in *U.S. News & World Report*:

As the economy has unraveled, stitching families together has become increasingly arduous. The weight of the evidence suggests that because of the recession, families in the United States will be fewer, smaller, and weaker.

The marriage rate fell in 1991 to its lowest level in more than a decade, and birthrates dropped after four straight years of increases. At the same time, financial uncertainty is driving couples apart, complicating already painful divorces. And adoptions of abandoned and unwanted children appear to be slipping.

Says Phyllis Moen of the Life Course Institute at Cornell University: "The literature across the board points to the fact that economic loss or the threat of economic loss is very stressful on families."

Little wonder the newsmagazine's headline read: "The dark shadow of recession is contributing to the breakup of hearts and homes all across America."

So you can line up your expert commentators and researchers and take your pick about what's happening to family ties. What may be the more empirical an assessment is the "iffy" results of a national survey done under the aegis of the National Commission on Children, a government panel chaired by West Virginia's U.S. Senator John D. "Jay" Rockefeller:

- Americans think the American family is falling apart — everywhere but in their own. Pollsters dub the paradox the "I'm OK but you're not" syndrome.
- 70% of nuclear families say they eat dinner together at least five times a week, but 81% of Americans say parents don't spend enough time with their children.
- 97% of all parents say their relations with their children are "good" or "excellent," even though nearly as lopsided a majority of all adults say

that parents have less influence over their children's values than do entertainment figures.

- Family ties may have grown stronger in the past two years, as measured by a 9% point increase in the number of people who say it's important to respect one's parents and one's children, and leave something for the next generation. Yet two of every three Americans say they think family traditions are growing weaker (Taylor 1991).

It was this study that led to a call for $40 million in tax breaks for families with children "in a harsh economy and hostile culture making family life both more difficult and more valued." It could be that people of retiree age have the most solid lock on family ties. At least, according to a sampling of 52 million people age 55 and over, conducted by the Gerontology Institute of the University of Massachusetts at Boston:

- 15 million provide unpaid care for a sick or disabled family member or friend — the equivalent of seven million full-time jobs.
- 23 million help care for their childen, grandchildren, or great-grandchildren.
- 9 million provide "sizeable" financial support for their children or grandchildren, while 2 million receive financial support from their children or grandchildren.

The Schoenfeld experience supports both the pessimists and the optimists, as may yours. For a time during the trauma of the Vietnam era, it looked like our family ties could go down the tube as three daughters each sought a rendevous with revolt that spread us to the four winds of geography and togetherness. Today, all three daughters are happily married and "settled down," as the saying goes. We all get together at least once a week via telephone conference calls, periodically by visits, and at least once a year at an annual rally, electrified by the presence of eight grandchildren and — in two cases — their significant others.

One reviewer offers this sound advice:

> By way of making family relationships agreeable and rewarding for all concerned, recognize that your children are now adults, and set on running their own lives. The relationship could change from those between children and parents to those among adults.

You no doubt have had your own family tensions and now have own means of cementing family ties. For retirees particularly, family ties are at once a link to the past and a leverage on the future.

ENJOYING FRIENDS AND FLOATING CRAPGAMES

Of all the activities Milletti's retirees say they're engaged in, far and away one of the most commonly mentioned is some variation of "enjoying relations with friends." You can look forward to that, too.

The reasons are simple. First, in retirement the world of getting and spending is no longer so much with you, so you have plenty of time in which to maintain, renew, or cultivate friendly relations. And second, nothing is easier or more satisfying than to share time and experiences with fellow human beings — except for one factor now entering the picture.

Just as retirement combined with growing older will represent a major shake-up in your regimen, so will it be with friends and associates. The more varied the friendships you develop over the years — in age, background, circumstances, shared activities — the more fortunate you will be in retirement, in that fewer ties with friends need be severed through changing lifestyles on the part of all parties.

It's not that you haven't already experienced this phenomenon. For example, all through the growing up of your children — from day care, to kindergarten, to elementary school PTA, to Scouts, to high school sports, to college dorm — you developed friendships, sometimes very close friendships, as you went along with fellow parents experiencing the same evolutions. Some of those friendships may have lasted, most of them faded as phases in life changed.

It will be so again as some of your present friends and you inevitably get out of sync — and as opportunities arise for making new friends. Be prepared for these changes, and take them in stride, viewing them as challenges rather than disruptions.

You may carry over into retirement close, almost automatic relations with many campus colleagues, or you may have none other than those you have built on a highly personal basis. That is why the more varied your friends and associates before retirement, the better the odds of lasting relationships.

For instance, in analyzing my closest friendships after six years of retirement, I discover some are old, some new, some borrowed. A couple of them date back to boyhood, a couple only from recent neighborliness. Some stem from old campus ties, some from new associations altogether. Some are professionally based, others on shared avocations or recreational activities.

The tightest — those developed through shared exigencies: a handful of old Army buddies, couples who were fellow inmates of a grad-student housing project, a foursome of golfers whose prowess on the course is declining apace, collegial co-authors now well-mellowed after times of writing and editing travail, the people who sponsored the unorthodox courtship of my much younger spouse and me.

As circles of friends fade or flame, so will their shared activities become modified. For example, my deer-hunting gang of 30 years longevity no longer performs exhausting drives over hill and down ravine; we're each now content to stand sedately beside a likely trail. And my once macho poker-playing club now deals party bridge with spouses.

However broad or narrow your friendships, however varied or constricted their nature, cherish them with all your heart. Retirement, thy name is fellowship.

One inevitability: sooner or later you'll pass from an era of weddings and baptisms to an era of funerals, and some of those departing will be close friends. Against those days of grief, store in your mind the sheer joy of friendships — good oak logs with which to light warm fires of memory in days to come, bereft of some companions.

LETTING THE TRAVEL BUG BITE

Right up there with relations with family and friends as a primary pastime in retirement years is travel — the two often being combined.

Travel agents have figured this out. Once you retire, if not just before, you'll be in receipt of all manner of invitations from commercial companies and fraternal organizations to join a tour to Australia or Zanzibar, Atlanta or Vallejo, the dinner theater down the road or a dog track in Florida, concerts in New York or tables in Vegas — wherever you want to go, somebody will be happy to escort you there — for a price, of course.

My colleagues and I debate the comparative advantages of joining a conducted tour or of taking off on our own, as do Milletti's retirees. For example:

"I highly prize my local senior citizens center. I find it much fun helping to plan the various activities. We join in enjoyable day trips as well as longer trips."

"It's such a pleasure to do what you want to do when you want to do it. We love to travel — but never on a conducted tour."

Some retirees are globe-trotting devotees; others enjoy more close-at-hand expeditions:

"Have visited every continent, including making 10 trips to Europe and three trips to Hawaii — plus Alaska — in the past 10 years."

"When I go, I go — Japan, Russia, Europe, South Pacific, New Zealand, Australia, Tahiti, Fiji."

"Just returned from a three-week ramble down the coast through the Carolinas, Georgia, Florida — back through the Blue Ridge Parkway."

"Retirement gives us freedom of mobility — to England twice in five years, to China last summer. Now we're going to settle down more and cruise the Midwest."

"I'm enjoying discovering my home state."

"We haven't traveled more than 300 miles from home. We cherish the leisurely pace and the lack of tension compared to a guided continental tour."

Tips for the Far-and-Wide Traveler

Wherever, however you plan on extended travel, here are some suggestions gleaned from personal and colleague experience, the sort of tips you won't find in an ordinary guide — listed in no particular order of priority:

Pay full fare only under duress — transportation fares, hotel/motel accommodations, restaurant menus, and so on.

"Isn't it nice to take advantage of senior citizens' rates both at home and abroad?"

"Without our cut-rate fares, we couldn't have gone where we've been."

"Most airlines sell books of coupons for older adults — one-way travel within the continental U.S. Each coupon currently costs only about $80, so it's cheap travel."

Exploit the seasons.

"Now I can vacation in the Vermont woods in fall, soaking up the beauty of the leaves, and then catch the almost-lavish color of the Arizona desert later."

"I travel with the seasons, staying always where the temperatures are within my comfort range, and where paths and pavements are safe for a walker in winter."

Exploit any expertise.

"I was lucky enough to get to know France and Italy occasionally during my working years, and now I can stay longer, dipping into their art, literature, music, language."

"As a Civil War buff, I'm tramping battlefields from Pennsylvania to Georgia and west to Texas."

If you're stiff in the joints, don't hesitate to ask for the special assistance the airlines provide ailing fliers.

"At one time I had to use a cane, and I enjoyed the wheelchair rides in terminals and the opportunity to board early. Now I confess I continue to carry a cane so I can still be among the first to board!"

"If it weren't for those redcaps with their motorized carts, I could never negotiate trips to visit my darling great-grandsons.

Get one of those two-wheel dollies for your luggage.

"I like to carry on the maximum number of bags, and I can get around terminals easily with that contraption."

"The airline pilots and hostesses use them, why not me?"

If you're a committed car driver, join an auto club.

"Those Triptiks not only give us clues to suitable accommodations en route, they make informative reading about the towns and cities we're passing."

"We once had to make a long detour because we hadn't checked for advice on highway construction."

"When you need a tow, you need a tow, and a club membership will give you an edge."

Whatever your means of transportation, join a hotel/motel club sponsored by a national chain.

"For a modest annual fee, we get a monthly guide about places to go and see — and stay at reduced prices."

"I feel like a big shot when I walk into a lobby and present my card."

Subscribe to a magazine like *Gourmet* or read it at the library.

"We photocopy articles and take them along as clues to fine dining."

"For one outstanding dinner in each city, domestic or foreign, we refer to *Gourmet*'s annual index."

Overseas travelers, remember the restrictions on Medicare and even on some Medigap policies.

"Marooned in a Paris hospital, I was glad I had taken out special travel coverage."

"When my wife took ill in Ireland, my Medicare card wasn't worth a plugged nickel."

Observe prescription drug protocol.

"I always take medications — and spare eyeglasses — in my carry-on."

"Ask your doctor to make out prescriptions for all your drugs and carry them in your purse or wallet — along with a photocopy of your passport. A mere list of your drugs and their numbers won't do it; you have to have a doctor's prescriptions along, or else ask the apothecary to call back to authenticate."

"Wherever you go, equip yourself with varied credit cards."

"My local bank credit card was unacceptable in New Orleans."

"There are indeed some places that honor only one type of card, and it isn't **that** one."

"Overseas, it's comforting to be able to go to a familiar office and exchange plastic for the coin of the realm."

On any tour contract, read the fine print carefully.

"We thought everything was covered; it wasn't, by any means."

"It turned out that when we had to cancel the trip, we didn't do it in time to get a refund."

"By reading the contract line by line, we knew enough to take along our own potent potables — and in plastic flasks."

Travel light, but not too light.

"When our bags didn't keep up with us, we had to go out and buy razor and hair drier."

"Once we were held hostage in an interior California town's high school gym when all roads were blocked by high water and mud slides, and we were the toast of the place because we had along a pocket TV!"

"We always take along small plastic jars of coffee, immersion heater, and converter plug. With local bread and fruit we can avoid $15 breakfasts."

Try Amtrak.

"I just love to go back in time by riding a marvelous train. "So what if it doesn't run on time. What's the rush?"

"The food and service are excellent, but don't get off except when you have to. The depots are abominable."

"This is the way to see the country — from sea to shining sea."

"When you use the facilities in a roomette, read the instructions on the wall carefully. The flush button and the shower button are side by side."

"If only access to Amtrak were easily available!"

If you take pictures, be judicious in showing them.

"I thought I would die, looking at one more foreign hotel facade!"

Keep your valuables, especially a passport, in a separate place on your person.

"I'm glad I bought that under-arm 'holster.'

"We lost everything to a street-snatcher in Rome."

"I always carry a supply of traveler's checks in my money belt."

Be judicious in making chance acquaintanceships.

"Some of our dearest friends today are people we've met on our ocean voyages."

"We carry along a small map of the U.S. to locate our city for friends."

When visiting family or friends in this country, consider staying at a nearby motel.

"It relieves the pressure on one-bathroom houses."

"I need psychic space — even from offspring and their offspring."

Bone up in advance on any country or strange states you're visiting.

"By listening to tapes, I was able to polish my limping command of German, especially the idioms."

"We use our public library for planning trips — and planning's half the fun. Good travel books will tell you the operating hours of museums, matters relating to visas, customs, and currencies, opportunities to stay in the homes of local residents, menu specialties, and things the typical tourist group doesn't get to see or do."

"By reading a guide to Australia, I made a hit by knowing about Boxing Day."

Keep track of your grad students.

"We've had some delightful times looking up former students hither and yon."

"One of my Ph.D.'s showed us sights and introduced us to people we would otherwise never have seen or met."

Get a good travel agent.

"This is the absolute key. One who knows you, your tastes and interests, and one who'll **work** for you. We have one such, and she doesn't cost a thing!"

"Especially for independent, international travel, he or she can find out-of-the-way hotels instead of the kind where you see only Americans, arrange train or bus transportation so you can really see the countryside, and pick flights with the most convenient arrival and departure times, plus notifying you of any late changes in schedules."

Investigate arranging for guest accommodations (faculty club, dining hall, library, and so on) on any campus you'll be visiting.

"The winter months we spent near Atlanta, we had campus privileges at Emory."

"The University of New South Wales was delighted to give us entree to the faculty rooms; in turn, I gave a guest lecture."

If you're a retired armed forces officer, remember your air travel and post/base privileges.

"We flew 'space available' to Spain at nominal cost."

"My wife and I are regular guests each winter at Fort Benning, and we play golf at Fort Knox enroute."

Leave an itinerary or mail drop/phone contact points with a friend or relative.

"You want to be able to be contacted at various points should there be an emergency at home."

"If one of your kids or elderly parents has an accident, you want to know, even if you're in India — and phone service works pretty well these days from even fairly primitive areas."

"A Western Union office makes a good point of call — in case you run short of funds."

No doubt you've acquired or will acquire your own travel tips. Keep the cards and letters coming to Magna Publications, and we'll include them in the next edition of *Retirement 901* for the edification of future retiree vagabonds.

Exploring Nearby Sideroads

Travel doesn't have to mean global or even continental expeditions. Particularly as you get older, you may find as rewarding in its own way the exploration of highways and byways in your own region.

Although one couple in my retirement complex is a veteran of worldwide travel, the infirmities that are the inevitable concomitant of reaching 85-plus have brought their globetrotting to a halt, but that doesn't mean they vegetate around their Madison living room fireplace. They've switched to that great old American pastime, the Sunday afternoon drive.

As their guide, they're using a Schoenfeld book titled *Down Wisconsin Sideroads*. Its opening pages include these thoughts:

> In the spirit of Thoreau, we all yearn for those old, meandering, dry, uninhabited roads which lead away from town, where our heads are more in heaven than our feet on earth, where travelers are not too often to be met, where our spirits are free, where we can walk and think with least obstruction, and which are wide enough — "wide as the thoughts they allow to visit you."

GOING BACK TO SCHOOL

The campus senior class is now just that — more than a million students aged 55 and over estimated to be involved in organized post-secondary education, some 320,000 of them enrolled in college courses for credit, including more than 65,000 at the graduate or professional levels, according to the Census Bureau's latest count.

Pursuing degree programs, auditing classes, forming retiree study groups, attending campus lectures, joining study-travel expeditions — this going-back-to-school boom is even turning some college towns into new retirement meccas.

Some older learners are preparing for late-life career changes, some are earning degrees for the first time, others are drawn back to a campus for the sheer pleasure of learning.

"I've never had so much fun," says one 86-year-old, who finally earned his Yale degree last year 65 years after being expelled — for getting married. He lived on campus and was a bit taken aback at first by the coed bathrooms, but, he says, "At my age, such things don't seem important; I'm more concerned with just standing up."

Attending classes can help fill the void left by a deceased spouse, grown children, or retiring from the working world. Once they begin taking classes, many older students find they want to keep going. One was a bored California woman dabbling in community-college courses when she discovered anthropology. Last June, at 66, she received her Ph.D. from Stanford.

There are a variety of formal and informal back-to-school arrangements you can consider:

Elderhostel

Elderhostel, the granddaddy of the field, was started in 1975 with five New Hampshire campuses hosting 220 participants. The Boston-based, nonprofit organization expects its 1991-92 enrollment to top 220,000, attending one-to-four-week programs at more than 1,600 colleges in the United States and in 43 foreign countries, taught by campus experts and housed in college dorms during vacation periods.

Each term Elderhostel publishes a thick catalog that offers an array of courses from the arts to zoology and adventures in Nepal studying the culture of the Sherpas. The average stay on a U.S. campus costs $270 a week, a month overseas up to $5,700, including airfare from a U.S. gateway city.

The Elderhostel address is 75 Federal St., Boston, MA 02100; 617/426-8056.

Institutes for Learning in Retirement

The Institutes for Learning in Retirement (ILRs) are usually on college campuses — study groups tailored specifically for older students. Members pay an annual fee and design their own courses, recruiting instructors from within their own ranks. The courses are usually semester-length.

The concept was pioneered by the New School of Social Research in New York. Some 160 ILR programs are now offered nationwide. Harvard's ILR, for example, has 430 members in 49 study groups. Delaware's "Academy of Life-Long Learning" is one of the largest, with 1,400 students participating in 110 courses in its own building on the Wilmington campus. There are no grades or exams, yet the courses are demanding and discussions can be electric. "I like to discuss WW II with people who lived through it, not with an instructor to whom it's ancient history," says one ILR fan.

Some ILR programs are highly selective. UCLA's 375-member PLATO Society (for Planned Learning and Teaching Organization) has a waiting list; members must have at least 20 years' professional experience and be prepared to give dissertation-style presentations in seminars of graduate-level quality. Mostly, though, ILR retirees relish each other's company as they pursue eclectic interests.

All told there are currently some 35,000 ILR participants. Information can be had from The Institute Network, 15 Garrison Ave., Durham, NC 03824; 603/862-3642.

Shepherd's Centers

Shepherd's Centers are not college-oriented but offer some academic courses as well as "how to" classes at about 100 senior centers in more than 70 communities. An informal headquarters is at Shepherd's Centers of America, 6700 Troost Ave., Suite 616, Kansas City, MO 64131; 816/523-1080.

Ad Hoc Independent Campus Programs

It's the rare community college, four-year college, or university these days that doesn't have at least one educational program, if not an array of programs, tailored to retiree proclivities. In fact, 36 states discount or even waive fees for older adults seeking degrees, auditing courses, or attending special non-credit, college-level "joy of learning" options at public institutions.

For example, when I was Dean of Inter-College Programs at the University of Wisconsin-Madison, I had under my recognizance (a) Special Students — adults with inadequate credentials testing their ability to pursue degree programs for credit, paying per-course fees, (b) Guest Students — adults auditing for free any courses of interest where they could find seating room, (c) PLATOnics in an ILR institute, and (d) assorted older people in varied non-credit programs designed for their physical and/or mental stimulation. (By the way, most of those returnees were an inspiration, but some were a pain in the neck with their ridiculous demands for custom treatment. So, watch it if you go back!)

Retirement Communities

For many years, active armed forces forts, fields, and stations have been the nuclei for retirement communities, attracting retired uniformed personnel desirous of availing themselves of associated prerequisites. Now the trend is catching on for real estate firms to build retirement facilities adjacent to college campuses — Green Hills near Iowa State, the Colonnades near the University of Virginia, Kendal near Dartmouth, Meadowood near Indiana, and similar developments projected for Oberlin, Lehigh, Cornell, and other campuses.

Most of these communities aren't officially affiliated with the institution, but their proximity gives their residents readier access to the academic and cultural life of the campus. For example, at Green Hills, a resident often walks by the house he and his wife owned on his way to the office the retired zoology and fishery professor still maintains at ISU. "Many of our friends thought we were giving up too early to move into a place like this," he says, "but we know too many people who waited too long."

(For more on the issue of where to live in retirement, see sections on "Staying Home on the Range" in this chapter.)

Learning Vacation Programs

Combining travel with a learning experience may be shaping up as one of the biggest trends of the '90s — retirees pursuing not only diversion but knowledge and understanding of the culture and habitat of a destination. Name a subject of interest and you're likely to find a learning vacation to fit it these days.

Excursions average one to three weeks and cost from $270 to $5,000, sometimes more. Participants usually pay their own transportation expenses separately, but fees for some programs may include round-trip airfare. Tour leaders are experts in their fields — geologists, archaeologists, ecologists, astronomers, sociologists, artists, and so on.

Here are some major study-tour operators:

Earthwatch

Programs involve a wide range of subject matter. Volunteers share costs of research-oriented expeditions, averaging $1,300 a person, tax deductible. Contact Earthwatch, 680 Mount Auburn St., PO Box 403N, Watertown, MA 02272; 617/926-8200.

TraveLearn

Arranges learning vacations for 122 university-sponsored programs with one faculty member for every 15 participants. Costs range from $2,000 to $5,000. For tour descriptions, dates, and prices, contact TraveLearn, PO Box 315, Lakeville, PA 18438; 717/226-9114.

Elderhostel

Publishes eight catalogs during the year. Cost of programs abroad includes travel to destination. Groups vary in size from 15 to 40 and are known to develop a camaraderie. A companion who is 50 years old or older may accompany a participant who is at least age 60. Contact Elderhostel, 75 Federal St., Boston, MA 92110; 617/426-7788.

Smithsonian Institution

Sponsors extensive study tours around the world, usually two weeks in length. Participants average 55 years of age. Contact Smithsonian Associates and Travel Program, 1100 Jefferson Drive SW, Washington, DC 20560; 202/357-4700.

Outward Bound

Offers courses at 50 schools and centers worldwide, specializing in climbing and wilderness-experience expeditions. Participants ages range from 14 to 70; 61% are men. For more information, contact Outward

Bound, 384 Field Point Road, Greenwich, CT 06830; 800/243-8520.

All told, the life of the mind needn't go out the window when you retire. Manifold opportunities will present themselves for continued collective mental stimulation. Or, you alone or you and your spouse can conduct your own independent learning regimen (Beck *et al.* 1991a).

ROLLING WITH CLOCK AND CALENDAR

Most academics have had to be creatures of schedule. With retirement you're off the treadmill. If promptness was almost a disease, you can now relax and let your blood pressure go down. Throw away your watch, if you wish, and your alarm clock. Enjoy the pleasure of turning over in bed for another snooze. Go on spur-of-the-moment shopping trips. Nobody will complain if you complete a task on Thursday you had planned to finish Tuesday.

Run if you feel like it, walk if you feel like it, or just sit and rock for a spell. Relish the tranquility that comes from being exempt from calls from a boss. Nap in the afternoon if you're so inclined. Take a hike before breakfast. Go swimming in the middle of the morning. Watch TV to all hours of the night. The only clock you need to punch the next morning is your microwave timer.

Enjoy freedom from calendars, too. If you live in a northern clime, one of the most delightful rewards of retirement is that you can just sit and watch it snow, snow, snow. No requirement that you get up at the crack of dawn to shovel out the driveway. Or if you live in the South, no requirement that you go out in the noonday sun. And at equinox time, you can take time off to sniff the fragrance of fringed gentians in spring or revel in fall's cavalcade of color.

And yet there's the possibility you could fall victim to too much freedom. Procrastination lurks. As a Scottish proverb goes, "What may be done at any time will be done at no time." Simply staying at home in front of the tube can be a trap. If you don't keep active, you'll go down hill physically and mentally. To be simply a creature of whim — doing just what you want to do when you want to — is what one retiree warns can be "a slippery slope to oblivion."

From the multiple comments he received from his survey of college and university retirees, Milletti concluded that there's a "strong need in retirement for 'time management' skills — the ability to plan the use of one's time productively," to stay reasonably well organized, to retain that measure of self-discipline to go by a clock and calendar you yourself set, but nonetheless by a schedule.

Explains one reviewer:

> Old habits can help. I am up at my regular 7 a.m. time, "work" at something until 5 p.m., then opt for a highball or two, read the paper, eat dinner, and then "recreate" — read, TV, listen to music, and so on — until bedtime. I even have a weekend schedule different from weekday.

Yet on any daily schedule, why not earmark some time just to look around and smell the roses, to savor those odd moments of ordinary existence within our daily grasp if we will but seize them — and appreciate.

KEEPING A DATE A DAY

Faculty and academic staff tend to be very scheduled, as we've said. So it's only natural that, when they suddenly switch to unscheduled retirement, a certain amount of stress develops, particularly when there's absolutely nothing on the calendar — just the opposite of the stress formerly engendered by running frantically from one campus commitment to another.

Fortunately there's a very simple solution for this insidious ennui: go out of your way to keep one major date — and only one — a day.

If you're importuned to attend more than one event or keep more than one engagement on a same day, try to stagger your schedule so that you ration your dates to cover a whole week. Not only will such a practice allow you to concentrate your undivided interest and attention on the date at hand, it will mitigate against any "dead spots" in your schedule.

If no invitations or announcements come your way, invent an event. Anticipate the calendar. Is your spouse's birthday coming up? You now have no excuse to forget it. Is it time to correspond with favorite former grad students? Make a special day of it. Is a grandchild a lonesome college student? Schedule a long phone call. The options are innumerable.

My favorite device is to continue to observe days that stand out in my past, even though I may no longer be able to do so in full former style.

You Can Go Home Again

I am — I'm proud to say it — a duck hunter. For the inveterate duck hunter, Opening Day is one of which memories are made — a combination of Christmas, New Year's, and Yom Kippur — a day to be observed religiously in perpetuity, whether you actually can participate full-bore or not.

For example, each opening day I make a sentimental journey to where it all began for me on Rock Lake at Lake Mills, WI. Sometimes I'm lucky enough to be a guest of a native in his blind on the marsh, but more likely I just take potluck by walking the railroad grade that separates marsh from lake.

In a way it's bad to go back. There are ghosts around an old hunting spot. Some Rock Lake ghosts died in their beds; some did not. One is an MIA in a stinking Buna swamp, another in the waters off Midway, another in a Netuno cemetery. Their names are inscribed with gold stars on the plaque in the city-square park, but I can't find them where they would like to be — on Rock Lake marsh on Opening Day.

So it's bad to go back. But it's good, too.

There's the same weatherworn railroad bridge which makes such a natural lookout for spying on the life of the marsh. There's the blue winged teal that cannonballs by just as did his ancestors. And there's the pair of whistling swans that invariably occupies Korth's Bay. Waterfowl don't change. With them you can get back behind the years.

Along the grade I can even meet myself — in the form of a youngster playing hookey from high school, toting a double-barrel as big as his hopes. I talk to him about the red sprays of sumac and the golden spires of tamarack. I point out how a wood duck cranes its neck when it flies, and how a hooded merganser will decoy without caution.

I talk and we wait and we watch together, and the decades wash away with the waves. There is shotgun-booming from Shultz's Bay to the north. I and my companion hunker down in the willows. Far out over the lake we spot them, low on the water — a gaggle of scaup. Will they give us a pass or will they swing off? It's a question as old as my years yet as fresh as my young compatriot's eyes. The birds keep coming. As they near the grade, they start to climb.

"Hold your fire," I caution, "they're out of range." My partner conforms.

Rock Lake has spawned a new duck hunter — and I've kept a date with yet another Opening Day, filling my retirement schedule with memories not to be forgotten. It's a nice feeling.

Try it, you'll like it — reliving your own special times.

WRITING YOUR MEMOIRS

Wondering what to give your grown children for Christmas? How about the gift of a lifetime?

You don't have to have discovered penicillin, parsed Shakespeare, or mediated the problems of a farm community to write your life story. A

75-year-old retiree lives quietly outside my city, but his life could fill a book. In fact it has — five books, to be exact.

The title of the first was a single word printed elegantly in the center of a plain white cover: *Reminiscences.* He sent copies to each of his four grown children, who live scattered across two continents.

Today, when many families are separated by years and geography and even issues, a sense of where we come from is a precious commodity.

"Whatever you lose as you age," this retiree says, "there is one thing you have — a monopoly on history. Whether it was Herbert Hoover being sworn in as president — to put a chicken in every pot and a car in every garage, or Franklin D. proclaiming that 'we have nothing to fear but fear itself' — or Harry Truman signing the Medicare bill, ... I was around."

He sent his first book as a Christmas surprise in 1970. In it he included both world events and personal stories about growing up in the 1920s. "I wanted to create a bridge between the personal and the national experience, about how the Depression and World War II affected daily life," he says.

Beyond checking dates in a history text, he didn't do much formal research. He relied on photos, clippings, phone calls to old friends, and his memories. But he once traveled to Kansas in search of his childhood home in a bustling town — only to find a stone marker. But it triggered a thousand memories.

Like many others, the family suffered a rift in the 1960s. The mending process began with the youngest daughter, 36, when the first book arrived. "It was a big deal for me — bringing the family back together," she recalls. Reading the book also gave her brother new insights into a father-son relationship: "I realized how values had been passed along."

Before beginning the project, this retiree never saw himself as a writer; he liked to write letters but nothing more. How he's completed five books is instructive for other retirees:

> After you start, then it's easy. You turn to it, and you don't want to leave it alone. In the midst of a busy life — church events, ushering at a civic theater, classes, square dancing, canoe trips, and so on — I stick to a regular writing schedule. I sit at my desk with a stack of cards and jot down thoughts about people, places, and events. Whatever comes to mind. Later we turn it all into a manuscript. Reliving the experiences is an enjoyable form of recreation.
>
> He admits he feels more at ease on paper than in person — simply a difference in style: "There's this notion you have something stored in

your memory that's worth passing on. Something that nobody else can supply. It's unique, by definition, by nature. That's what it's all about" (Pritzi 1991).

As you can see, this retiree is a pencil-and-paper person, which may be the very best way to let your thoughts flow but which complicates enormously transmitting those thoughts into manuscript form. As a Milletti correspondent says, "Those who are retired can have trouble getting a letter typed. You can see by this typing that my working life was spent where there were good secretaries."

The answer, of course, is to master an electric typewriter, a word processor, or a personal computer — in order of complication and finished product. If you propose to write your memoirs, that is.

As you might assume, the writer of this book has also written some memoirs — on a rudimentary Brother word processor that looks like standard Royal.

The first was a book-length tome titled *Ribbands of Blue* (see *The Old Testament*, Numbers, 15:38). To lend scope and sequence to his personal reminiscences for his three daughters, he got permission from William Manchester — adjunct professor of history at Wesleyan University and scintillating author of (among other titles) *The Glory and the Dream: A Narrative History of America — 1932-1972* (Boston: Little, Brown, 1974) — to precede each chapter with an extended excerpt.

The first chapter, titled "Ten-hut" (which is the way a regular Army sergeant calls his troops to attention) starts out like this:

> To put you in the proper mood for this book, let me just say:
>
> If you were I, you would have been born on 16 December 1918 in an upstairs bedroom in the Congregational parsonage on a back street in Mineral Point, Wisconsin. A maiden aunt heated the legendary hot water on a coal-and-wood stove in the kitchen below, and a proverbial country doctor made the required house call without, I assume, batting an eye. I will undoubtedly expire in an intensive care unit of a carpeted and chrome hospital in Madison, Wisconsin, bathed in solar-heated water and attended by a reluctant intern in lieu of the resident specialist who is surfing at the moment in Hawaii. In between 1918 and whatever I will have put in a full and fascinating life, garlanded by exciting or excruciating exploits. So I span two eras.
>
> But this book isn't about me at all. It is about the friends, Americans, country persons, who have made life meaningful, folk who wear Biblical ribbands of blue, individuals who symbolize what faith, hope, and charity are all about. We hear and see a lot these days about "the bad

> guys." This book is a sentimental tribute to "the good guys" — of both sexes — who can save us from ourselves. ...
>
> *Ribbands of Blue* is about the people who have picked me from lonely strands, and with whom I have lived, however briefly, within the charmed circle of humanity. So, just come along with me through a portfolio of real people — good people, famous people, folks next door — the sort of blue-ribband personalities with whom we all may weave the tapestries of our lives.
>
> Here is also a gallery of mid-America scenes — a trout stream in the first shy days of spring, summer sights at country fairs, the riot of color and sound on a college campus in autumn, winter memories of bleak battlefields — all the panorama of a great region to sense and savor.
>
> As a story that spans the past 60 years, this memoir is a dramatic reminder of how much our lives have changed in the memory of living people — from Round Oak kitchen wood stoves to Amana microwave ovens, from Overland Six touring cars to Winnebago RV's, from a vision of a chicken in every pot to the reality of a TV dinner. Yet this book also tries to remind us that what really counts doesn't change — the music of humaneness, dramatized here in true situations you may recognize.
>
> This book doesn't pretend to be anything but what it is — a nostalgic visit with the kind people who've touched its author. Yet in a larger sense it is a picture of a particular America, a time-capsule of us human beings AD 1918-1982 in the provinces north of Chicago — in our growing up and growing out, our living and loving, working and dreaming, fighting, dying, and rising again — all set against a background interpreted by that incomparable writer, William Manchester.

You see how easy it is?

Because that volume was received with so much acclaim, I decided to do a sequel for my eight grandchildren, titled *Around the Calendar with Grandpa Clay's Bedtime Stories for Boys and Girls*.

But you needn't be a writer to put your life into words. Comments one reviewer:

> Please include something about taping memoirs. Some people who may not be adept at manual writing are nonetheless natural storytellers, and whose stories are actually best told orally. These types should never bother to struggle with a keyboard when it's so easy for them to talk into a microphone. For a recipient to hear the voice adds real authenticity and personal touch to the narrative.

Another reviewer concurs:

> I agree with a previous reviewer's remarks that you should cover *taping* one's memoirs in addition to writing them. Words flow easily

from your mind to paper; others may not be adept. In fact, you ought to include *videotaping* as a possibility as well."

Done.

Sharing Your Expertise

If writing your memoirs isn't your thing, at least not for now, perhaps continuing your scholarly writing is — only this time for a larger audience.

It may be significant that in spring 1992 at least two leading figures in higher education pled with their colleagues — active and retired — to share their expertise on key national issues with a general public hungry for ideas:

Speaking to the American Association for Higher Education in Chicago in April, Derek Bok, president emeritus of Harvard and now a fellow at the Center for Advanced Study in the Behavioral Sciences at Stanford, said one reason the nation's higher education institutions are being bashed is because they're not seen as taking part in a national agenda.

"We must associate ourselves more prominently with solving the problems that concern Americans most," he urged.

The very same week Jeffrey Boutwell, associate executive officer of the American Academy of Arts and Sciences, was sounding the same theme in an "Opinion" essay in *The Chronicle of Higher Education*:

"Among the many ways in which citizens can become better informed on the myriad issues facing the body politic, ... a resource readily at hand" — the million-plus personnel, those still working and those retired, associated with more than 3,500 colleges and universities who "must not ignore their responsibility to help continue the education of all our citizens."

Two examples of what they were talking about cropped up within a month in the wake of Los Angeles riots:

- Peter Edelman, associate dean and professor of law at the Georgetown University Law Center, appeared on the editorial pages of *The Washington Post National Weekly Edition*, offering a five-point program "if the administration and the Congress were actually going to do something."
- Peter Morris, emeritus professor of urban planning at UCLA challenged his younger colleagues in the social sciences on a "Point of View" page in *The Chronicle of Higher Education*:

> Research has to become engaged with the moral issues that its findings address, such as racial and gender discrimination, inequality of opportunity, and what responsibility our society should take for political and economic decisions that affect our most vulnerable citizens. ... It could at once inform the discussion of policy and reconnect sociology to its roots in social idealism and reform.

As Emeriti Bok and Morris demonstrate, just because you retired doesn't mean you'll have nothing more to say. You have perspective. You've been there! And now you'll be free of those institutional and disciplinary constraints that can muffle younger faculty.

So, when the spirit moves you, sound off! It doesn't have to be in the columns of a national daily; a community group may appreciate your thoughts even more.

Writing of Other Kinds

If sounding off isn't your thing, but writing is, there are plenty of options.

For instance, that tome your discipline has always needed. Emeritus University of Wisconsin-Madison Professor of Wildlife Ecology Robert McCabe contributed to the literature of his profession a remarkable personal account of his long-time close collaboration with the profession's founder, Aldo Leopold.

Or The Great American Novel.

Or then again, do what Emeritus University of Minnesota Twin Cities Professor of Scandinavian Languages and Literature Allen Simpson is doing — writing for fun and profit — in his case, murder mysteries.

"I no longer believe in literary analysis," he says. "I like writing mysteries 648 times better."

His latest, *A Gift for Murder*, was Avon Book's lead mystery title in December 1992. Its setting: the rivalry-ridden world of academe, specifically a university with an "ivy-covered old campus" and a "new campus, home of the hard sciences," the two separated by a river. Any resemblance to UM is of course accidental. As if he could really fool his old colleagues, Simpson writes under the pen name of M.D. Lake (from the nearby real Medicine Lake) And it's therapeutic medicine for the second-career author. Simpson notes, "I dump all my prejudices into my books" (Weglarz 1992).

READIN,' ROCKIN,' AND REUNIONS

No, I'm not going to close this chapter without saying a few words about three of the most ubiquitous of retirement diversions.

Readin'

For those so inclined, there's no retirement blessing more blessed than new-found time for reading — occasional or omnivorous.

Whether it's today's newspaper, this week's newsmagazine, this month's digest, or a parade of books, you have practically all the time you wish to devote to reading. What the mail carrier doesn't bring, you can get at a nearby library, thanks to exchange programs tying even rural reading rooms to continental resources.

If your sight begins to fail, there are large-print books, chapters-a-day on public radio, and books on tape.

A couple of suggestions:

- You may find it stimulating to keep up with trends in higher education via *The Chronicle of Higher Education*, or *Change*, *Academe*, and *Academic Leader*.
- Your disciplinary association may offer reduced rates for retirees that will continue to bring you your journal(s).
- Your campus library will likely have a reference desk with an unending supply of information.
- Rereading old favorites can be as fascinating as delving into the newest best-sellers.

One caution: applying the seat of your pants or skirt to the seat of a chair sans exercise can be dangerous to your health.

Rockin'

Rockin' and watching TV or listening to music, that is.

Some emeritus professors eschew the tube, but many professional/technical types know better: there's a wealth of fine programs.

Take PBS, for example "MacNeil and Lehrer" each weeknight, "Washington Week in Review" and "Wall Street Week" each Friday, "Great Performances" on occasion — television at its best. On cable, CNN and C-Span are equally elucidating.

If you can't adjust to current fare on your local channels, they're likely to offer an array of "golden oldies" for your entertainment. It's hard not to find at least one show that will bring back pleasant memories of family times around the tube.

If you're hearing ebbs, you likely can find closed-caption programs accessible with a special adapter.

A couple of suggestions:

- While Saturdays tend indeed to be that celebrated "wasteland," Sunday mornings offer a potpourri of programs from the inspirational to the recreational to the enlightening.
- For sports fans, ESPN is a gem.
- If you don't regularly watch at least one local and national newscast, you'll be out of a lot of conversations.

That VCR is a great device for recording what you can't watch and for showing a bewildering choice of videotape movies.

Rockin' can also involve hours of listening to music on records, tapes or compact discs.

That caution again: Rockin' in the absence of exercise is that slippery slope to physical decay.

Reunions

Some dread reunions. Some thrive on them, as a chance to rediscover their past. They're there for retirees to pass up or participate in.

I myself pass up some, but there's one I always go to: the annual get-together of the Lake Mills (WI) high school class of '36.

I really only lived in Lake Mills from 1933, when my father answered a call to become pastor of the local Congregational Church, until 1937, when I took off for the University of Wisconsin. But no years of my life were so formative or fun — thanks to the good folks there.

Lake Mills people are special to me. They have had the grace to reach out to a prodigal with affection and regard. I've even become considered as something of a "native." To the itinerant son of an itinerant preacher, that is everything.

Lake Mills is a good town. Not many very famous people have ever come out of it, but there aren't any skeletons in the closet, either. Whisking past Lake Mills on the interstate between Madison and Milwaukee, it's easy to ignore the place, but if you turn off and drive around the picture-postcard town square or stop in at a local spa, you can catch the flavor of America's backbone.

So once a year I savor that annual Lake Mills High reunion, renewing precious friendships with living classmates, paying silent tribute to those up there in the cemetery. While I'm enjoying my adventures in the present, it's nice to take an occasional journey into my past.

STAYING HOME ON THE RANGE?

We've left one of the more vexing self-fulfillment questions to the last — Do you move or stay?

Actually, the question is more complicated than that; it's multifaceted:

Do you stay in the same geographic site where you are? Or do you move to a different area of the country entirely?

In either case:

Do you continue to live in the same type of physical facility you're used to? Or do you change to a different category of housing?

For instance, let's say our prototype 55-year-old professor, contemplating retirement at 65, owns, together with spouse, a single-family dwelling, a condo, or an apartment not far from campus. Do they stay put indefinitely upon retiring, do they move to a similar accommodation in a different clime, or do they change to another type of housing, either in their immediate vicinity or away somewhere?

Their answers to these questions will depend on a host of variables, not the least of which is: What point on the retirement continuum are they talking about — age 65? age 85? or somewhere in between?

In answering your own questions about your address in retirement, if you want to go by demographic statistics, here are some for you to chew on:

- According to U.S. Department of Agriculture data, once you turn 65, the chance of your moving is only 1 in 100 ("moving" not defined).
- According to an American Association of Retired Persons (AARP) survey, most older Americans want to stay in their homes.
- According to U.S. Census statistics on geographic mobility, 47 out of 50 people older than 60 stay at their present address.
- According to Milletti's survey of 1,500 academic retirees, on the other hand, 45% **had** moved geographically coincident with retirement. (Which may tell us something or other about a peculiar peripatetic nature of academics.)

Whatever the statistics, the choices are obviously, in most cases, yours.

Crucial Considerations

In deciding whether or not to stay on the range, here are some key factors to throw into your mental hopper, adapted from Peter A. Dickinson (1990) and organized under our three "triple-A retirement essentials":

Adequate Income Stream

- Housing costs, availability, variety
- Food and household goods costs
- Taxes
- Energy supply and costs
- Dwelling services availability and costs
- Opportunities for earning money
- Senior citizen discounts or tax breaks

Affordable Health Care

- Hospital availability and costs
- Dentist/doctor availability and costs
- Nursing services and facilities
- Clinic types and costs
- Specialists
- Temperature, humidity, temperature-humidity index
- Sunshine or clear days
- Elevation
- Water quality
- Air quality
- Noise
- Municipal and business services
- Police and fire protection
- Wellness facilities
- Highway, road, street, and sidewalk conditions

Activities for Self-Fulfillment

- Opportunities for continued scholarly endeavor
- Proximity to family and favored friends
- Cultural facilities
- Social activities

- Educational opportunities
- Library resources
- Outdoor recreation
- Peer groups
- Senior centers or clubs
- Offices and counseling on aging
- Special programs or services for seniors
- Public transportation

Make your own checklist, choosing among those items (or others you add) which are most important to you, and rate them: 3, vital; 2, important; 1, of some concern. Use a minus sign if the answer is no. Use the same rating scale for each community you're considering, then add up each score. Be sure to rate your present community; you may find you're better off not moving, or that you'd better start packing.

Changing Geographic Venue

Why might you indeed move cross-country? Milletti's data, drawn from retired academics who did, suggest the following reasons, alone or in combination:

- To be nearer family and friends, 30%
- To enjoy a better climate, 29%
- To reduce home and maintenance responsibilities, 17%
- To live in a nicer area, 17%
- To get a home of more appropriate size, 16%
- To reduce cost of maintaining home, 15%
- To reduce property tax, 12%
- To improve health, 9%

What this chart doesn't indicate, of course, is that for some retirees, dominant factors were such as: to be nearer better health care personnel and facilities, to facilitate continued research, or to participate in a particular form of recreation or cultural amenity.

These data are merely for your information; don't let them sway what must be a highly individual decision. Notice, too, that some of these considerations don't necessarily require a major geographic move.

Testing the Waters (Literally and Figuratively)

If, for one or more reasons, you're contemplating a geographic move,

Dickinson recommends these steps in preparation:

- Try to pinpoint the area you'd like to settle in. A good guidebook like Dickinson's will help immeasurably. Or you can write to the U.S. Departments of HEW and HUD for suggestions. (You can use your Congressman or Congresswoman as an intermediary.)
- After you've pinpointed the area, write to the specific state units on aging, located in the state capital, asking specifics about location and availability of housing, cost of living and taxes, climate and environment, health care, and services/facilities for seniors.
- Then write to the chambers of commerce of the various cities and towns you're interested in. All you need is the ZIP code. Again, ask specific questions uppermost in your mind.
- Subscribe to weekly or Sunday papers to learn more about the area's gestalt and cost-of-living.
- Vacation there — off season as well as in. Take the pulse of the place. Get to know the people — mail carrier, grocer, real estate agent, neighbors, association members.

- Rent before buying. Leave an anchor to windward by renting out your abode at home.
- Think twice before buying into a development with no track record of solvency.
- Do a double-check on long-term supply, quality, and price of water, energy, air, and waste-disposal services. Ditto for affordable, quality health care facilities and services, short-term and long-term.
- Put into the equation such environmental factors as insect infestations, violent storm tracks, flooding, and neighborhood stability.
- Rate all such factors against the dominant factor influencing your move.

For example, primarily to escape Wisconsin winters, my spouse and I rented a condo on Florida's west coast. The weather was great, but it didn't make up for multiple culture shock — in our case, at least.

An emeritus reviewer who relocated from Michigan to Florida says he and his spouse used vacation time in preretirement years to select a place to which to retire later on, and that one thing of particular importance was the availability of "rapid and easily accessible air transportation to help keep us in touch with distant family members and friends."

Voices of Experience

You may find it useful to check out what experts and/or experienced retirees recommend about where to locate, based on whatever of the three retirement essentials has your top priority.

Cost of Living

U.S. News & World Report (Wiener 1991) asked a number of retirement experts for their best guesses of where the cost combined with quality of life would draw retirees of the future. The spots named again and again are small town and rural: "You won't find the natives rocking the paint off their porches, though. At least physically speaking, there's plenty to do. All eight of the towns are within an hour or two of a medium-sized to large city."

(In case you're curious, from east to west, here are the experts' picks: Hanover, NH; Charles Town, WV; Hendersonville, NC; Clayton, GA; Guntersville, AL; Eagle River, WI; Prescott, AZ; Sequin, WA.)

Bill and Paula Woodward (1991), writers who themselves chose a ranching community in northern Wyoming in which to retire, offer this comparison of housing costs between metropolitan and small-town America:

	Baker, OR	**Herndon, VA**
House Purchase Price	$80,000	$170,000
Housing-Related Monthly Costs		
Mortgage payment	$411.63	$1,399.35
Property taxes	$120	$181
Heating	$80	(see power)
Power	$40	$150
Sanitation	$9	$15
	Baker, OR	**Herndon, VA**
Total	**$660.63**	**$1,745.71**

Health Care

With some exceptions, a rural small town is just where you won't want to go if your top priority is readily accessible, varied short- and long-term health care. When Dickinson rates Sunbelt sites on the basis of medical facilities, every one is at least a medium-size city. The same would hold for any other part of the country.

Amenities

Again, if your activities for self-fulfillment center around the cultural and educational, a metropolitan area will likely be your choice.

Listen to these comments from some of Milletti's retirees:

> "The richness of cultural endeavors — music, opera, ballet, theater, senior citizen college programs" ... "Don't let the glamor of a new move to a vacation area blind you to the reality of the situation; I'm considering moving to another site with a more cosmopolitan make-up and more cultural activity" ... "It was a very expensive proposition to repack and move back to New York" ... "We picked the city because of its mental stimulation" ... "We retired to a place that's almost ideal with respect to climate, but it lacks people with similar intellectual and cultural interests to our own" ... "I really miss abundant library facilities" ... "My retirement enjoyment comes from opportunities unique to New York City."

On the other hand, if your wont is for the outdoors — its recreation and scenery — then of course you'll head for wide, open spaces.

The Woodwards in Wyoming:

> The pluses (in rural living) far outweigh the disadvantages for us. We realized that one morning last spring. We had stepped outside with our first cups of coffee to check on the progress of the garden. It was one of those classic Rocky Mountain mornings when the sun bakes the dew from the grass and the sky sparkles above. We talked for awhile about whence we might travel on our vacation. Then we looked west to the Big Horns towering above us. A lush sea of bright wildflowers flowed from town upward to a forest of lodgepole pine. The tops of the mountains were still wrapped in snow and, as we watched, the wind blew fresh powder from the ridges in long trailing wisps of white.
>
> We realized then that there was no need to search for a perfect vacation spot. We lived there.

It's not that way at all for many retirees, says Deborah Ersland, a developer who specializes in housing for the elderly: "We've found that seniors want to be close to action — grocery stores, bus lines, shopping, churches. Seniors don't want to look out their windows and see trees, meadows, and bunnies" (Erland 1992).

As in the case of this retiree:

> We enjoyed the warm summers in central California so much we retired in a quiet little town there. But soon we began to miss the interaction of a bustling community and dread the days of doing nothing. What had been a pleasant summer escape when we were working became a boring gulch of sameness.

We realized we are outgoing people who thrive on mingling with others. So we moved to a small city across the lake where we are active in the community, I in the politics of the water control board, my spouse in service programs for the elderly (Glaser 1992).

A reviewer:

I have a retired friend (age 69) who, with a new husband of two years (age 71), has traveled continuously since their marriage — to Alaska, Hawaii, and so on, living mostly in a van. The home of one of the husband's sons serves as a headquarters where I can always reach them by mail. The couple makes frequent stops outside of all of their children's homes. Most summers they work together at a Boy Scout camp in the Upper Peninsula. Parts of most winters they spend with daughters in California and Arizona.

What about mentioning this sort of "perpetual motion" as an option?"

Another reviewer:

"If you live in a stable neighborhood, know and are known — have roots — why move? Besides, to move and get settled costs 10% of the price of the new digs."

In many a retiree's case, of course, the inescapable bottom-line consideration in debating whether to go or stay may well be health (Longino *et al.* 1992).

Staying Put Indefinitely

Let's say, like so many people contemplating retirement, you've opted to stay in your present abode as long as you can.

But that doesn't mean you shouldn't adapt it to the inevitable claims of your aging.

Here are some — what architects call "**retrofitting**" — ideas you might well consider assigning to a remodeling contractor, or to yourself if you're that handy (Schlapak 1991):

- If you can, collapse your living onto a ground floor.
- If you can't, install powered stair-lifts.
- Widen all door apertures (except for closets) to 36 inches wide to accommodate easy movement of walkers and wheelchairs.
- Install lever-handle hardware on all doors for when arthritis makes turning a knob tough.
- Bring all kitchen cabinets and shelving down to easy-to-reach height.
- Move all electric outlets to 48 inches up, to eliminate bending.

- Lay cushioned sheet vinyl, soft and warm, on kitchen and bathroom floors.
- Eliminate all ceiling lighting fixtures and substitute indirect lighting to reduce shadows. The light level should be about twice that in a unit for younger people.
- Eliminate all throw rugs and high-pile carpets in living areas; replace with low-pile carpet plus a thin pad.
- Install illuminated light switches in bedroom and bath.
- Locate an emergency call-switch, if such is available, in both bedroom and bath.
- Post emergency and commonly called numbers near your phone(s).
- Investigate a "panic button" arrangement which automatically calls for help.
- Install smoke alarms throughout, and a handy fire extinguisher.
- Swing the bathroom door(s) outward to facilitate emergency access.
- Install a fiberglass tub and shower unit with slip-resistant finish and single-lever mixer faucets with a pressure-balanced anti-scald system. Add grab-bars and a phone extension. Convert sink and bowl faucets to the single-lever mixer type. Secure towel racks to studs to afford "grab-bar stability."
- Get a remote control for your TV.
- Install sturdy railings and non-slip surfaces on porches and steps.
- Install an automatic garage door opener.
- Remove door sills to avoid tripping.
- Equip the kitchen with helpful gadgets like a battery-powered jar-top opener.
- Substitute touch-button appliances for those with knobs.
- Equip the living room with a powered easy-rise chair and a heat/massage chair.
- Operate lighting fixtures and TV with clap on/clap off controls.
- Contract for lawn, shrubbery, tree, sidewalk, and driveway maintenance year-round.
- For when the time might come, investigate the availability of home health care, from simple meals-on-wheels to more extensive practical-nurse help.

With such well-conceived modifications, you can help make it easier to stay home on the range as long as possible. Or, if you change your geographic venue, you can arrange in advance for or make such alterations wherever you settle.

A reviewer notes:

> Modifications like that will actually enhance the salability of property to a young family. For instance, doors wide enough to accommodate wheelchairs are ideal for moving a crib or playpen from room to room, bathroom grab-bars are great for tots, and a teenager will positively love that phone in there.

Choosing an Alternate Retirement Haven

Whether you opt to stay on familiar terrain or to pull up stakes, you have a choice among varied accommodations. In general they represent a continuum from independent living to some services provided to total nursing care. Which you choose will depend, as we've said, on what stage you're at on your own retirement continuum.

In ascending order of assistance provided, you have five broad options — NORC, DRC, SSF, ISF, and FSF. We'll go into each of them now in general descriptions.

An NORC

A naturally occurring retirement community (NORC) is what sociologists call accommodations that have, by accident, attracted a preponderance of older people, either because longtime residents have stayed put or new retirees have been lured by location, amenities, whatever. They offer no special features other than compatible neighbors and, if you're lucky, a sympathetic manager/custodian who serves as a *de facto* social worker. Typically they're sets of condos or apartment buildings near main areas or routes of trade.

Down the avenue from my residence there's one such NORC that was written up recently in *The New York Times* (Lewin 1991). Once upon a time it was alive with new university hires, complete with sandboxes and swings. Now some of those faculty have moved back in from their too-big homes, along with other retirees, although there's still a smattering of grad students and younger people to lend diversity to the environment.

Michael Hunt, a University of Wisconsin-Madison professor who has made a specialty of studying NORCs, says they attract older people who like a familiar area and social connections:

> The people who come to NORCs are often widowed women who feel isolated in their homes after their husbands die, but they don't want to

> leave the pharmacist and the grocer and the friendships they know. They sell their house, giving up the space and the memories, and move to a NORC nearby, where the tradeoff is gaining social ties and having other people to watch out for them. In some of these places, it's like a college dorm. You can go down the hall in the afternoon, and all the doors are open.

A couple I know who moved into the NORC apartment building near me after selling their home a mile away — "so we didn't have to shovel snow any more" — have started a Thursday breakfast club in which a dozen residents car pool to a nearby restaurant — making sure to invite any newcomers.

A DRC

A designed retirement complex (DRC) is a layout of separate homes, cottages, condos, or even trailers adjacent to a swimming pool, golf course, community building, or shopping/service center, with a wide range of professionally or self-organized activities but no other support services besides perhaps yard and building maintenance. You either pay an entrance fee and then rent, buy and pay a service fee, or a combination thereof.

Many retirees like DRCs, especially as an interim address. The advantages are much the same as those of an NORC, plus the customized activities. One hazard: the developers may sell out, and new owners may be less than accommodating.

Here's a sampling of representative DRCs near campuses:

Chenal Valley, Little Rock, AR — Home ownership on 2,500 acres. World-class, 18-hole golf course.

Village at Skyline, Colorado Springs, CO — Home ownership available, single family and duplex, on 36 acres.

The Villages of Orange Blossom Gardens, Central Lady Lake, FL — Homes from the low $30s. Homesites from $15,000. Golf courses, country clubs, medical facilities, shopping centers nearby.

Crystal Cove at Sandestin, Destin, FL — Rental fees start at $1,250. Located within security gates of Sandestin Beach Resort. Private access to Gulf of Mexico beaches, a deep-water marina, and a full range of resort-style amenities and services.

Pinewild Country Club, Pinehurst, NC — 2,100-acre private residential country club community. Championship 18-hole golf course, 24-hour security. Homesites 3.4 to 2.5 acres from $26,000 to $85,000.

Penn National, Fayetteville, PA — Single-family homes and townhouses starting at $90,000. A golf course recreational community.

The Highlander of Kerrville, Kerrville, TX — Home ownership with buyback option from $89,000. Customized interior plans for garden homes on 35 acres. Near good medical care in the hill country northwest of San Antonio.

Atlantic Shores, Virginia Beach, VA — Condominium ownership starting at $85,000. Midrise apartments and villas on 201 acres.

An SSF

A self-service facility (SSF) is much like a DRC, except that while the latter is usually a community of resident-owned homes or condos, the former is usually a building of rental apartments.

I'm looking at a brochure for a new SSF going up in my community. It reads like this:

> Greentree Glen will be Horizon Investment & Development Corp.'s fifth senior apartment project. Greentree Glen is conveniently located on Madison's west side next to Woodman's Supermarket and across from the site of the new post office, with a major mall nearby. The complex will have beautiful one and two-bedroom apartments specifically designed for mature adults. Security locked, elevator, underground heated parking, community room, emergency call system, on-site resident manager, and social and educational coordination are some of the amenities.
>
> Each unit features washer and drier hook-up, storage room, all appliances, including dishwasher and self-cleaning oven, patio or balcony, central cable TV, emergency pull cords, intercom security system.

That's a fairly typical description of an SSF. Some may have more features, like a fireplace in each apartment; some less, like no covered parking.

You'll notice the brochure doesn't specify whether heat and light are included in the rent, whether there's air conditioning, or whether there's an entrance fee — things to check on before you'd sign up, along with the amount of monthly tariff — probably about $800 to $1,000 a month in Madison, depending on the size of the apartment.

All told, an SSF is something to consider. It's more cramped than a house, but then you relieve yourself of all sorts of maintenance chores and costs without sacrificing much independence. Yet an SSF doesn't give you the support services you may need, now or in the future.

An ISF

An intermediate service facility (ISF) I can tell you about exactly, because I live in one (when I'm not at our cabin retreat with my wife).

An ISF is like an SSF, except that it adds these support services (for an added fee in many instances):

- The dinner meal in a dining room or tray service in your apartment, and with an option to entertain guests at dinner.
- Breakfast and lunch by tray in your apartment at your convenience, or in a dining room.
- Apartment cleaning — very thorough — every other week, to include dishes and laundry, if you're so inclined.
- A nurse on call around the clock.
- Assistance in daily living, if you need it.
- In-house beauty/manicure/haircut parlor.
- In-house dentistry and podiatry attention.
- In-house physical therapy room.
- In-house worship services.
- A bewildering array of intellectual, cultural, recreational, and shopping services, in house and by bus, courtesy of the management.
- An in-house craft room.
- A Residents Council, to buffer complaints and proffer suggestions.

The nearest thing to it is a combined sorority/fraternity or, in my case, a combined officer's quarters/club.

For a blueprint for volunteering your time, read *Time Dollars* by Edgar Khan (distributed by St. Martin's Press, 1992). Says Ralph Nader, "This book could sweep the nation to higher levels of care, compassion, and enjoyment."

Since my ISF is associated with a nursing home, I have priority of access to that facility — which is no small advantage, given the shortage of good nursing homes. But an ISF is not a FSS, a full-service facility, or, as they're often called, a CCRC — a continuing care retirement community.

An FSF

A full-service facility (FSF), sometimes called a continuing care retirement community (CCRC), is the ultimate in long-term housing and health assurance. You can enter hale and hearty and leave on a stretcher, in the meantime experiencing a full range of attention from virtually none at all to intensive nursing care.

An FSF adds to the services of an ISF such features as these:

- Three meals a day.
- Assisted living for residents who need personal care with activities of daily living (ADLs) such as bathing, dressing, eating, and taking medications.
- Intensive nursing care.
- Psychological counseling.

Residents of FSFs usually pay for health care in one of three ways: on a fee-for-service basis, with a one-time entrance fee and monthly service fee, or a combination of the two. As health care costs continue to rise, fewer FSFs are guaranteeing the total cost of health care in exchange for the entrance fee and monthly service charge.

Living in a FSF with an on-site nursing home offers couples a special advantage: if husband or wife enters the nursing facility, the spouse remaining in another unit can make frequent visits without the added stress of commute.

Examples of FSFs near campuses:

Concordia Retirement Community, Bella Vista, AZ — Entrance fees start at $26,962. Includes 30 days of free nursing care. Apartments and townhouses on 22 acres. On-site health care center. Assisted living units. 117 holes of golf nearby.

Las Brisas San Pedro, Oceanside, CA — Entrance fees start at $100,500. Nursing home care at no additional cost. Apartments on 17 acres. On-site health care center. Personal care center.

The Medallion, Colorado Springs, CO — Entrance fees start at $33,753. Highrise apartments. On-site nursing and health care, including home care. Monthly rentals also available.

Green Ridge Village, Newville, PA — Entrance fees start at $35,000. Thirty-eight independent living apartment homes, 56 independent living cottages, 33 personal care apartments on more than 130 acres. On-site 66-bed health center.

The Forum at Lincoln Heights, San Antonio, TX — 150 apartment residences, 30 assisted-living suites, and a 60-bed skilled health care center. One- and two-bedroom apartments start at $1,420 a month.

Rappahannock Westminster-Canterbury, Irvington, VA — Entrance fees start at $87,150. Nursing care provided at no additional cost at on-site health care center. Apartments and cottages on 113 acres.

Bunking with the Kids?

Most older people prefer to live independently, either in their own homes or in a retirement facility of their choice. But what if you can't care for yourself, yet you're not incapacitated enough to be in a nursing home? In such a situation, some people opt for moving in with their adult children. But that can lead to unpleasantness, even grief.

Here are some questions to consider, posed in a Mayo Clinic Health Letter:

1. Do you and your son or daughter really want to live together?
2. Can your family afford it?
3. How easily can you adapt to their lifestyle, and they to yours?
4. Will you feel like a visitor?
5. Frankly, what are the strengths and weaknesses of your relationship?
6. Can you continue to pursue your hobbies?
7. Can you keep in touch with friends?
8. How much time do you expect your family to spend with you?
9. Will you have your own private space?
10. Can you bring along favorite furniture?
11. Will you have to depend on your family for transportation?
12. Do you want to help with cooking and cleaning? Will your family let you?
13. Can your family accommodate to any needs for personal care?
14. Can you help with household expenses?
15. If you can't manage your own financial affairs, who will assume this responsibility?

If you and your children have reservations about living together, think twice. At least consider a trial period (Landers 1992).

Some Fiscal Implications

As you might expect, Professor Emeritus Doug Osterheld (1992) points out there are fiscal implications to the decision of where to live in retirement.

First off, if you plan to sell your current home, you may want to take right away any one-time-only capital gains tax break or, if you are downsizing to a new accommodation, you may want to postpone taking the tax break now and, instead, pay a tax on the difference in cost be tween a more economical new home and the higher selling price of your old home.

Second, it's possible to significantly increase your disposable income by moving to a state with a more favorable tax climate. For example, you may avoid state income taxes.

But Osterheld recommends that, given the volatility of tax laws, you consult an expert before you dive off the end of the pier, and never make a move solely on the basis of taxes (Osterheld 1992).

(What did the Osterhelds themselves do? Well, their winter address is now in south Florida, although they retain a summer cottage in northern Wisconsin. I told you he was money-smart.)

A front-page headline in *The Wall Street Journal* Jan. 22, 1992, summarizes the plight of some retirees who weren't as smart as they thought they were:

Senior Squeeze: A Retirement Haven Struggles with Curse of Low Interest Rates

Datelined Sun City, AZ, the story reads:

> The extended interest rate decline has set off alarms all along the quiet streets and lush fairways of this sprawling retirement haven, shocking residents whose security is backed by safe and simple interest-bearing investments, principally CDs.

The moral: Don't peg your retirement housing costs to abnormal, unrealistic, or risky investment returns.

The Down-Sizing Issue

With few exceptions, whenever and wherever you relocate, you'll likely move into smaller accommodations. You accumulate "things" all through your life, and you now have to decide what to take along and what not. It's not an easy task.

The worst thing you can do, probably, is to keep every blessed piece of furniture by crowding into already cramped quarters so you can scarcely turn around. It may almost be better to part with everything except a cherished chair or rug or whatnot and start from scratch with custom furniture tailored to the space available.

Regardless, you'll likely have to walk away from some things. What to do with them?

One reviewer lists these options:

> Give some to your family, friends, and/or neighbors (if you can do it without producing a row). Put on a garage sale (preferably with the aid

of a professional pitch person). Sell appropriate items to an antique dealer. Sell other items, like appliances, to the new owner of your former home. Contribute still others to Goodwill, the Salvation Army, or a like charity. What's left, contribute to a solid waste disposal site. Or, if in the trauma of moving you simply can't decide about some things, put them in a rented storage locker until a moment arrives when you're calm and collected (or when monthly rental fees prod you into making up your mind).

From my experience, don't expect to be infallible in your triage. Some keepsakes I discarded 10 years ago I'd give my eyeteeth to have now, and some things I retained I've never even looked at, much less used. But perhaps you'll be more astute. Whatever, relax in the knowledge that many others have survived downsizing.

Housing Pros and Cons

Because, I've lived in an ISF for seven years, I've had an opportunity to chat with a variety of retirees, many of them with campus associations, about the issue of where, when, and how to live in retirement.

I thought you might like to share in some of their more pointed or poignant comments:

"Most younger adults change housing accommodations over the years in a natural progression — single room, apartment, starter house, larger home. Older adults should think nothing of experiencing the same sequence, only in reverse."

"You must have sensed that I'm unhappy here. I was very content in a California condo until my daughter persuaded me that I should come to Wisconsin — where I've never been — so she could look after me. I left cherished friends and a halcyon climate to be 'warehoused' in this place, and now, because she thinks I'm secure, my daughter neglects me."

"The big disadvantage of moving into a facility like this — as fine as it is — is the size constraint on your quarters. We've had to parcel out a host of cherished family heirloom furniture pieces in order to fit into our apartment."

"Relief from snow shoveling and lawn mowing is worth the price of admission here!"

"Giving up my pet in order to get in here was the toughest thing!"

"We have the best of both worlds. We're here in summer and in a New Mexico retirement complex in winter, without a maintenance care in the world."

"I'm a very private person, so I resent the togetherness I'm supposed to participate in."

"I've made firmer friends here than anywhere else in my life."

"We had a fine time for a while down in the Sunbelt, but family ties finally drew us back here."

"My department has kindly continued to provide me with an office, and I'm close enough so I can walk to it."

"We've been in a whole series of retirement setups since we sold our house, and we've found something to like about them all, but I can tell you this: there's no *Shangri-La*."

"I wish we could have stayed in our home longer, but infirmities denied us the privilege."

"My husband passed away shortly after we moved in here. I know he's content knowing I'm secure here."

"The big advantage of going into a retirement tower is that you're guaranteed access to a good nursing home if and when you need it — and I consider that a real bonus, having experienced the trauma of trying to find decent accommodations for an ailing parent."

"We wouldn't have considered this place if it hadn't been in existence for a dozen years, with a triple-A rating. We lost our shirts on an apartment we bought for my mother in a continuing care community in Louisiana when the outfit went broke, and it was church-related, too."

"You can't imagine the relief we feel when we travel, knowing we don't have to worry about the furnace failing or the water softener overflowing."

"I'd like it better if there were more of a mix of residents. The preponderance of older women gets on my nerves. I'd love to eat dinner with a young grad student occasionally again."

"The range of cultural and educational and recreational activities the management provides is outstanding. I'm going all the time!"

"I guess I'm considered sort of an oddball, because I studiously avoid all these activities somebody is always staging. I'm just not that type. I do like the library services, though."

"We're glad we came in here when we did. So many of our friends wait until they need to come, and by then they're ready for intensive care — no interim period of winding down."

"If I had to do it all over again, I'd never come into a place like this; I'd shoot myself instead. To be surrounded only by old people is stifling."

"I've got a lot of role models here. Take Mrs. Blank: she's 97 and still driving, still walking a mile a day, still going north to fish every summer. That's a real inspiration to somebody like me who's only 67."

"You remember last summer when the tornado touched down nearby? Well, I was talking to one of our residents, and she said she was in a natural disaster when she was a child. It turned out to be the San Francisco earthquake early in the century! Now that's perspective for you! You couldn't get it if you were living alone."

"When my spouse came home from the hospital with a hip replacement, boy was I glad for the pull-chain that summons a night nurse in a minute."

"The staff of this place is really cloying. I hate being told to have my blood pressure taken every week, and those exercise sessions — ."

"These people are really with it when it comes to current events, thanks to CNN. I never lack for a stimulating conversation."

"I get so tired of rehearsing the Depression and World War II! I wish I could still converse with my cat."

"Am I happy here? Yes, because I've finally learned life is what you make it."

While it hardly is a scientific sample of retirees, at least the responses are honest. In evaluating them, remember these are all people age 67 to 99, all in a particular stage in the retirement continuum, all white-collar types. And, as you can see, for just about every plus there's a minus.

The Staging-Area Site

If you can't decide between seashore or mountain view, perpetual summer or four seasons, metropolitan culture or bucolic charm, or some other debate, why not consider what real estate people call a "staging-area site"; that is, one that has no special setting in itself but which is within easy commute of a variety of attractions and amenities. (Such sites tend to be less expensive than those located in the heart of a boom area.)

For example, our cabin retreat isn't "on" or "in" anything but a stretch of rural countryside, yet we're only 4 miles from a grocery store/meat market, 5 miles from a country church, 6 miles from a comprehensive health care clinic, 7 miles from a world-class restaurant, 8 miles from a ski tow, 9 miles from a major river, 10 miles from a lake/swimming beach, 11 miles from a Shakespearean theater, 12 miles from a championship golf course, 35 miles from campus and capital — 5 miles from a Greyhound bus stop leading to Minneapolis or Chicago, 16 miles from an I-highway leading to Seattle or Washington, DC, 30 miles from an Amtrak depot leading to New York or San Francisco, 40 miles from an airport leading to Timbuktu — and 10 feet from a busy songbird feeder, 100 yards from deer, grouse, and wild turkey cover, 1 mile from trout water. The mail carrier comes by daily, the sheriff periodically; trash pickup once a week, highway patrol in season.

The range of nearby scenery is neither spectacular nor challenging by national park standards, but it is here, comfortable — and America in microcosm. We think of our front window as a charmed, magic casement, opening in our mind on rocks and rills, woods and templed hills, fruited plains, and foaming seas.

For example, the frontispiece of the scene from our cabin den is a magnificent American elm, not yet struck down by beetles. It's xylem and phloem "bloodline" is identical to that of the New England tree under which General Washington bid a solemn farewell to his victorious Continental troops. At the base of our elm runs J. Jones Road. A sideroad has its own natural appeal as it snakes along the nap of the earth, and it offers periodic reminder that nobody can really make it alone in this world; we can count on at least two vehicles to come past every day. One is that U.S. mail carrier, a friendly wave signifying that all's quiet along the Potomac. The other vehicle is a truck carrying milk to a cheese factory, from whence, perchance, a package will wend its way to Sydney, Australia, where relatives of ours will pay a premium for a slice of America's dairyland.

Beyond J. Jones Road we can see the west end of our pond, sparkling under the massage of a brisk breeze. The wind has come from Montana ranges, across fecund fields of Iowa corn.

At the edge of the pond is a sand-blow, the remnant of an eroded beanfield. In our mind's eye it is one of Indiana's famous Dunes, where a pioneer botanist propounded the theory of plant succession.

Beyond the dune is an old pasture, now studded with invading sumac and poplar. A redtail is cruising the field. He is not an endangered golden eagle soaring above a Wyoming wilderness, but our hawk adds his own wild grace to our cabin view.

Beyond the field the ground pitches sharply upward to form a rugged ridge. We know it to be 800 feet in elevation, but from the perspective of imagination it is an 8,000-foot Colorado mountain.

Sandstone castles and mural escarpments punctuate the skyline. Geologists tell us these pockmarked rocks mark the shores of a paleolithic sea. When we thrust our heads into a mini-cave aperture, we imagine we can hear the pounding, pounding of ancient surf. Lichens lend a marine-green touch to the stone outcroppings, as if in memory of undulating weeds and waves.

Birch and cedars mingle with oak and hickory on the sharp slope. At their feet is a seasonal parade of wildflowers. This evening a cautious doe may lead her fractious fawn down to the pond, and a cock grouse will certainly drum the announcement that an acre or two is his territory, no matter what our abstract of title may say.

At night our casement will open on a sea of stars, and that sight may indeed become a wonder. For millions of smog-ridden Americans, a starstudded sky is a rarity. To see a clear moon they must watch television.

So, without even leaving our staging-area site, the whole of a continent is within our minds' grasp.

Quickie Quiz

SECTION 1

1. List the jobs or spare-time activities you've always wanted to do but never had the time. Score them 3 for an obsession, 2 for a real desire, 1 for just a yen.

2. If married, list the jobs or spare-time activities your spouse has always wanted to do but never had the time. Score them 3 for an obsession, 2 for a real desire, 1 for just a yen.

3. List the special skills you have. Score them 3 for top-notch, 2 for above average, 1 for pretty good.

4. If married, list the special skills of your spouse. Score them 3 for top-notch, 2 for above average, 1 for pretty good.

5. On the basis of the lists, write down all the things you might do after retirement. Score them 4 for great, 3 for might be the thing, 2 for worth a try, 1 for only fair.

6. On the basis of that list, write down all the activities and interests that stimulate you most and have business possibilities. Score them 3 for best bet, 2 for worth exploring, 1 for outside chance (Otte 1976).

SECTION 2

To determine the degree in retirement to which you'll surmount the influence of time pressures, answer each of the following 10 questions by circling the number of the alternative that best fits you.

- Compared with your life five years ago, would you say you'll now have more or less leisure time?

  1. Less 2. About the same
  3. A bit more 4. A lot more

- How would you compare the amount of time you spend running errands today with the amount of time you spent five years ago?

  1. More 2. About the same
  3. Somewhat less 4. A lot less

- How many hours do you sleep during an average weeknight?

  1. Five hours or less 2. Six hours
  3. Seven hours 4. Eight or more

- How good are you at glancing at your watch or a clock without anyone noticing?

  1. Very good 2. Good
  3. Fair 4. No good at all

- When talking on the phone, are you more likely to:

  1. Do paperwork, wash dishes, or do some other chore?
  2. Straighten up the surrounding area?
  3. Do small personal tasks?
  4. Do nothing else?

- In an average week, how many evening or weekend hours do you spend on work at home?

  1. 16 or more 2. 11 to 15
  3. Six to 10 4. Zero to five

- During a typical weekend, do you engage primarily in:

  1. Work for pleasure or profit
  2. Household chores and errands
  3. Leisure activities
  4. Catching up on sleep and relaxing

- How often do you find yourself wishing you had more time to spend with family members or friends?
  1. Constantly 2. Often
  3. Occasionally 4. Almost never
- Which statement best describes your daily schedule?
  1. There aren't enough hours in the day to do everything I want to do.
  2. On the whole, I have just about enough time to do what I have to do.
  3. I can usually do the things I have to do, with time left over.
  4. The day seems to have more hours than I'm able to fill.

SCORING: Add up the total of all numbers circled. A score of 10 to 17 indicates you are still **timelocked**; 18 to 25, **pressed for time**; 26 to 23, **in balance**; 34 to 40, **time on your hands** (Keyes 1992).

Recommended Readings

Boyer, Richard, and David Savageau, 1989. *Places Rated Almanac* (New York: Prentice Hall).

Boyer, Richard, and David Savageau, 1988. *Retirement Places Rated* (New York: Prentice Hall).

Dickinson, Peter A., 1990. *Retirement Edens Outside the Sunbelt (Washington, DC: American Association of Retired Persons).*

Howells, John, 1991. *Where to Retire* (Ashland, OR: Gateway Books).

Options for Senior Housing, 1991. (Kensington, MD: Marriott Information Center).

Retrofitting Housing for the Elderly, 1991. (Upper Marlboro, MD: National Association of Home Builders).

Polniaszek, Susan, 1991. *Long Term Living* (Washington, DC: United Seniors Health Cooperative).

The Continuing Care Retirement Community: A Guidebook for Consumers, 1990. (Washington, DC: American Association of Homes for the Aging).

References

Anderson, Paul, 1992. "Elderly Undervalued, Study Says," Knight Ridder Newspapers, June 25.

Associated Press, 1992. *Wisconsin State Journal*, June 8, p. 6A.

Beck, Melinda, *et al.*, 1992. "Finding Work After 50," *Newsweek*, March 16, pp. 56-60.

Beck, Melinda, *et al.*, 1991. "School Days for Seniors," *Newsweek*, Nov. 11, pp. 60-65.

Bigger, Joanne, 1991. "Retirees Going Back to College," *Maturity News Service.*

Bjerke, Aaron, 1992. "Tapping into Volunteer Resources," *Wisconsin Week*, May 4, p. 8.

Bowen, William G., and Neil L. Rudenstine, 1992. *In Pursuit of the Ph.D.* (Princeton, NJ: Princeton University Press).

Bumpass, Larry, 1992. "A Trend Revived," *Wisconsin State Journal*, April 5, p. 1A, 9A.

Crohan, Susan, 1992. "Constructive Conflict Leads to Stability" *Wisconsin Week*, Feb. 5, p. 12.

Culp, Stephanie, 1992. "How to Uncomplicate Your Life," *Bottom Line Personal*, Jan. 30, p. 11.

Culp, Stephanie, 1992. *Streamlining Your Life: A Five-Point Plan for Uncomplicated Living* (Cincinnati: Writer's Digest Books).

Dickinson, Peter A., 1990. *Sunbelt Retirement* (New York: E.P. Dutton).

Ersland, Deborah, 1992. Quoted in Chris Martell, "Senior Housing Boom," (Madison) *Wisconsin State Journal*, June 26, pp. 1I, 3I.

Glaser, Vera, 1992. *Maturity News Service*, "Plotting the Good Life," Jan. 13.

Griffin, W.E.B., 1991. *Battleground* (New York: Jove Books), p. 291.

Houston, Patrick, 1991. "A New Breed of Retirement Community," *Newsweek*, Nov. 11, p. 62.

Keyes, Ralph, 1992. "Do You Have the Time?" *Parade Magazine*, Feb. 26, pp. 22-25.

Kinney, Donald P., and Sharon P. Smith, 1992. "Age and Teaching Performance," *Journal of Higher Education*, May-June, pp. 282-302.

Landers, Ann, 1992. "Questions for Those Who Are Aging," (Madison) *Wisconsin State Journal*, April 25, p. 4D.

Lewin, Tamar, 1991. "Retirement Communities Offer Comfort, Convenience," *The New York Times*, July 22, p. 2C.

Longino, Charles F., Jr., *et al.* 1991. "The Second Move: Health and Geographic Mobility," *Journal of Gerontology*, July, pp. 218-224.

Milletti, Mario A., 1989. *Voices of Experience: 1500 Retired People Talk About Retirement* (New York: TIAA-CREF).

Moore, Lisa J., with Richard J. Newman, 1992. "Still Working," *U.S. News & World Report*, May 22, pp. 80-83.

NonProfit Times, 1992. "Taste-Testing Seniors Keep Chef on His Toes," January, p. 28.

Osterheld, Doug, 1984. *Financial Planning for Retirement* (Madison: University of Wisconsin System).

Osterheld, Doug, 1992. Personal correspondence in author's files, Feb. 14.

Otte, Elmer, 1976. *Retirement Rehearsal Guidebook* (Indianapolis: Pictorial).

Palmer, Thomas, 1992. "New 'Family' Takes Hold," Boston Globe, Feb. 23, pp. 1, 8A.

Price, Tom, 1992. Cox News Service, March.

Pritzi, Penny, 1991. "Gift of a Lifetime" (Madison: *Wisconsin State Journal*, Nov. 21, p. 1C.

Rice, Marc, 1992. Associated Press, "Hotel Chain Tops in Hiring Senior Workers," Jan. 12.

Rowell, Rainbow, 1992. "Run with It," *The Nebraskan*, Feb. 25, p. 1.

Ruebhausen, Oscar M., Ed., 1990. *Pension and Retirement Policies in Colleges and Universities* (San Francisco: Jossey-Bass).

Ryan, Michael, 1991. "Here, They See Age as an Asset," *Parade Magazine*, July 14, pp. 4-5.

Saltzman, Amy, 1992. "Books for the Job Hunt," *U.S. News & World Report*, March 16, pp. 66-68.

Santovec, Mary Lou, 1992. "Retired Faculty Volunteers Replace Paid Advisors," *Academic Leader*, April, p. 5.

Schlapak, Elaine, 1991. "Designs for Living Well," *The Retired Officer Magazine*, September, pp. 29-36.

Schoenfeld, A. Clay, and Robert Magnan, 1992. *Mentor in a Manual* (Madison, WI: Magna Publications).

Taylor, Paul, 1991. "Family Life: Shelter From the Storm," *Washington Post Weekly Edition*, Dec. 16, p.37.

Walsh, Kenneth T., 1991. "The Retro Campaign," *U.S. News & World Report*, Dec. 9, pp. 32-4.

Weglarz, Jennifer, 1992. "U. Professor Works in Mysterious Ways," *University of Minnesota Daily*, June 2, pp. 1, 4.

West, Hollie I., 1992. "Second Careers Fulfill Many," *New York Daily News*, Sunday, March 1, p. 3D.

Wiener, Daniel P., 1991. "Retirement Hot Spots," *U.S. News & World Report*, Oct. 21, pp. 102-107.

Woodward, Bill, and Paula Woodward, 1991. "The Small Town Alternative," *The Retired Officer Magazine*, September, pp. 24-27.

5

"A" Is for Attitude, "Z" Is for Zeal

Conventional wisdom holds that professors are given to being dull and long-winded. In my early faculty years, I never thought I was guilty, until one morning around the family breakfast table, when I announced that I'd be in Wausau that day, an 8-year-old daughter asked:

"Mommy, what's Daddy going to do in Wausau?"

"Why don't you ask your Daddy?" her mother replied.

"Because," Laurie said, "I don't want to hear that much about it!"

I trust that in this retirement seminar I've been lively and concise. Yet, now that the class bell is about to ring, there are still a couple of things yet to be said about putting any retirement picture all together.

In the retirement tower where I now reside part-time, we have a dining room ground rule:

"No organ recitals!"

That's to protect us from the residents who dote on reciting their ailments and operations, those from 20 years to two weeks ago.

Some retirees simply insist on looking on a glass as half-empty, not half-full. They seem to thrive on misery. How much better to look on your retirement years, not as the beginning of the end, but as the end of the beginning. In short, retirement can be a substantial part of your life, a phase not to be dreaded but eagerly anticipated. It all depends on your attitude and on your zeal and enthusiasm to take on a change in lifestyle with zest.

I never think of enthusiasm without recalling a World War II experience while on a Naples R&R from the Anzio front. I had taken along my platoon sergeant, a Texas cowboy, and we were at an observation point overlooking the volcanic Mount Vesuvius, which was smoking away.

"Now, tell me, Eddie, even though you're a Texas booster, you can't tell me you've got any natural wonder like that in Texas," I said.

Eddie thought a moment, then said, "No, Lieutenant, I can't. But I can tell you this: the Dallas fire department could put it out in half an hour!"

In like manner, being a retirement booster is a lot healthier, mentally and physically, than being a retirement grudge.

To explain away any lack of zeal for staying active in retirement, no longer can you use as an excuse that maturing years of necessity cause a person to "run out of gas."

Who says so? A bevy of researchers, that's who. Here are the headlines of news releases from two campuses in spring 1992: "Age Appears

No Barrier in Leadership" and "Study Finds Chronological Age Not Good Predictor of Job Performance."

The first story, from Eastern Montana College, reports on a study of some 1,600 managers in 17 organizations by Professors Ronald Collins and G. Ronald Gilbert that indicates "no significant differences" between young and old supervisors in terms of leadership capabilities.

The second story, from Pennsylvania State University, reports on a study of public safety officers in 182 police departments, 165 fire departments, and 102 correctional facilities around the country by a panel led by Professor Frank J. Landry to the effect that "public safety might actually be enhanced by virtue of allowing the experience of public safety officers to accrue" because "age is not a good predictor of important aspects of their job performance."

So there you have it. Reaching retirement age is no signal to roll over and play dead. Your future is now.

What, Oh What, Does the Future Hold?

As chair of BrainReserve Inc., of New York, Faith Popcorn makes her living as a trend analyst for such firms as American Express, IBM, and Polaroid.

Here's what she predicts in her latest book, *The Popcorn Report*:

- **Cocooning.** The need to protect ourselves from the harsh, unpredictable realities of the outside world.
- **Fantasy adventure.** Modern age whets our appetite for roads untaken.
- **Small indulgences.** Affordable luxuries and ways to reward ourselves.
- **Ergonomics.** The sterile computer era breeds a desire to make a personal statement.
- **Cashing out.** Working men and women, questioning personal/career satisfaction and goals, opt for simpler living.
- **Down-aging.** Nostalgic for their carefree childhood, Baby Boomers find comfort in familiar pursuits and products of youth.
- **Staying alive.** Awareness that good health extends longevity leads to a new way of life.
- **Consumerism.** The consumer manipulates marketers and the marketplace through pressure, protest, and politics.
- **99 lives.** Too fast a pace, too little time forces us to assume multiple roles and adapt easily.

- **SOS (Save Our Society).** The country rediscovers a social conscience of ethics, passion, and compassion (Popcorn 1992).

You may have your own crystal ball, tuned to your own personal wavelength.

KEEPING UP WITH THE TIMES

While we've tried to make this book as current as possible, the retiree environment is changing as fast as the maps of Europe and the former Soviet Union. So unless you personally make a point of keeping up with the times, you'll find that information in this manual can become passé.

For example:

Adequate Income Stream?

As you know, your annual Social Security cost of living adjustment (COLA) is calculated by the U.S. Department of Labor on the basis of the rise in the Consumer Price Index (CPI), which in turn is calculated on the basis of a market-basket of goods and services. If and when the Labor economists change the market-basket mix, that could directly affect the CPI and, in turn, your COLA. For instance, were the mix to tilt toward the service sector of the economy, where prices are mounting, and away from hard goods, where prices are stabilizing, that would lift the CPI. On the other hand, a shift toward durable goods could lower the CPI.

In a related switch already under way, the U.S Commerce Department is recalculating the government's principal economic scorecard, the gross national product (GNP), by converting to a new gauge, the gross domestic product (GDP). Commerce economists are shifting because GDP measures production of goods and services in just the United States, while the GNP includes the amount by which earnings on American-owned investments in other countries exceed earnings on foreign-owned investments in this country, causing GNP figures to give a misleading reading of the U.S. economy's health.

For instance, using GDP data instead of GNP data, the Commerce Department now says the American economy grew a little more slowly in the 1980s than officials had thought. The change in arithmetic "will give the public and policy makers a better sense of how the economy is doing, so officials and political leaders will be in a better position to make policy choices" (Berry 1991).

You can use the same new measuring-rod in making your own policy decisions about how to protect your retirement income stream.

Pension Plan Problems

Just about when you're chortling that your pension plan is as solid as the gold in Fort Knox (or as solid as it *was*), you may pick up the paper one morning to read that, hard hit by lingering recession, some states and institutions are looking at ways to control pension costs, like cutting back on contributions to pension plans, freezing pension plan contributions, or even raiding pension funds.

For example, early in 1992 the state of New York reduced contributions to its own Teachers Retirement System in the face of a $4.5 billion budget shortfall and called a three-month halt on contributions to optional pension plans like TIAA-CREF. Also in 1991 the state of Virginia reduced its contributions to optional retirement plans and the state of California dipped into its pension fund to finance an early retirement "buyout" program.

Recession-weary states and institutions are apt to keep a watchful eye on faculty and staff pensions, says Murray Rosen, an employee benefits consultant with the American Association of University Professors (Devaries 1992).

Writing in 1992 about "crisis in the Northeast," Professor David D. Palmer in the School of Business at the University of Connecticut, and Cynthia H. Adams, professor of allied health professions at the same institution say:

> Pensions have become the "golden egg" in the eyes of desperate governors — the glittering hope for recovery from deficit problems. The under-funding of pensions leaves future retirees with reduced security, no assurance that the state can cover their pension requirements if a significant number of employees retire simultaneously, and no guarantee that money "borrowed" by states today will actually be paid back with enough interest ever to regain intended funding levels (Palmer 1992).

Palmer and Adams cite a Maine governor's proposal to defer two years of payments into the state's pension fund, and a Connecticut governor's plan to defer payments of $215 million to the already underfunded state pension reserve.

Those are apparently not isolated instances. Eugene Lehrmann, formerly head of Wisconsin's vocational school system and now president of the American Association of Retired Persons (AARP), told a conference of state and local government retirees that a third of the states have delayed or cut contributions to their retirement funds or debated doing so. The "most insidious threat" to public pension funds is a move to divert them into economic development programs that promise to build a state's economy, he says, "a move that violates an overriding principle of fund management that the funds are to be managed solely for the benefit of plan participants" (Lehrmann 1992).

Pension funds will continue to make a tempting target, Lehrmann warns, in the eyes of both public officials and private employers.

As if that sort of news weren't bad enough, the first issue of the AAUP's quarterly, *Academe*, under new editor Eugene Arden teed off on TIAA-CREF itself, the "Rock of Gibraltar" of private pension funds in education.

In the lead article, Professor Emeritus Gerald H. Rosen of Drexel University reported that "while its ratings remain high, TIAA's returns have fallen — and its CEO received a total compensation package of $1283,650 in 1990, an astonishing figure for the not-for-profit community" (Rosen 1992).

In a follow-up article, Richard T. Garrigan, professor of finance at DePaul University, worried that as of year-end 1990, more than half of TIAA's assets consisted of investments in depressed commercial mortgages or real estate.

"Much as participants might like to sit back and not think about their retirement savings, the realities of today's investment world do not permit such a luxury," says Garrigan (1992).

By way of rebuttal, Robert Perrin, TIAA-CREF executive vice president for external affairs, says "the TIAA portfolio rate of return continues to out-perform the average of the life insurance industry year after year" (Perrin 1992); Thomas W. Jones, TIAA-CREF executive vice president for finance and planning, is proud that "today TIAA is one of only eight U.S. life insurance companies that hold the highest ratings from Moody's, S&P, and A.M. Best" (Jones 1992).

All of which simply means that keeping up with the times means keeping our fingers crossed about our pension funds.

Social Insecurity?

Fear of a collapsing Social Security system may be no joke, according to Dorcas Hardy, former Social Security Commissioner, and her co-author, C. Colburn Hardy, investment counselor. They say Americans born after 1937 are in for a jolt because around the year 2010 the system will begin running a deficit — because the government is using SSA trust funds now to pay for government operations.

There's no problem at the moment because now there are 3.4 workers to support each retiree, but by 2025 there will be fewer than two workers per retiree — which would mean taxes will have to be raised, benefits cut, or both (Hardy 1991).

Other demographers, economists, and politicians either dispute the Hardy Jeremiad or hold to a Dickensian belief that "something will turn up" in the way of system reform. Incidentally, the Hardys blame "the power of the old-age lobbies, which have made meddling with Social Security taboo."

It'll be well to keep your eyes open for stories about Sen. Patrick Moynihan and other Congressional leaders as they play watchdogs over the SS Trust Fund.

Social Security lobbyists may think the system is immutable. Guess again. It has been revised 14 times since its inception in 1935. Favorite reforms in some quarters: (1) change the age of eligibility from 65 to 70 or higher on the grounds that average longevity has changed significantly since 1935, and (2) index benefits in some manner so the well-to-do receive lower monthly checks.

Either or both departures could manifestly affect your retirement planning.

And the First Shall Be Last

You heard about them in Chapter 2, you're hearing about them again now, and you're well advised to keep them on your planning agenda at all times.

Yes, we're talking about taxes.

In keeping up with the times, nothing is any more important than reviewing changing tax regulations in the light of your changing status.

For example, in the years immediately preceding retirement, your income and your tax bracket may well be at their highest, leading you to invest in tax-free municipal bonds. If your tax rate declines along with income in post-retirement years, as is possible, then you may want to review the efficiency of those municipal bonds.

At the point of retirement, tax implications may well determine how and when you take distribution from an annuity. Tax implications can likewise impact on any decision about disposal of a home. A remunerative second career also can carry tax baggage.

"Before taking steps to implement any changing tax strategy, speak with a tax and/or legal advisor," recommends financial consultant Gregory Baker (1992).

Affordable Health Care

"Our Unraveling Health Care System" and "Health Care Costs Soar," announced daily newspaper headlines from Washington, DC, to the state of Washington in 1992.

If there's any topic about which you'll need to watch your "P's" and "Q's" in retirement, it's this one — health care. Ten years ago, about 9 cents out of every American consumer dollar was spent on health care. Today, it's 12 cents — and climbing. Some type of state/federal intervention will probably be necessary to keep the country from spending itself into a sickbed.

Here are some of the remedies being proposed, any one of which could significantly affect your retirement:

- Get rid of Medicare and replace it with a universal health-care plan that covers all those who cannot afford their own insurance, including the "uninsured."
- "Means test" Medicare benefits. Medicare barely distinguishes between a well-to-do 65-year-old retiree and someone who is 85 and penniless.
- Phase out the Veterans Administration hospital system and give veterans vouchers to be used at any public or private hospital running at less than capacity.
- Curb the practice of "defensive medicine" by setting limits on malpractice awards and hence on questionable tests, treatments, drugs, or even surgeries.
- Regulate the pharmaceutical industry better, to end the "Keep up with the Joneses'" competition.
- Ration duplicate buildings and equipment among hospitals and clinics.
- Steer medical school graduates into practices and geographic areas where there are shortages, via various bonus offers.
- Require insurance companies and doctors to play fair in compensation and billing.
- Regulate health care providers in a manner similar to that of public utility commissions.
- Cap insurance premiums and ban insurers from dropping a group based on claims experience.
- Cover the uninsured by hiking Medicare rates.
- Push people into "managed care" networks by offering tax rebates.

- Prevent insurers from denying coverage to an insured person changing jobs.

Some of those proposals are pretty draconian measures that, right or wrong, will have a tough time running the gauntlet of pressure groups onto the floor of Congress. But with health care emerging as a national political and social issue, you're apt to see "action, and action now!" sooner or later. And every action is likely to have an impact on your own health care situation. Stay tuned.

Group Health Woes

Don't assume any group health insurance plan under which you're covered by your institution is immutable. Several factors are operating to cause boards of trustees very real concerns.

First, of course, health care costs in this country are skyrocketing.

Second, new reporting requirements from the Financial Accounting Standards Board mandate that institutions of higher education calculate all future expected costs for post-employment health benefits and include those liabilities in their annual financial statements. Hitherto, most institutions funded retiree health benefits on a current year, pay-as-you-go basis and didn't estimate or report future liabilities for retiree benefits. With four-year U.S. colleges spending an average of $1,794 per employee, active and retired, on health insurance in 1990, up from $279 in 1977, you can readily see how reflecting such future accumulative costs as a liability in an annual financial statement will throw a lot of campus operating budgets out of whack.

Third, the proportion of health insurance spent on retirees is increasing at a faster rate than for active employees, because the ratio of retirees to active employees is increasing every year as more people opt for retirement and then live longer.

This triple whammy is causing boards of trustees to look around very hard for cost-containment strategies, short of abandoning health benefits for their retirees.

Dean Craig E. Daniels of the School of Arts and Sciences at Eastern Connecticut State University, and Associate Dean Janet D. Daniels of the Graduate School at Bryant College in Rhode Island, say we can well expect to see such modifications as these in health care programs:

- Shift a portion of insurance costs to retirees by raising premiums, increasing deductibles and maximums, and/or eliminating double payments from multiple plans.

- Establish flexible-benefit (cafeteria) plans which allow you to choose among a list of benefits or accept cash in lieu of benefits.
- Require your switching to a health maintenance organization with its lower costs for less individualized care.
- Coordinate benefits with Medicare by including Medicare payments in the college-provided benefits calculations.
- Link retiree health benefits to length of service; for example, a service-linked plan might pay 100% of a retiree's health insurance premiums after 25 years of service and prorate the institution's contribution for a lesser number of years (Daniels 1992).

In short, you'll have to live with both macro and micro concerns about the viability of whatever health care program covers you now. Daniels and Daniels call it "a ticking bomb."

Activities for Self-Fulfillment — and Public Relations?

The University of Wisconsin System Board of Regents struck a minor blow against discrimination in spring 1992. Despite a loud letter and phone protest on the part of senior citizens, the Regents voted to end a policy of letting persons age 62 and older audit campus courses for free.

Ex Officio Regent Burt Grover, state superintendent of public instruction and ever ready to stick his head in a lion's mouth, stated the argument that carried the day:

> Non-need-based entitlements are taking America down the tube. This System has a moral obligation to take the high ground on this issue. ... We ought not to persist with policies that discriminate among the generations.

In my book, Grover is absolutely right. Today's real "welfare queens" (and "kings") are relatively well-off senior citizens simultaneously clipping bond coupons, cashing Social Security checks, getting a cheap ride on Medicare, and enjoying a staggering array of commercial perks reserved for the "golden oldie" generation, meanwhile reaping handsome salaries or generous pensions — or even both. And that cohort includes some senior college and university faculty and administrators, either still active or retired.

When the freebie audit policy was introduced some 20 years ago during my tenure as UW-Madison Dean of Inter-College Programs in charge of those "guest students," we were happy to make a small gesture to honor our fathers and mothers. But times have changed. Similar gestures — some midget and some gross — have multiplied like coat hangers in a closet, and now an ever-growing phalanx of the elderly partakes of varied gratuities and perks — all at the expense of our children, grandchildren, great-grandchildren, and their peers.

That those younger generations are hurting, recent news stories attest.

- In the 1980s, families with a head under 35 years of age lost 20% of their buying power, while families with a head 55-64 years of age gained 8.2%.
- Big Gains went to many living out their golden years. Brandeis University economist William Crown figures that the wealthiest 20% of American households with at least one member 65 or older — families with an average net worth of $320,000 in 1988 — did well because of their generous pensions, high returns on financial investments, and hefty home equity. In fact, he says, large increases in those areas — not Social Security benefits — are the reason the share held by working-age Americans shrinks (Dentzer 1992).
- Paul R. Kruegman, economics professor at the Massachusetts Institute of Technology and a *U.S. News & World Report* contributing editor, writes, "The growth in inequality in America" between young and old, rich and poor, between 1977 and 1989 "is greater than anybody expected," as revealed alike by Congressional Budget Office, Federal Reserve, and Census Bureau studies in mid-1992 (Kruegman 1992).

While it's perfectly true that many elderly are at the poverty line, it's also true that many others defy the stereotype with a flourish — and among the more fortunate are those academics nearing or past retirement age who have well-funded, secure pension plans.

Their numbers are mounting. All the academic personnel brought on in the 1955-1964 decade to staff an exploding higher education establishment, these graying faculty are now entering the retirement zone, so that in the 1994-2003 decade the number of academics retiring or contemplating retirement will considerably exceed the figure for any previous decade, as we've frequently pointed out in this book.

As people over the age of 65 constitute an ever larger segment of the population, drawing on federal and state fiscal resources and on perks supplied by the private sector, and as Federal Insurance Contribution Act (FICA, better known as Social Security) taxes bear ever more heavily on younger wage-earners, there could come a backlash against seniors.

As a matter of fact, a backlash is already beginning. Founded in Irving, Texas, in 1989, an American Association of Boomers (AAB) has over 21,000 members and is growing by 150 a week. Taking its name from the baby boomer generation born between 1946 and 1964, the AAB is out to get its piece of the pie, like restoring the tax incentives for retirement savings their parents enjoyed, instituting an affordable health insurance plan for young self-employed, and garnering the same sort of discounts their elders collect on all manner of consumer goods, as we noted in chapter 2.

But those perks are really small potatoes compared with a couple of big-ticket items rigged in favor of senior citizens.

First, Social Security. In the total absence of any means-testing, too many Americans over the age of 65 are drawing monthly SS benefits whether they need them or not. True, in general if a person's adjusted gross income is over a set amount (and the ceiling is the same for everybody, regardless of the extent of that gross income), he or she will pay taxes on the SSA income, but only on *half* of it. And yes, I know, it's our money — we put it in there during our working years; but most of us will run out of "our" SS money long before we die.

Playing to the American Association of Retired Persons lobby, one of my U.S. Senators proclaimed the other day: "Social Security is a pension program; it is not welfare. All who contribute should be entitled to their full benefits." But without paying taxes on it, Senator? And irrespective of the size of our personal investment portfolio?

Second, Medicare. Here again, in the absence of means-testing, a lot of Americans who could otherwise afford it are getting a cut-rate ride on hospital and medical care. True enough, you prepay your Part A hospital insurance through FICA payroll taxes based on work covered by Social Security, and you pay for Part B medical insurance by monthly premiums deducted from your SS allotment. But those are payments the government has to supplement from general revenues in order to keep the system solvent. With health care costs now more than $200 billion a year and mounting at more than twice the overall inflation rate, it's problematic how long the system can work in the absence of some means-testing of beneficiaries.

But even Social Security and Medicare are themselves pale perversions compared to the gross strategy practiced by some well-to-do Americans who deliberately bequeath, transfer, or otherwise hide their assets — "spend down" — in order to reach the level of poverty that qualifies them for long-turn nursing home or hospice health care at public expense under Medicaid. As Jane Bryant Quinn writes, "The huge loopholes in the Medicaid law, exploited by greedy seniors, are creating a legion of false poor, collecting public money they don't deserve" (Quinn 1991).

"Taken all together, the small and large largesse bequeathed upon today's generation of the elderly constitutes a major component of that "culture of contentment," John Kenneth Galbraith writes in his latest book by that title — what he calls "underenlightened self-interest": "Doing well, many wish to do better. Having enough, many wish for more. Being comfortable, many raise vigorous objection to that which invades comfort" (Galbraith 1992).

Closing the Generation Gap

Scholar/author Michael Barone assesses the situation this way: "Americans today ... are less interested in minor supplements to one year's income than in accumulating enough wealth for a comfortable retirement. That is why ordinary voters these days are so sensitive to any changes threatening their primary sources of wealth — real estate and pension and Social Security and Medicare entitlements" (Barone 1992).

Discussing the matter with colleagues around the country, I find I'm not alone in my antipathy to elder perks and my concern about a growing econo-social generation gap.

Writes Rudolf J.H. Schafer, recently retired California state department of education administrator:

> I call it 'eldergreed.' I'm appalled at the attitude of many older people who seem to want everything from the younger generation and give nothing in return. They vote down school bonds, civic improvements, and so on, and yet are constantly asking for more themselves. I hate the unfairness of some of the deals offered seniors — for those, that is, who can afford to pay their own way. Let's be fair about our demands and let's support necessary social expenses — even if they might reduce us to only three cruises a year (1992).

Charles O. Kroncke, dean, University of Texas-Dallas School of Management, concurs:

> The elderly have been encouraged to band around the Claude Peppers to fear and fight for their financial security instead of providing America with much needed leadership and vision. It doesn't seem proper that the elderly should be encouraged to focus all their energies on the conservation of economic privilege instead of thinking through their social and spiritual as well as economic priorities and taking advantage of their stage in life to act on them.

Their sentiments were to be aired in a remarkable interview by Ted Koppel on his ABC *Nightline*, June 3, 1992, in which six leading U.S. Senators — three Republicans and three Democrats — called for an end to "platitudes and poppycock" once and for all on the part of politicians about a U.S. deficit that's rising at the rate of $11,600 a second and now puts every citizen over $11,600 in debt just to pay the interest (1992).

"My parents borrowed *for* me; they didn't borrow *from* me," one senator said in calling for an end to an "eat, drink, and be merry and let our children pay" mentality, and for a clear recognition of the absolute need to cap entitlements in concert with raising taxes.

Another senator called for a crash adult education program to confront American citizens with their collective dire fiscal straits and inescapable individual responsibilities.

Is it in the realm of possibility that phalanxes of university extension/outreach/continuing education professors, aged 40 to 80, could muster for such a task the same energy they have routinely devoted to counseling adult students on how to fill out forms for handouts — from agricultural subsidies to enterprise zones? And is it possible that social science researchers would respond to the challenge posed by Professor Peter Harris-Jones (1991) in his book, *Making Knowledge Count*, a call for "advocacy in social science?"

But the crucial role for senior academic faculty in closing the generation gap can be a very direct one. Andrew Hacker, publicized professor of political science at Queens College of the City University of New York, aims at fellow academics a striking suggestion:

> A little altruism would help. ... Full professors could opt to retire at 65. ... At a time of (campus) budget freezes and firings, can senior faculty members really feel comfortable about absorbing so large a share of shrinking resources? ... Now is the time (to share) some of our financial good fortune with those who want to carry on our calling (Hacker 1992).

Most of us elder academics have indeed been favored with good fortune. Good fortune in profession, friends, experiences, goods. Most of us have benefited from the interest of others. There's a kind of natural justice that expects most of us now to share some of that good fortune.

Listen to the plaint of David Awbrey, young editorial page editor of the *Wichita* (KS) *Eagle*:

> For the World War II generation, the GI Bill meant free college tuition and low-cost housing. The incredible prosperity of post-war America kept taxes relatively low while providing a cornucopia of government benefits — from highways that opened up suburbia to mortgage deductions to farm supports.
>
> As today's senior citizens, the World War II generation consumes the greatest share of the federal budget through Medicare, Social Security,

> federal pensions, and other entitlement programs. The most politically savvy of the generations, the elderly are not shy about demanding more from government. ...
>
> The short end of the demographic stick is held by today's twenty-somethings and the rear end of the baby boom generation. Not only must that group pay for many of the social and fiscal excesses of their parents, grandparents, and older siblings, it is the first U.S. generation to face stiff foreign economic competition within its peer group.
>
> Put simply, Americans born in the late 1960s through the mid-1970s were cheated. Their schools were disasters as educators dumbed-down the curriculum. College tuitions have soared, forcing many of them to seek burdensome student loans. Their job opportunities are scarce as the country undergoes an economic dislocation unmatched since the Depression. ...
>
> Moreover, the youngest adults could be crushed by the federal deficit. Since their elders refuse to pay fully for their own government programs, much of the bill is being left to the twenty-somethings. That is one reason those folks will likely not have a lifestyle enjoyed by older generations.

There are abundant opportunities to identify at least one self-fulfilling activity that can directly help close the generation gap — in same small way or other — with another person or persons or in an institutional setting (Awbrey 1992).

Increasingly, some emeriti are coming to the volunteer aid of their own college or university — its younger faculty and students. We detailed several of these in chapters 2 and 3. Several others merit a few words here, as examples of enlightened senior citizenship at work on campus:

- Universities in Minnesota are matching emeritus faculty with regions in the state where the professors are well-known by virtue of birth or association, equipping them with computer-driven scripts and videotapes detailing the specific services the institutions render citizens in those regions, and scheduling the emeriti for appearances before varied community organizations.
- At the University of Wisconsin-Madison, some retired staff are helping operate an Employees Assistance Center, counseling employees with personal problems, and retired faculty are sharing their experiences and expertise with state K-12 students and their parents at assembly programs, in classes, and at evening forums.
- A senior mentoring service at Temple University pairs retired faculty members with new hires "to enhance the junior faculty's teaching ef-

fectiveness in the Temple setting." The assistant professors can discuss their teaching problems more openly with seniors "who are no longer participants in the process of tenure review," the program director says.

Such efforts aren't for everyone, to be sure. And, of course, volunteer public service doesn't have to be with one's institution. For those senior academics willing and able to help personify an image of a caring elder class, challenges are there for those interested in beginning to close the generation gap. Not the least of which could be pressing for equity reforms in Social Security, Medicare, and Medicaid that would lower the tax burden on the coming generation.

A practical approach: instigate a letter-writing campaign to members of Congress, urging them to start taxing all the Social Security benefits of all recipients with gross incomes over $55,000. If such an activity is too draconian for anybody's tastes, how about simply staging a personal boycott of all those "golden oldie" perks?

You would not be alone. Led by George Washington University sociologist Amitai Ezione and his journal, *The Responsive Community*, a nascent national "communitarian" movement is beginning to ask Americans to balance veneration of individual rights with responsibility to the community at large.

A goodly number of Americans are responding. Based on a 1992 sampling of the 54 million people over 55, researchers at the Gerontology Institute of the University of Massachusetts at Boston conclude that:

- By taking care of relatives or friends, older Americans work the equivalent of 7.1 million full-time jobs.
- Their work with religious institutions and public-service organizations equals 1.1 million full-time positions (Anderson 1992).

The generation gap out there will take that sort of citizenship, and more, to bridge. Will senior academics — active and retired — be, as the saying goes — a part of the problem or a part of the solution?

My country preacher father had a sermon that was a perennial bell-ringer with rural congregations.

"Are you like an ear of corn moldering in the bin?" he would ask from the pulpit. "Or are you like a kernel planting itself in the soil of service?"

I guess that sort of sums up the message of the day.

LOOKING OVER YOUR SHOULDER

Investigators, prosecutors, and social service agency officials say there are signs that money or property are being stolen or coerced from

America's elderly at a disturbing rate, and that a large proportion of the crimes are committed not by professional criminals but by neighbors, household workers, service persons, and even family members.

That was the lead of a 1991 *New York Times* article.

Exploitation and deception of older persons are likely to continue to grow as the number of older Americans who are most vulnerable to it — the lonely and those in poor health — rises, the story goes on to say.

"There has been an alarming increase in reported cases of such crimes, and I'm afraid it is fast becoming the crime of the 1990s," according to Joanne Matlatt, program administrator of adult protection services for the state of Colorado. "And, like child abuse, many crimes against the elderly are never reported because the victims are ashamed as well as traumatized" (Nordheimer 1991).

All that may be so, but it'll never happen to me, you may well say. Guess again.

In the last two years at our cabin, Sheryl and I have been visited by handypersons peddling aluminum siding, painting, pointing, roofing, lightning rods, and driveway blacktopping. We might have bit on one or more except for an experience we had when getting our city home ready for sale.

It needed a coat of paint badly, so we looked in the want ads of the weekly shopper for a likely crew. One ad particularly intrigued us: "Skilled university grad students working on their Ph.D.'s, looking for summer work, will paint your house at bargain rates." When it turned out the students were in the department of philosophy, we should have had our suspicions, but who were we not to help subsidize the writing of an interpretive biography of Max Otto?

To make a long story short, that paint job was not only cut-rate, it was cut-quality. We had to have the whole house done over again by professionals. Now we never employ service persons who can't display a license and references.

In the retirement apartment tower where I now reside, there have been several cases of disappearing jewelry and cash, even though the building is security-locked. Itinerant aides are suspected (although the "culprit" could be the absent-minded resident).

"Material exploitation of older Americans is expected to grow in company with recession and drug abuse," says Professor Karl Pillemer of the department of human development and family studies at Cornell and author of *Helping Elderly Victims* (1989).

Health-Care Scams

Sad to report, the most insidious threats lying in wait for the elderly are a variety of frauds associated with health care:

- Poorly managed health insurance companies that fail — an estimated 120 in the past three years. However, chances are good that your institution's carrier will be insured by a state fund or by the institution itself.
- Poorly managed health maintenance organizations (HMOs) that fail — around 130 between 1986 and 1990. Here again, however, all federally qualified HMOs have "hold harmless" clauses that prevent health providers from dunning you for bills your HMO should have paid (Quinn 1992).
- For-profit mental health facilities that pay "bounty hunters" to bring in patients, hospitalize patients against their will, tailor treatments to maximize insurance payments, take kickbacks for recruiting patients, and over-bill for services. Crackdowns really depend on smarter, more vigilant consumers.
- Phone solicitations peddling cut-rate health equipment like special beds or recliners. Don't give out your Social Security, Medicare, or insurance policy numbers.
- Rolling labs and health fairs that offer a battery of tests rather than a single test like one for cholesterol or skin cancer or a mammogram. Don't provide a detailed medical history or sign multiple insurance forms that assign reimbursement to a provider.
- A scenario that goes like this: The provider says your insurance will probably cover only $500 of a treatment for which the usual charge is $1,000. He or she proposes to submit fees of $2,000 — expecting to get reimbursed for around $1,000 — and waive your part of the bill. These lies could prevent you from getting life or health insurance down the road.
- Home-care agencies that try to sell you services or equipment your doctor hasn't specified. It's best to choose a home-care provider licensed by the state, certified by Medicare, and accredited by a national organization.

You can find fraud fighters in most state attorney general's offices, and Medicare recipients can file suspicions by calling a toll-free fraud hotline: 800/368-5779 (Finlay 1992).

GROWING OLDER GRACEFULLY

As we've said, in addition to growing into retirement, you're going to grow older.

This reality may first come to you when you roll out of bed one morning and there's a strange cramp in your left leg.

It may come to you when your fingers are no longer so nimble in knitting a pair of Christmas mittens for a granddaughter.

The TV screen may become progressively blurred or the telephone ring indistinct.

Or it may come to you when you're suddenly short of breath climbing the hill on the eighteenth fairway — and you acquiesce to that ultimate symbol of degeneration, a rented golf cart.

Don't bridle; it's inevitable and honorable. Fighting the problem will only make you despondent. Relax, adapt, and enjoy all the many less exacting pursuits.

Grace, according to *Webster's*, has an abundance of meanings, including:

- A charming trait or accomplishment.
- Fitness or proportion of line or expression.
- Charm of bearing.
- Sense of propriety or right.
- Divine assistance.

Surely, out of all those definitions, you can select one or two that'll help you grow older gracefully.

The alternative, to hole up and vegetate, is certainly unbecoming to anyone who has devoted his or her life to being a professional role model for generations of college students.

> Grow old along with me!
> The best is yet to be,
> The last of life, for which the first was made: ...
> Youth shows but half ...

FOLDING THE TENT

Part of growing older gracefully is preparing just as gracefully to die, whatever your faith or fashion. And the law now encourages you to prepare.

As of December 1991, patients admitted to hospitals or nursing homes joining an HMO, or signing up for hospice or home health care will be asked whether they have made out a *living will* specifying exactly what treatments they would accept or reject as the end of life draws near. In addition, medical institutions must give new patients written information about medical rights and institutional policies regarding treatment. While not everyone considers this progress, the congressionally mandated procedure is a powerful reminder of the rights of Americans to refuse unwanted medical treatment.

While the law doesn't force anyone to make out a living will, the assumption is that more people will opt to forgo costly, life-sustaining technology if recovery is hopeless, thereby letting a bit of air out of the nation's ballooning health-care bill. On the other hand, you're perfectly free to say something like: "I want my life prolonged to the greatest extent possible without regard to my condition, the chances I have for recovery, or the cost of the procedures."

But because in some states living wills take effect only when a physician certifies that the patient is terminal, and because state laws vary in their acceptance of living wills, health officials, lawyers, and trust officers increasingly encourage people to appoint a proxy to stick up for their medical wishes.

That's accomplished by making out a legal document known as a *power of attorney for health care*. Most people choose their spouse as their proxy, but the main requisite is that the proxy be tough enough to fend off doctors and family members should they be at odds over a living will's provisions.

Of course, your proxy won't know what your wishes are unless you discuss them with him or her in detail in advance. To help people do that in a clear and convincing manner, there are questionnaires that can be filled out and attached to a living will and to a power of attorney for health care. A typical form prompts people to clarify their underlying values and guide loved ones who might have to make medical treatment decisions for patients temporarily or permanently incapable of making or communicating their own decisions.

A model *Values History* form, developed at the University of New Mexico's Institute of Public Law, asks such questions as these:

Attitude Toward Health. If you have medical problems, in what ways — if any — do they affect your ability to function? How well are you able to meet the basic necessities of life: eating, food preparation, sleep, personal hygiene?

Independence and Control. How important are independence and self-sufficiency in your life? If you were to experience decreased physical and mental abilities, how would that affect your attitude toward independence and self-sufficiency?

Personal Relationships. Do you expect your friends, family, and/or others will support your decisions regarding medical treatment you might need now or in the future? Have you made arrangements for your family or friends to make medical decisions on your behalf? What, if any, unfinished business or legal matters are you concerned about?

Attitude Toward Illness and Death. What will be important to you when you are dying — for example, physical comfort, no pain, family members present? Where would you prefer to die? How do you feel about the use of life-sustaining measures in the face of terminal illness? Of permanent coma? Irreversible chronic illness? What, if any, is your attitude toward death?

Religious Beliefs. How do your religious beliefs affect your attitude toward serious and terminal illness? Does your attitude toward death find support in your religion? How does your form of worship view the role of prayer or religious sacraments in an illness?

Finances. How much do you worry about having enough money to provide for your care? Would you prefer to spend less money on your care so that more money can be saved for the benefit of relatives and/or friends?

The further away anyone is from contemplating the occasion for a living will, the more likely the answer to many such questions will be, "It depends." That is why a living will, a durable power of attorney for health care, and any codicil should be reviewed annually with spouse, lawyer, physician, and proxy; and **all three documents should be filed with all four**.

If proper forms aren't easily available to you locally, here are sources:

- For a **values history**, send $3 to the UMM Public Law Institute, 1117 Stanford NE, Albuquerque, NM 87131.
- For a **free living will** suited to your state, write Choice in Dying, 250 W. 57th, New York, NY 10107.
- For a **free health care power of attorney**, write for Stock No. D13895, AARP Fulfillment, 1909 K St. NW, Washington, DC 20049.
- For a videotape with program guide (rental $18, purchase $48), send to "In Your Hands," Modern Talking Pictures, 5000 Park St. N, St. Petersburg, FL 33709 (Podolsky 1991, Schreter 1991).

If you make out both a living will and a durable power of attorney for health care, make sure their overt and covert instructions are not in conflict. As a matter of fact, the latest opinion of the Wisconsin Center for Public Representation is that you should *not* have both because of the possibility of misinterpretations.

Doctor Talk

This may sound a little gruesome, but understanding the following terms will help you discuss these issues with your physician, either personally or via an advance directive.

Brain death. The absence of brain activity, which may be documented by the patient's total lack of response to pain and absence of reflexes. When this occurs, the patient is legally considered dead, although other vital organs may continue to function briefly.

Cardiopulmonary resuscitation (CPR). A medical procedure that helps the heart start beating after cardiac arrest. It generally involves compressions to the chest, artificial respiration, medication, and electrical

---

HE'S GOT A "NO-CODE" TATTOO

On his 65th birthday in 1984, Dr. Douglas Lindsey, a UA professor emeritus of surgery/emergency medicine, went out and got tattooed.

The design he chose, slightly larger than a quarter and near his left aerola, shows a defibrillation paddle with the international symbol for "no" crossed over it.

The defibrillation paddle is used to restore normal heart rhythm when someone suffers a heart attack. By getting his tattoo, Lindsey hopes that if he ever suffers from an attack, the medical people called to help will not try to resuscitate him.

"If the paramedics don't re-establish the pulse before getting to the hospital, resuscitation can be a waste of time," Lindsay says. The patient may survive, but he will frequently suffer massive neurological damage.

Research indicates fewer than one percent of patients with prehospital cardiac arrest who lack restoration of vital signs by the time they reach the emergency room ever leave the hospital alive.

"I don't mind dying, but I sure as hell do not want to spend days, months, or years in a nursing home bouncing beach balls in a parachute blanket," Lindsay says.

—*Arizona Alumnus*, University of Arizona

---

shocks to the heart. Patients who undergo successful CPR may need to be placed on a ventilator afterward. (Don't be too hasty in renouncing CPR. I had to have CPR in 1982 — five grandchildren, two national board directorships, and seven books ago.)

Do not resuscitate/no blue cart. An order directing staff to refrain from CPR if the patient's heart stops.

Intubation. Placing a tube into the nose or mouth to help a patient breathe.

Palliative care. Pain relief to make a seriously ill patient as comfortable as possible.

Persistent vegetative state (PVS). A form of permanent unconsciousness in which the patient's eyes are open and he or she is periodically awake, but is at no time aware of himself or herself or environment.

Tube feeding. A method of giving food and water to a patient who can't eat or drink. The patient may be fed through a tube placed directly into the stomach or through the nose and throat into the stomach.

Ventilator. A machine that breathes for a patient who can't breathe naturally (U-Care 1992).

OBSERVING LAST RIGHTS

We don't want to sound maudlin or alarmist, but the fact is you may someday have to face a scenario that goes something like this:

Your spouse is dead. Your children are scattered around the continent, you're in failing physical and/or mental health.

Hence, the following checklist to point you to actions you can take well before the moment of truth:

Finances

- Make out that **durable power of attorney**, giving a trustee the right to manage your money in an exigency. Regular powers of attorney are no good in such a case; only a durable power stays in force if you become incapacitated. Ask a lawyer to draw one up (the fee should be low). Then get it approved by all the financial institutions that you use — bank, insurance company, broker, TDA fund, pension fund(s), and so on, because some institutions won't accept a power of attorney not drawn up on their own forms. On the other hand, some states have legislated an approved form. Check it out. Whom to appoint as your trustee? It should be somebody (a) in the vicinity, (b) younger than you, (c) with money management skills, (d) whom you trust implicitly.

- As a guide for your trustee, make out a complete, detailed list of all **your income, assets, and liabilities**. Consider now squeezing more liquidity and cash out of your savings by moving money out of a passbook into a short-term certificate of deposit or by taking out a loan on an insurance policy.
- Consider a **joint bank account** with your trustee for paying minor bills. But this apparently simple strategy isn't without risk. Were your trustee to die first, any trustee's creditors might try to tap the account. Or if your trustee is a child and you die, what's left of the money will normally be paid to the trustee-child — cutting out any siblings you might wish had a share. Ask your bank if it offers joint accounts "for convenience only," not for inheritance.
- Set up **automatic receiving and paying**, if you haven't already. Certain income, like pensions and Social Security benefits, can be wired directly to your bank account. A bank can pay many bills automatically, like mortgage or rent, insurance, utilities.
- Double-check your **supplemental short-term health care and long-term health care insurance policies**, and ask the companies to send duplicate bills to your trustee to make sure premiums get paid on time.
- Under the law, your doctor has to enter Medicare claims, but it's up to you to collect on any private insurance, as we've said. If your doctor and/or hospital won't help by filing **insurance claim forms for medical bills**, prepare your trustee for the chore.

Health

Against the day when you may need health and/or household help:

- **Make a safety check of your abode**, and if you haven't done so already, carry out that "retrofitting" plan discussed earlier in Chapter 4.
- Make out that living will, power of attorney for health care, and codicil. As we've explained, the will expresses your wishes about life support systems and so on; the power of attorney appoints someone of your choice to make medical decisions on your behalf if you become unable to do so; and a **values history** codicil gives explicit guidance to your proxy.
- Identify to your trustee, your proxy, and your next of kin in your current and/or potential support system — doctor, lawyer, banker, church or temple, friends, neighbors, building manager — people who can check with each other if something's amiss. Remember, too, the advantage of switching professional horses, described in Chapter 3.

- Reconnoiter **personal care professionals**. Fortunately, most communities offer a web of services, public and private. But it takes time, personal visits, and counsel to get a line on all the help you might need someday. Start by calling the office for the aging in the capital of your state. Get the phone number of the local area agency on aging, a mother lode of good advice about Meals on Wheels, adult day care, senior citizen discounts, transportation, visiting nurses, traveling libraries, and so on.
- Consider a private care manager — a rapidly growing field peopled with nurses, social workers, psychologists, and gerontologists. For a fee, they'll arrange support, pay regular visits, and handle emergencies. Warning: this field so far is utterly unregulated, so don't choose anyone without checking up on references carefully (Quinn 1991).

Fulfillment

Work out some sort of entente to eliminate or at least reduce any chance of your heirs fighting over possessions. You've undoubtedly spelled out the disposition of big-ticket equities, but what about your matched set of Ben Hogan irons, a favorite flyrod, the stemware you inherited from Aunt Tilly, and so on?

"It's seldom a major item that sets family members at loggerheads," says my attorney. "It's more likely to be a patchwork quilt."

SUMMING UP

Let me recite another story about that eight-year-old daughter. She was growing up in a boy-less neighborhood and already was starved for male attention, so one day I was happy to tell her that Beverly across the street was "expecting" and that it might be a boy. In a flash, Laurie raced over to tell Beverly's husband, Ted, "Please, Mr. Wamelink, have a baby boy!" "I'd like that, too, Laurie," said Ted, "but about all we can do is pray."

Of course Laurie prayed. She prayed for a week and nothing happened. She prayed for another week and nothing happened. So in frustration she stopped praying.

After another week, Laurie got a phone call from Ted.

"Beverly's back from the hospital, Laurie, and I want you to come over and see what she brought home."

Ted led Laurie around to one side of the bed and said, "Laurie, here's that baby boy for you to play with!" Then he led her around to the other side of the bed and said, "And, Laurie, here's another baby boy for you to play with! Now aren't you glad you prayed?"

"Yes!" Laurie exclaimed, and then after a pause: "But aren't you glad I quit!"

You, too, are likely glad this seminar is about over. But first, a final word before the bell: Milletti's 1,500 academic retirees told him in concert that, "like full-time work and probably any other aspect of our lives, the retirement experience can be a blend of both the pleasant and unpleasant — opportunity and pitfall, joy and tedium, challenge and drudgery, rewarding social experiences and some decidedly otherwise."

There's an even louder voice coming from those retirees: that what we make of retirement "depends in good part on how (and how much) we prepare for the new lifestyle."

Based on his assembled data, Milletti says "preparation for retirement actually involves some rather simple notions":

Build up retirement savings. Income from Social Security and your pension are unlikely to be anything but barely adequate, so you'll need some margin to fund a retirement the way you'd like.

Get firsthand knowledge of people and places — particularly helpful if you're thinking of relocating, and useful anyway in getting a feel for what it'll be like not going to the campus every day. Talk to peers who've been there.

Tap specialists. If your campus doesn't offer retirement counseling, you can energize some seminars, utilizing scholars or practitioners in the field.

Ask questions of yourself. Given the trend toward earlier retirements and longer lifespans, you could easily spend half as many years in retirement as you spent in working. So don't just drift into it. The quickie quizzes at the end of Chapters 1-4 are designed to encourage some introspection. Also, please complete the "Seminar Evaluation" at this chapter's end.

If married, involve your spouse. By cooperatively thinking about retirement's opportunities and constraints, you can help defuse potential tensions.

Take action far ahead of actual retirement. Early planning allows you to adapt to your needs as much information as possible — and to initiate a savings program.

View retirement in perspective. Don't associate retirement necessarily with aging. You'll grow older and experience waning energy levels whether you retire or not. Look on retirement as does Milletti's benedictory retiree: "Retirement is a very valuable time of life. There is time to know and grow in a different way" (Milletti 1989).

References

Anderson, Paul, 1992. "Elderly Undervalued, Study Says," Knight Ridder Newspapers, June 25.

Awbrey, David, 1992. "Issue of the Week," *Wichita* [KS] *Eagle*, July 11, p. A4.

Baker, Gregory, 1992. "Income Tax Planning for Retirement," *Management World*, Winter, p. 9.

Barone, Michael, 1992. "The New 'Save the Wealth' Voters, *U.S. News & World Report*, June 22, p. 45.

Berry, John M., 1991. "Calculating the Economy," *The Washington Post Weekly Edition*, December, p. 7.

Daniels, Craig E., and Janet D. Daniels, 1992. "Retiree Health Care: A Ticking Bomb," *AGB Reports*, March/April, pp. 17-19.

Dentzer, Susan, 1992. "A Wealth of Difference," *U.S. News & World Report*, June 1, pp. 45-47.

Devaries, Charles, 1992. "Recession Prompts Some Change in Faculty Retirement Plans," *Community College Week*, April 13, p. 10.

Finlay, Steven, 1992. "How to Thwart Health-Care Fraud," *U.S. News & World Report*, February, p. 43.

Galbraith, John Kenneth, 1992. *The Culture of Contentment* (Boston: Houghton-Mifflin).

Garrigan, Richard T., 1992. "TIAA's Commercial Mortgage and Real Estate Investments," *Academe*, January-February, pp. 13-17c.

Hacker, Andrew, 1992. "A Bloat of Well-Heeled Profs," *Sacramento* (CA) *Bee*, March 8, Forum pp. 1-2.

Hardy, Dorcas R., and C. Colburn Hardy, 1991. *Social Insecurity* (Bristol, VT: Basic Books).

Harris-Jones, Peter, 1991. *Making Knowledge Count* (Montreal: McGill Queen's University Press).

Kroncke, Charles O., 1992. Personal correspondence in author's files.

Kruegman, Paul R., 1992. "Ignorance and Inequality," *U.S. News and World Report*, June 1, pp. 48-49.

Jones, Thomas W., 1992. "We Stand on Our Record," *Academe*, January-February, pp. 18-19.

Lehrmann, Eugene, 1992. Quoted in William R. Wineke, "Incoming AARP President Sees Pension Fund Dangers" (Madison: *Wisconsin State Journal*), June 26, p. 6C.

Milletti, Mario, 1989. *Voices of Experience: 1500 Retired People Talk About Retirement* (New York: TIAA-CREF).

Nordheimer, Jon, 1991. "Elderly Victimized by People They Know," *New York Times*, Dec., 15, p. 9A. *Academe*, January-February, pp. 20-22.

Palmer, David D., and Cynthia H. Adams, 1992. "Crisis in the Northeast,"

Perrin, Robert, 1992. "The TIAA Portfolio Rate," *Academe*, January-February, pp. 11-12.

Pillemer, Karl, 1989. *Helping Elderly Victims* (New York: Columbia University Press).

Podolsky, Doug, 1991. "A Right-to-Die Reminder," *U.S. News & World Report*, Dec. 2, p. 74.

Popcorn, Faith, 1992. *The Popcorn Report* (New York: Doubleday).

Quinn, Jane Bryant, 1992. "When Health Plans Fail," *Newsweek*, Feb. 24, p. 45.

Quinn, Jane Bryant, 1991. "Policies for Old Age Care," *Newsweek*, April 30, p. 61.

Rosen, Gerald H., 1992. "TIAA-CREF Declining Revenues," *Academe*, Jan., Feb., pp. 8-11.

Schafer, Rudolf J. H., 1992. Personal correspondence in author's files.

Schreter, Carol, 1991. "Beyond the Living Will," *The Retired Officer Magazine*, November, pp. 30-34.

U-Care, 1992. *Answers to Questions About Advance Directives* (Madison, WI: UW Faculty Physicians and Hospital).

Seminar Evaluation

We're the optimistic type, so we're already contemplating a second edition of *Retirement 901*, and we're inviting you to collaborate by providing brief answers to the following questions and mailing them to the author personally at 602 North Segoe Road, Apartment 601, Madison, WI 53705, or to Box 67B, Barneveld, WI 53507.

1. What feature of this guide did you find most helpful? Least? Why?

2. What knowledge or experience of yours supports the guide? Contradicts the guide?

3. What's missing from the guide? What's superfluous?

4. Has anything transpired since publication that renders something obsolete?

5. Did you find any language inappropriate or offensive? What?

6. If you sign your quiz, do we have your permission to quote you by name?

Index

WHAT THEY'RE SAYING ABOUT *RETIREMENT 901*

"Jam-packed with helpful information, not only for staff and faculty who are just beginnning to think about retirement but also for those who are already out to pasture. Very readable and on target throughout. My experiences of the last year have made me aware of the value of a book like this."

—**DAYLE MOLEN,** *recently retired as professor and former chair, Journalism, California State University-Fresno.*

"An outstanding concept, useful for non-academic professionals as well as university faculty. The points made about diet, exercise, and prevention are correct and well made."

—**Dr. DAVID WATTS,** *Clinical Professor of Geriatrics, University of Wisconsin Hospital and Clinics.*

"Comprehensive and worthwhile. Particularly strong in discussing what might be called 'the psychology of retirement' — loss of status, relations with spouse, family relationships, the need for feelings of accomplishment."

—**RUDOLPH J. H. SCHAFER,** *recently retired as director of energy/environmental education, California State Department of Education.*

"A great 'course.' Dull but important material expressed in fascinating ways. Personal references give the data reality and vitality."

—**ROBERT DICK,** *recently retired community development communications specialist, University of Wisconsin System Extension.*

"Packed with charm, wisdom, and insight."

—**ROBERT J. GRIFFIN,** *professor, College of Communication, Journalism, and Performing Arts, Marquette University.*

"Clearly written and filled with much good information. While pitched to the senior end of the age spectrum, the book is personally relevant to every single academic. I learned a lot."

—**ROBERT F. MEIER,** *chair, sociology, Iowa State University.*

"Very helpful in setting attitudes for those about to make a new journey. I do not find any fatal flaws. Makes the case that it is the elderly that can provide America with much needed leadership and vision."

—**CHARLES O. KRONCKE,** *dean, School of Management, The University of Texas-Dallas.*

"This is a very fine piece of work. Nothing missing, nothing superfluous."

—**JOHN F. DISINGER,** *professor, School of Natural Resources, The Ohio State University.*

"It's a pleasure to read this magnificent book; it surely derives from a most massive research effort. Could I have read it 15 years or so ago, it would have saved me a lot of hassle."

—**WILLIAM E. HAIGHT II,** *retired professor of mass communication, Michigan State University.*

"An excellent 'course' for the inevitable future we all face. 'Happiness/Unhappiness' is the equivalent of 'Pass/Fail.'"

—**JOHN C. HENDEE,** *dean, College of Forestry, Wildlife, and Range Sciences, University of Idaho.*

"A classic summary on the subject, filled with both gusto and depth of research. It will vastly ease any pain."

—**JOHN LONG,** *retired adjunct professor of English, Loyola University.*

"Both Yvonne and I read the manuscript, enjoyed it immensely, and will certainly recommend the book to our friends who are contemplating retirement. ... The book is so comprehensive each chapter could be a guide of its own."

— **LARRY D. CLARK,** *dean, College of Arts and Science, University of Missouri-Columbia.*